Dear Brendan,
Thanks for
your advice
and companionship.
Take care
Alexander
munenson

10.11.95

AFTER THE FALL

AFTER THE FALL

The Pursuit of Democracy in Central Europe

JEFFREY C. GOLDFARB

BasicBooks
A Division of HarperCollins*Publishers*

Library of Congress Cataloging-in-Publication Data

Goldfarb, Jeffrey C.
    After the fall: the pursuit of democracy in Central Europe/
Jeffrey C. Goldfarb.
      p.   cm.
    Includes bibliographical references and index.
    ISBN 0–465–01605–7
    1. Europe, Eastern—History—1989– 2. Central Europe—
History. 3. Democracy. I. Title.
DJK51.G65 1992
943'.0009717—dc20   91–55465
                                          CIP

For Naomi

CONTENTS

vii

PART V: THE ECONOMY

PART VI: CULTURE

PREFACE

In the late summer of 1989, I received a call from my New School colleague David Gordon. As the organizer of our General Seminar for the coming academic year, he asked me to present a paper. Since its founding in 1933 as The University in Exile, such presentations have been recurring responsibilities of the New School's Graduate Faculty. The faculty comes together once a month to talk about each other's work. David knew I had just published a book on the political culture of the Soviet bloc and thought it would be timely to discuss the issue. I agreed. This book is an extension of that agreement.

Little did I realize the challenge I had agreed to take on. I had assumed I would simply reshape a chapter from *Beyond Glasnost: The Post-Totalitarian Mind* and discuss it with my colleagues in a normal academic fashion. Instead, I found I had committed myself to the project of trying to understand the most dramatic and radical change the world has experienced in my lifetime, as it occurred. Between August 1989 and December 13, 1989 (the date of my seminar presentation), the world was transformed. Eastern and Central European Communists were pushed aside; the Berlin Wall fell; negotiated transitions to democracy were put into place in Hungary and Poland; a "Velvet Revolution" took place in Czechoslovakia, followed by a violent revolution in Romania. My task for the seminar program, as I understood it, was to provoke a discussion about the broad theoretical, comparative, political, and cultural implications of the events in the "other Europe." I knew that whatever implications I chose to highlight were bound to be controversial.

I argued that we live in an entirely new political epoch, one in which the polarity between socialism and capitalism has become meaningless. The contrasts between left and right have to be fundamentally rethought, and the ideology of Marxism, along with other modern ideologies, must be frontally rejected. As expected, my forceful critique of Marxism and socialism provoked strong reaction from my academic colleagues on the left. Yet it was not the reaction I had expected and feared. It took on more the character of a passionate exploration of new cultural territory than a deadening reiteration of old ideological battles. The meeting of that seminar, which had been initiated by German scholars exiled by Nazi totalitarianism, confronted what I took to be a possible end point of modern tyranny.

In this book I explore the ground beyond this end point. I attempt to show how revolutionary challenges are being addressed by enfranchised citizens and their political leaders. The political present is being shaped by past experiences and accomplishments, and future expectations, hopes, and fears. As in my General Seminar presentation, I argue against ideology and the overly facile distinctions between socialism and capitalism. Thus, centrally, I criticize those who seek easy cures for complex problems through "the magic of the market." Without minimizing the importance of a market economy (I don't think there is any alternative economic system in a complex modern society), I show how those who are working for a civilized social order in Eastern

and Central Europe must frontally address the dilemmas of constituting a democratic order, the complexities of political leadership,
and the thorny issues of nation and religion, along with the difficulties of constructing a sound economy from an economic scrap
heap. The creativity of individuals, the vitality of independent civil
institutions (neither dominated by the state nor the economy),
and the ideal of Europe, I maintain, suggest that democracy is a
practical possibility in the newly independent nation-states of
Europe. Their roads to democracy, moreover, I believe have broad
implications for us: how we attempt to think and act democratically. If they are detoured, democrats everywhere will be weakened. If they reach their destinations, we will be strengthened.

I take the issues raised in this book very personally. I have
matured as a scholar and as a citizen through my continuing associations and friendships with democratic activists in Europe. They
have taught me the importance of democratic commitment and
that idealism can be the most practical form of realism. As much as
possible, I have tried to capture this educational experience in
these pages, particularly as it has progressed after the fall of communism. For their exemplary lives and invaluable advice, I would
specifically like to thank Adam Michnik, Jan Józef Szczepański,
Jan Lityński, Kostek Gebert, Jan Urban, Fedor Gal, Jan Langoš,
György Bence, Pavel Campeanu, and Rumyana Kolarova. I am
honored by their friendship, and humbled by their achievements.

I would also like to acknowledge the assistance and support I
have received at The New School for Social Research. It has been
my great good fortune that my intellectual and political commitments are shared by many of my colleagues, and that we have
been supported by our university. Andrew Arato, Ferenc Fehér,
Ira Katznelson, Aristide Zolberg, Vera Zolberg, Elżbieta Matynia,
José Casanova, and Alice Amsden have been the most active members of our democracy seminar in New York. Because they realize
that political ideas and serious discussion matter, I have learned a
great deal from their work and from their criticisms of mine. We
are indeed fortunate that in the tradition of the University in
Exile, the support of intellectual freedom and human rights in the
old Soviet bloc has become a university commitment. With the

assistance of the Ford Foundation and Mellon Foundation, we have established The International Democracy Seminar, a network of democratic intellectual activists throughout the region, and our East Central Europe Program, a project to help rebuild the social sciences in the region. My association with these university endeavors has made this book possible.

June 15, 1991

Then and Now

At the time, the circumstances of my arrest in Poland seemed trivial. I hardly thought about them afterward. But now, when I consider the fall of 1989, and the fall of communism, my little run-in with the Polish authorities seems highly suggestive of how things were then and what has since come to be.

Clearly, we now live in a new political epoch. The changes were apparently quick and revolutionary. We have seen the lifting of the "Iron Curtain"—that seemingly permanent barrier dividing the political East from the political West, the socialist bloc from the capitalist bloc, the free world from the totalitarian world. Not surprisingly, many feel disoriented; while others, with absolute certainty, foolishly proclaim future scenarios for the new world stage. But the banalities of my brief detention remind me of how fundamental the political changes have been, how they developed over a very long period of time, and how political "wisdoms" should always be doubted, at least a little bit more than they usually are.

Disorientation is what I remember about that April afternoon in Lublin, in 1974, when the People's Militia detained me for a couple of hours. I was attending a Festival of Youth Theaters. Because such theaters were an important arena for cultural experimentation and critical political expression, I was writing my Ph.D. dissertation about them. But the bulk of the theater presentations in Lublin were not very interesting. Some of the best theater groups of the Polish youth movement were not represented at this relatively minor festival, and others of mediocre quality were there in great number.

Veteran theater critics, journalists, directors, and actors were generally dissatisfied, particularly with one performance I attended, billed as a "happening." It took place in a gymnasium and consisted of little more than a rock soundtrack, a colorful slide show, and some student actors playing with an orange and yellow sheet. When it ended, a group of Polish journalists wanted to make things more interesting. They grabbed the sheet and spread it over themselves. They stood on one another's shoulders, made pyramids, and horsed around. And then they decided to go outside with their merrymaking and turn the pseudo-happening into the real thing.

The journalists under the sheet led the other members of the audience, along with the actors of the failed performance, down two flights of stairs onto a busy thoroughfare in downtown Lublin. And as soon as they hit the street, their act of ordinary horseplay became a public event. Traffic stopped. Crowds formed on both sides of the street. Theater participants mingled with shoppers, clerks, and workers in marveling at an open, spontaneous public event.

Most seemed to enjoy the break in the normal order of things. But a few others, particularly one middle-aged man in an oversized trenchcoat, seemed to be offended. He and a woman companion started shouting at those under the sheet: "You will hurt yourselves!" "Not only yourselves, but others!" "You can't breathe properly under there!" and the like. With a refined, cosmopolitan sense of what happenings were supposed to provoke, the theater people laughed and enjoyed the couple's contribution to the show. Others just scoffed at them and shouted back at them to leave the kids alone. The couple left. With that the interest of the passersby dissipated, and the happening moved on. The sheet-being turned up a side street and draped itself over a small Italian Fiat 850-S with German tourist license plates: my car.

Some friends coaxed me into the car with the sheet performers. When it was clear that the next logical step was to start the engine, at my Polish colleagues' instigation I turned on the ignition. Ten seconds later, the man in the oversized trenchcoat swept the sheet off my car and, with a paddywagon behind him, showed us his identification. He was with the People's Militia, and he politely indicated that we were to follow him.

At the militia headquarters, we had to hand in our papers. The Poles presented their personal "Legitimacja," I my American passport. Then we were taken to a secured lockup area. I presented unanticipated problems. They hadn't expected an American to be at this provincial performance, let alone at a place where the divide between theater performance and political order had been breached. They wanted to put an end to the event in as uncompromising a way as possible. But the officers on duty did not seem to have the authority to either release us, or further process our detention.

Our guard told us that they had to confirm our story with the theater festival's organizers. But first, he confiscated film from the cameras of the journalist photographers. And then we waited.

I was nervous and angry with myself. Like other American scholars visiting Poland, at the very beginning of my year-and-a-half stay in Poland I had been warned by the security chief of the American embassy not to take part in illegal political activities. Now, just as I was about to finish my research, I had disobeyed his advice and gotten myself arrested. But the advice had not been easy to follow. Aside from the fact that the American official's cloak-and-dagger speech had been hard to take seriously (in a safe room in the embassy), it was difficult to realize on the day of the happening that something political was developing.

As it happened, geopolitics were a key to that day's events.

Lublin is in eastern Poland, close to the Soviet border. It had been the first seat of the Soviet-supported provisional government, formed under the cover of the Red Army in opposition to the Western-backed government in exile. On the day of the theater festival, a special delegation from the Soviet Union was commemorating Soviet-Polish friendship. And so the Polish authorities, who usually demonstrated little tolerance for unsupervised public activity, were especially touchy. Ordinarily, their attitude to youth theater involved a typically socialist sort of repressive tolerance. Youth theater was viewed by those at the top as a carefully controlled safety valve for critical students. It kept them off the streets, out of politics. The students could create a fictive world of critical judgment, but through censorship and controlled publicity, that world was contained, and at the same time its mere existence gave an appearance of liberalism. If it hadn't been for the Soviet delegation on that day, the militia might very well have ignored the public disorder, or dispatched uniformed police to stop it gently. After all, even in the free West, street performers and demonstrators need permits. But on that day, an open use of undercover police was necessary to show the Soviet comrades that Polish life was appropriately sovietized; the Polish game of control and tolerance, repression and freedom, was not appropriate.

Now, after the fall, the less subtle Soviet totalitarianism, as well as the much more subtle Polish variety have come to an end. The means to such an end explain both the nature of the end and where it may lead. In Poland and the other countries of Eastern and Central Europe, there was some real tolerance contained within the socialist repressive tolerance, and it led to the development of dynamic movements of political transformation initiated by citizens as autonomous agents. In the Soviet Union, when the repression was lifted, first the change came from above and then there was confusion and disorder below.

While we were locked up in the militia station, my Polish friends, veterans of Poland's subtle politics of cultural life, assured me that nothing serious would happen. They realistically assessed our situation. If I weren't there, they told me, some greater unpleasantness might ensue. Maybe they would be detained for the permissible forty-eight hours without being formally charged. But our little escapade on the street was not really significant, and the city would not want to risk an international incident over it. Indeed, the provincial party hacks of Lublin might have been afraid their actions would meet disapproval in Warsaw. It was the era of détente. Poland was experiencing an apparent economic boom based on loans from Western governments and banks. Tensions were to be relaxed, and political muscle was not to be flexed. Therefore, the Poles predicted that we would wait for a few hours and then be warned and released. And they turned out to be right. After two hours our papers were returned (though not the film), and we were released with a warning not to take part again in an unauthorized theatrical event.

In spite of the Polish assurances, when I returned to the festival, and later to my apartment in Warsaw, I was shaken up. I had not intended to become involved in Polish politics except to study its relation to Polish culture. I knew the relationship was intimate, but I hadn't expected to be caught up in it. Of course, I was aware that I really wasn't very deeply caught up in it. The whole adventure almost immediately became the subject of jokes, and I soon forgot it. But I was to be reminded of it again.

A photographer in our group, it seemed, had somehow managed to retain a roll of film documenting what had happened. And months after the event, a weekly newspaper in Kraków published an account of it—not as a news story, but as a comic-book rendition of Little Red Riding Hood. The sheet-being was depicted as Little Red Riding Hood, and the city street became the forest in which we met the Big Bad Wolf: the undercover agent who finally showed his teeth when we were in Grandmother's House—my car. The newspaper didn't reveal all of the circumstances of the arrest, but it clearly showed the political police doing its work.

Thinking back, I realize that this happening was more successful than any other I have observed or read about. It crossed the divide between the aesthetic and the social, and it also developed a life of its own, encompassing a large and formidable territory. (Maybe these reflections should be included in that territory.) It began inside its own repressive context: it was forced to occur in a gymnasium, not outside on the street, because the authorities did not permit performances outside of conventional settings. The authorities wanted only channeled innovation, knowing that without proper channels, public autonomy might not easily find acceptable limits. But those in the world of theater, as well as in other arts and sciences, pushed limits as a matter of fundamental principle; and in Lublin that day, they did it spontaneously.

There was certainly a telling banality about those events in Lublin. The performance was mediocre. The fact that passersby paid attention to a group of kids fooling around on a city sidewalk in a closed society could be understood as little more than a totalitarian version of rubbernecking on a busy American highway. When the man in the trenchcoat intervened, trying to maintain the appearance of order for the special Soviet guests, I doubt if he or his colleagues had in mind any grand principles, political projects, or ideals. They certainly did not consider themselves henchmen of totalitarian control, or guardians of the socialist revolution. They were probably just doing their jobs, following the orders of their superiors. Possibly they didn't even like what they were doing. As individuals of independent judgment, they may very well have known that there was much ado about next to nothing that afternoon on the Lublin streets. In the end, it was just a little ripple of disorder on a very calm sea. But they had to fulfill their responsibilities and exercise their duties in at least a minimally successful fashion. In this way they were paid, supported their families, even received promotions. Their roles in the repressive apparatus were probably small, but their little decisions to enforce and comply with the despotic order actually made the order work.

It was with reference to this social configuration that Hannah Arendt, the major critical theorist of totalitarianism, coined the term "banality of evil" in her controversial essay *Eichmann in Jerusalem*. One of the most evil men in world history, Adolf Eichmann, appears in Arendt's account as a modern-day Everyman, concerned about his career, family, and social advancement, apparently not even cognizant of his responsibility for genocide. With less horrific implications, the same process was evident on the day of my detention. But the banal evil, the enforcement of total control without reflection, was met in Lublin by a complex though submerged political good. The police enforced a totalitarian control of public life with banal motivations. The public who reacted to the happening joyfully opened up, even if fleetingly, an autonomous alternative. When they saw our arrest and did nothing (although of course they couldn't do much), they acquiesced to the totalized order. But the journalists were fighting back. This was not their first run-in with the authorities, which was made evident by their cool appraisal of the situation. And more significantly, even while we were locked up, they were forging on: the photographer hid his pictures, and an editor was imagining a way for our little escapade to be brought to the attention of a broad public.

This activity of the young intellectuals was part of a long struggle with totalized political regimes over the issue of the freeing of public space. The happening revealed the nature of the battlefield. On the one side were the soft and hard totalitarians (as the Hungarian writer Miklós Haraszti puts it): those who feigned a modern, liberal appearance while maintaining complete control, the soft; and those who were more open about who and what they were, the hard. On the other side were those who provoked the rulers, who couldn't help struggling for room to act on their own, and those who saw the room so created, enjoyed it, and became collaborators with the resistance.

For the authorities, youth theater was a safety valve. For those involved in these events, well understanding their situation, it was a base of resistance, to be expanded whenever possible. They were not dissenters, they were oppositionists. They were the precursors of Solidarity, *glasnost*, and the fall of communism.

The situation in the "previously existing socialist societies"—in other words, the old Soviet bloc—has often been fundamentally misunderstood. When the old order was firmly entrenched, ideological accounts, communist and anticommunist, liberal and conservative, overlooked the complexities of political, cultural, and social existence. Those who, in my judgment, properly perceived totalitarianism as the distinctively modern form of tyranny, often didn't

notice that within the belly of the despotic beast, genuine opposition was not only a possibility but a reality. On the other hand,
those who wanted to minimize the distinctively tyrannical nature of
totalitarian orders mistook the success of their oppositions as a sign
of liberalism, or as an indication that the politics of the East were
not really that much different from those of the West.

Ever since the early 1970s and my days in the Lublin streets, I
have strongly argued that the authorities confronting my Eastern
European friends were fundamentally different from those in liberal societies. Just as strongly, I have argued that the struggles of
my friends, that is, the regime's opponents, should not be understood as lending legitimacy or normalcy to the abhorrent thing
communism was. To get these two points, one must understand
that the striving for an autonomous public life—a certain public
freedom—was an ongoing challenge to the old order. Now that
this opposition has prevailed, in order to comprehend the fall of
communism, we must appreciate that it is to a large degree the
achievement of the oppositionists.

For almost two decades, I have maintained that the emerging
free oppositional civil society in Eastern and Central Europe was
providing a point of view from which to understand the old
regime *in a nonideological fashion*. Now, in order to understand
the emerging political order, it is even more crucial to make such
an intellectual, nonideological move, based on the recognition of
the centrality of civil society. As I write these reflections, Western
observers, along with many citizens of Central Europe, have experienced moments of wild elation and deep pessimism. Boundless
hope about "a new world order" has been followed quickly by the
realization that the most ancient of problems are still with us, and
sometimes with a vengeance. The euphoria of liberation, which
was very real, has often been overshadowed by despair over political tension, nationalist conflict, religious fundamentalism, and economic breakdown. I believe, and will try to demonstrate, that
between euphoria and despair we can perceive grounds for cautious optimism, if we look closely at the unfolding developments
as they can be mediated in a free society, abandoning ideological
preconceptions.

The odds are always high against a humane democratic order, but the nonviolent method of the democratic revolutions of 1989 has real promise. If we give up too quickly on democratic hopes, our fear of failure may help democratic failure become a reality. We will define the situation as hopeless; and as a consequence, it will be hopeless. As we will see, the potential tragedy of this perspective goes beyond the borders of Central Europe. The first victim will be the ideal of a nonviolent and prosperous Europe. It is striking how democratic forces throughout the region, from Estonia to Albania, have used the slogan of joining Europe as an important support for their democratic appeals. But it should be clear as well to their Western neighbors that a spread of political, religious, and national hatreds and economic chaos will not easily be confined to the old Soviet bloc. A new Berlin Wall and new Iron Curtain will not suffice to contain it. Europe, indeed, is now in the same house. But this does not just mean Europe in the geographic sense. It means the Europe of the great Western ideals of freedom, culture, and democracy. All modern politics, economics, and cultures are implicated in some way in the fate of Central Europe.

Before we proceed to examine this claim more closely, I want to underscore my central themes concerning civil society in a post-totalitarian world. I will try to show that the appreciation of the importance of public life in civil society was central not only to the democratic challenge to totalitarianism but also to the democratic transition and the fall of totalitarian power. The appreciation of this role of civil society is important not only for political understanding and action in the developing democracies of Europe and around the world, but, as well, for a renewal of political thinking and democratic action in the established and often overly rigid democracies of the developed West. After the fall of 1989, a post-totalitarian, anti-ideological politics is possible.

The embedded opposition culture of the seventies, the politics of Solidarity in Poland and of its admirers throughout the bloc in the eighties, and now the ascendance of democratic politics throughout the old bloc, all indicate that we live in a world where modern ideologies have reached their limits. This, not the end of history (Fukuyama) nor the victory of liberal capitalism (Brzeziński), is what the fall of communism most fundamentally reveals. But to say that now we are really perceiving an end of ideology does not indicate an end to modern political accomplishments and aspirations, or the resolution of modern problems. Quite the contrary, the hallucinogen of ideology has obscured more than it has illuminated, frustrated more than it has fostered. Although fundamental principles at the center of modern political theory (freedom, equality, and democracy) were purportedly addressed by prevailing ideologies, our most recent past has clearly demonstrated that it just was not so. Ideological accounts of the world presented veils of ignorance and illusion. They rationalized political actions but had little to do with solving human problems or promoting human creativity. Further, ideological politics were not only of the communist or Marxist kind. They were the politics of our age, of the Cold War, of the free world versus the totalitarian world. The end of ideology means the collapse of the dominant ideological dichotomies, of the communists and the anti-communists, Marxists and anti-Marxists. These easy ideologies have defined a great deal of our political, economic, and sociological expert opinion and common sense. I believe that we must struggle to overcome them in order to understand the post-totalitarian situation, in Central Europe and beyond.

I

POLITICS

CHAPTER 1

Civil Society "As If"

For me, the development of a post-totalitarian politics, from the half-hidden battle for a free public life in the politics of culture (such as the Lublin happening), to the more open struggles of the democratic opposition and Solidarity (above and below ground), to the constitution of democratic practice throughout the old bloc, is best represented by my acquaintance with Adam Michnik. In and through our developing friendship, I came to know about the dense social relationships of a besieged but emerging independent civil society which eventually overwhelmed the coercive powers of totalitarian orders. This, to my mind, is where the end of communism began.

I had heard about Michnik even before I had any special interest in things Eastern and Central European. He was 1968's student from Poland. The French had Daniel Cohn-Bendit, Danny the Red; we Americans had an extensive cast of characters from Tom Hayden to Abbie Hoffman; and the Poles had Michnik. But he was a more sober sort of student leader than the ones in the West. He did not directly attack the fundamental norms and ideals of the existing socialist system; rather, he called for their full realization, along with fundamental liberal rights including freedom of speech and free university life. He led student protests against the closing of a production of Adam Mickiewicz's nineteenth-century classic *Forefather's Eve,* which escalated into broader protests against political interference in the university, which in the end included protests against Michnik's own arrest for so-called "antisocialist agitation."

A significant difference between liberal and totalitarian regimes was revealed by this arrest. While critical Western youth faced imprisonment for crimes committed, Michnik served years in jail only for his reforming beliefs. His fate was decided by a totalitarian government that conflated its interests with reason in history. He became an "antisocialist element," a label drenched with ideological terror. His choice was either to accept the existing social order and his place in it, as defined by the authorities, or to live a life outside political and social convention as an unemployed, or underemployed, political deviant and crimimal. Michnik's only escape from such a choice was the breakdown of the totalitarian system, which was a most unlikely prospect twenty years ago. To be sure, in the liberal West radical political critics have been harassed and persecuted, and systematically disadvantaged minorities have experienced the force of state oppression. But the injustice of such practices as American racism and the FBI surveillance and control of dissent have never been as severe as in the political East. Furthermore, they can be opposed by using the very political resources that the dissenters sometimes denigrated (the so-called bourgeois legal order) and officials often undermined (as most strikingly publicized in the Watergate revelations). The relatively humane treatment of dissenters in the liberal West depends on indigenous liberal traditions. The humane treatment of dissenters in the totalitarian East required the fall of communism. I had learned these hard facts over the span of two decades, as I observed our own dissenters choose lives of commitment or compromise to varying degrees, while the dissenters of 1968 in the political East escalated and sustained their critique to the point that it fundamentally transformed their and our political world.

In the mid- and late 1970s, during intervals when he was out of jail, I bumped into Adam Michnik twice. The first time was at a legal theatrical adaptation of *The Master and the Margarita*. The second was at an illegal but open reading of Stanisław Barańczak's poetry in a large private apartment. At both performances the audience represented a cross section of Warsaw's cosmopolitan intelligentsia, which included actors and philosophers, political economists and lay Catholic theologians, students and venerable, distinguished independent scholars, both those who identified with the secular traditions of the left and those who identified with the religious and nationalist traditions of the right. Michnik's presence at these events indicated their shared political and cultural character, which he came to see as a common ground for the transformation of the communist regime.

In the 1970s Michnik argued strongly for two complementary positions: first, that the only possible way to transform the totalitarian order fundamentally was through reform from below; and second, that all those seeking such transformation should recognize their common democratic commitments as more important than their political, cultural, or religious differences. By reform from below he meant a strategy of real and symbolic secession from the existing order. People should act as if they lived in a free society, and in the process they would constitute moments and places for a free existence. They should speak primarily to one another, not to their political overlords, expressing their differences but with mutual respect. In this way, at least some aspects of an independent social existence would be created.

In fact, this is what occurred on the Lublin streets, at the officially accepted cultural adaptation of *The Master and the Margarita*, and at the illegal poetry reading. This kind of activity later exploded in Poland, and it had repercussions throughout the Soviet bloc, from the pope's visit in 1979 to the strikes of August 1980, which culminated in the creation of Solidarity. Although the implications of critical cultural life—free but hidden from the general public (whether officially accepted or not) and in so-called *samizdat* publishing—were not fully appreciated before the fall of 1989, both communists and anticommunists knew that the pope's visit and the rise of Solidarity were historic events with complications for the whole world. Of course, they may not have realized at the time that it was the beginning of the end of the postwar period.

Nevertheless, the explosion of religious belief, ceremony, and demonstration in an officially atheist state and bloc, and the open constitution of an independent social movement and politics in a highly controlled political order, were understood to be of major significance, and people of many different political stripes in the West expressed admiration. With it came a clear sense that the Soviets would have to react. Some ideological anticommunists in the West even seemed to hope for a Soviet invasion, in order to prove that communism was unreformable. Indeed, Soviet patience seemed to be challenged. The Soviets did engage in threatening troop movements and naval maneuvers, and the escalation from threat to action was a course well known to the authors of and enforcers of the Brezhnev Doctrine. Jaruzelski's declaration of martial law put an end to the first period of legalized Solidarity. Liberal Polish communists, who were martial law's primary instigators, claimed that it was a last-ditch effort to maintain Polish national independence.

It was against this background of repression that my university, The New School for Social Research, granted Adam Michnik an honorary doctorate, along with five other human-rights activists from around the world, as a way of commemorating the fiftieth anniversary of The New School's Graduate Faculty. Founded in 1933 as the University in Exile, it was made up of scholars forced to flee Hitler's oppression. At the time of the ceremony Michnik was in jail, victim of a harsh repression, Jaruzelski's attempt to "normalize" Polish life. Czesław Miłosz, the Polish Nobel laureate, accepted Michnik's degree and read a moving letter from Michnik to General Kiszczak, Poland's minister of internal affairs, in which he condemned the general's offering him a comfortable exile instead of continued imprisonment with a chance to defend himself in an open courtroom:

> To admit one's disregard for the law so openly, one would have to be a fool. To offer a man who has been held in prison for two years the Côte d'Azur in exchange for his moral suicide, one would have to be a swine. To believe that I could accept such a proposal is to imagine that everyone is a police collaborator.

In 1984, Michnik was out of prison as part of a general amnesty.

He had not been released but had been forcibly evicted from his prison cell, and he was demanding the right to disprove the charges against him. He wanted to use the occasion of his trial to put the regime on trial. But the regime understood his purpose and had given him and his Solidarity colleagues their "freedom."

This freedom presented real problems. Open Solidarity had been destroyed as a mass social movement. The population was dispirited. Social and economic life was proceeding normally under the Communist Party's and the military's domination, and there did not seem to be much the union leadership or intellectual opposition could do. But Michnik was resolute in his message: continue to act as if Poland were a free society.

At this time, I met Michnik again. I was in Poland as part of a New School delegation to present him with his honorary degree. A week after the illegal ceremony, held in Edward Lipiński's apartment (without lights, thanks to the authorities, who had cut off the electricity), Adam and I became friends and coconspirators. The week we spent together taught me a great deal about the texture of an extraordinary social movement, the unusual sensibilities of a political hero, and the fundamental force that led to the downfall of communism.

In December 1984, I went to Warsaw with Jonathan Fanton, the president of The New School, Adrian DeWind, a member of our board of trustees, and DeWind's wife, Joan, to present Michnik with his degree. We traveled via West Berlin, where a celebration was held honoring the fiftieth anniversary of the University in Exile. But I was not in Berlin primarily to enjoy the occasion. Rather, I was there to pursue a moral and historical continuity. As a relatively junior member of the faculty, I had been asked to go to Berlin only as a stopover on the way to Warsaw, an example of a present-day totalitarian order. President Fanton and I had planned that I would go ahead to Poland before the others, to try to iron out the details of the formal activities there.

It was snowing when I got to Warsaw. My arrangements had been made through a number of intermediaries, including some old friends and contacts at Helsinki Watch in New York, and I had been given instructions to call a Polish scholar, Professor Jan Kielankowski. But since it was a time of martial law and direct contact was difficult, I wasn't certain if he would know about me or about the planned ceremony for Michnik. Although my close and old friend Roman Stachyra had taken me to his apartment, where he had a telephone, my instructions were to make all arrangements from public pay phones, and so, bundled up against the snow, I went out with Roman to find a public phone.

To my relief, the professor was in the first time I called, and he seemed to be expecting me. He appeared glad to hear from me, and suggested that I come right over. I agreed, found a taxi, and, with my friend, drove to a small street of elegant prewar apartments. Again following instructions, we did not leave the taxi in front of the exact address, but instead got out in the snow to look for Number 4B Opoczyńska Street. As we were searching, we saw a man of medium height in a ski parka turning in to what seemed to be the address we needed. I wondered momentarily whether this adventure would end before it started.

When the man opened the door for us, though, I was able to take a closer look, and I recognized Adam Michnik. He greeted us warmly and introduced himself. I realized very quickly that all plans were indeed in place. A major event was scheduled; all in opposition circles knew about it—as, surely, did the authorities. An invitation to Lipiński's apartment for the ceremony was highly sought after. The symbolic meaning of the event was widely appreciated.

I had met Adam briefly once before this meeting, on December 9, 1984, when we had simply exchanged pleasantries. But on that day we began what has become a sustained conversation. We walked up to the third-floor apartment, and Adam sincerely thanked me and The New School for the honor of the degree. I was surprised by his enthusiasm. I knew that American universities bestowed honorary doctorates rather freely. To be sure, his commemorated the fiftieth anniversary of a political-academic enterprise of particular importance—but still. I explained to him that to my mind, it was he who honored us by accepting the degree more than we who honored him.

We had reached Kielankowski's apartment. The professor was a man in his late sixties, and I was struck by the way Adam interacted with him. In Poland's somewhat old-fashioned society, even if two people were friends and used the informal "you," the conventional pattern of deference and demeanor required that the distinguished, elderly gentleman lead the conversation with a guest. But part of Adam's charm and authority was (and is) that he regularly transgressed such conventions.

Adam boisterously requested cognac for everybody so that he could toast The New School, and then explained why the degree was important to him. For him personally, it meant recognition as a scholar. It had hurt to be expelled from the university in the middle of his studies in history, so the academic legitimacy of the doctorate was especially appreciated. (At the time I viewed this statement with skepticism. It seemed to have been made to fulfill the requirements of decorum. But later I realized that Adam was being deeply sincere.) His second reason was more immediately convincing. Political, cultural, and intellectual opposition to totalitarianism was a lonely and isolating activity. Although the Poles had had the eyes of the world upon them in 1980 and 1981, Michnik and his colleagues were well aware of the short attention span of the popular media and their audience. Probably they were inflating the importance of Western recognition and support, but it did help sustain their activities.

In 1984 and 1985, remember, this point had particular significance. Jaruzelski seemed to be a political winner. Solidarity's activities were severely limited. Some economic reforms were in place. The West—especially West Germany—interpreted the policed order as social peace. The Polish populace was largely overwhelmed. Ordinary people felt that they could do little else but survive the system. A major theoretical and practical project for many intellectuals was to account for the "mistakes" of the Solidarity period. Some pessimists sank into hopelessness. Others argued about strategic mistakes: not setting up a contingency plan in case of a crackdown, for example, had been a crucial error. Still others wanted to rethink the general form of opposition, as extreme nationalist and Catholic positions gained favor. The very idea of building political opposition around a trade union movement was losing its appeal. Various forms of elitist programs, some promoting a more resolute anticommunism, others favoring a more subtle compromise with the communists, were formulated in the opposition press.

Michnik, who had spent most of the martial-law period in jail, was not subjected to such strong swings in mood and judgment. In prison, isolated from the pressures of daily involvement in the struggle, he was free to write letters and books in support of his theory that if citizens acted together *as if* they lived in a free society, a free society would be constituted. The award to Michnik was an important affirmation of this position, greatly appreciated not only by its recipient, but by his friends and admirers.

During that week, I met many of those friends and admirers: people who had been involved in the Solidarity underground and Michnik's journal *Krytyka*, others at the university and the institutes of the Academy of Science, and others in official and unofficial journalism. They all respected Adam for his intelligence, bravery, and conviction. Although some warned me that he was out of touch with the most recent developments because of his imprisonment, others viewed this as his great advantage. Adam was (and is) a strong personality, and even some who admired him didn't particularly like him. His humor and irony were subtle, and could be hard to take. His steadfastness could be overwhelming. His complicated approach to morality and politics convinced some and repelled others.

By the same token, many seemed to like him a great deal, even when they strongly disagreed with him. He seemed to bring together people of widely different experiences and sensibilities—not so that they could come to agree with each other, but just so that they could meet each other. I base such judgments on the various people I met through Adam, either directly or indirectly. The most famous included Lech Wałęsa and Tadeusz Mazowiecki. Less famous were people in almost every occupation and region of Poland. In the mid-1980s, the striking thing about these people was that they represented the real Polish society (in the Platonic sense). The so-called "actually existing socialist Poland" was ordered by the military and the Party's repressive apparatus. Economic rewards were doled out through the commands and statutes of Jaruzelski's party-state and geopolitically confirmed by the Soviet Union. But the self-determined Polish society, with all its conflicts and complexities, was represented in various "underground" activities.

The Michnik degree ceremony was held in the apartment of the late Edward Lipiński. The economist, a grand old man of the secular opposition and a lifelong socialist, then ninety-six years old, had provided his lavish home with a private art collection that rivaled many national museums. The setting served as a kind of Free Warsaw Kennedy Center. Afterward, we visited the monuments of oppositionist martyrdom: a statue to the heroes of the Warsaw Ghetto Uprising, and the tombstone of the Solidarity priest Jerzy Popiełuszko. Then we went to an odd "state dinner" at a hotel restaurant. Attending were my New School colleagues, as well as Michnik and his future wife, Basia Szwedowska; Michael Kaufman, the *New York Times* correspondent; Jacek Kuroń; and Bronisław Geremek. Kaufman and I served as linguistic and political-cultural translators.

At this dinner it was most obvious to Fanton and the DeWinds, my New School colleagues, that they were meeting with people who, in any normal situation, would be leaders of their country. And in fact, six years later, with the first semblance of a free election in Poland in sixty years, they were all elected to Parliament. In addition, Kuroń became one of the most important ministers in the first Solidarity government, minister of labor and social welfare. Geremek became the head of the Solidarity caucus in Parliament, and Michnik became the editor of the major newspaper.

All of these meetings displayed an apparently normal but in fact deeply layered social structure, significantly distorted by the absurdities of totalitarian political life. Lipiński's apartment was lavish because, as a former communist, he had once dutifully served the powers of the "bright and happy future." The Ghetto monument was not a normal stopover for official visits, and it wasn't usually considered in oppositional circles. But Michnik and Kaufman, both sons of Jewish communists who were once imprisoned in the same cell during the prewar period, had decided jointly to bring our New York delegation to this largely ignored Warsaw site. And the martyr Popiełuszko had been assassinated not by some foreign enemy, or an oppressive order from the distant past, but by the then-ruling regime. Our "state dinner" was an open act of oppositional display against that regime, noted by all in the hotel restaurant, from the waiter, to some visiting foreign dignitaries from Western Europe, to the secret police, who were no doubt observing.

• • •

After my colleagues left Warsaw, Michnik and I began a serious political and theoretical discussion, one outgrowth of which was my book
Beyond Glasnost. We talked about his letter in support of the struggle
of Chilean copper workers against Pinochet's dictatorship. In some
opposition circles, this letter, written from prison, aroused controversy. For the most committed anticommunists, it was a fundamental
mistake to undermine a good anticommunist like Pinochet. Adam's
firm response was, "Hitler was also an anticommunist." We talked
about the notion of totalitarianism, and about a thinker we both
highly admired, Hannah Arendt. I explained my critique of totalitarianism as a model of society. He explained his conviction that the
notion of "totalitarianism" still properly characterized Polish social
existence.

I learned that in prison Michnik wrote; out of prison, he organized.
He took me to the Warsaw Cardiac Hospital to visit Jan Józef Lipski,
a leading oppositionist and historian and author of the most extensive
history of Poland's democratic opposition of the 1970s. Because of a
serious heart condition, Lipski hadn't been able to attend the ceremony. We talked about interwar Polish history. I learned that for
Lipski, the difference between martial law and the general amnesty
was that after the amnesty there were no longer two soldiers posted
outside his hospital room.

When we left the hospital, while walking about the streets of
Warsaw, Adam suggested we organize an international seminar on the
topic of democracy, with centers in Warsaw, Prague, Budapest, and
New York. And these centers actually came into existence. They were
places where people talked about the meaning of totalitarianism, the
writings of Hannah Arendt, and the problems of democratization in
Latin America and their parallels with democratization in Eastern and
Central Europe. Between 1984 and 1989 they existed clandestinely,
but now, after the fall, they exist in all of the capitals of Eastern and
Central Europe. Many of the former underground participants in
Budapest and Warsaw are leaders of the new democracies.

The discussions of those earlier democracy seminars, like much of
the old oppositionist culture, had antipartisan discourse as their first
political principle. Ideologies of the left and right seemed to be part of
the political problem, not bases for democratic life. That position

brought together those of the traditional left and right and those of secular and religious orientation, both in the seminars and in the politics of the democratic opposition and Solidarity. When it was initially formulated, the notion of acting as if one lived in a free society had narrow appeal. It was the intellectual and practical exercise of a relatively small circle of oppositionists. The pope's visit, and legal Solidarity, changed all that. Six months after our week of conversation, when I attempted to visit Michnik again, I realized that the change had persisted despite years of systematic repression.

Michnik was on trial in Gdańsk for a capital crime, along with Bogdan Lis and Władysław Frasyniuk. Supposedly, a taped conversation in a private apartment among former leaders of the Solidarity movement indicated sedition. From his jail cell, Adam issued an open letter to friends of human rights in the West, asking them to come and observe the (il)legal proceedings. His intention was to put the regime itself on trial. In the meantime, through clandestine channels, he asked me to come to Gdańsk.

When I received Michnik's note, I immediately went about the business of trying to arrange a trip to Poland, though I was doubtful whether the Polish government would issue me a visa, in view of my very public and recent association with Michnik, and my scholarly writing about the political and cultural opposition. Five weeks after submitting a visa application, I went to the Polish consulate in New York to see about it. On that very day, Michnik's open letter was published on the op-ed page of the *New York Times*. I felt like a character in an absurdist play. There I was, reading a Western publication with strong anti-Polish propaganda calling for antisocialist agitation (from the point of view of the Polish authorities), and attempting to engage in the agitation myself by traveling to Poland. I was sure the woman in the caged visa window would halt the performance and stop the play. But she didn't. She issued me a visa.

The flight was uneventful, but Polish passport control at the Warsaw airport heightened my sense of absurdity. When the line I was in was moving particularly slowly, the woman in front of me turned to her colleague and exclaimed in exasperation, "Who do they think we are, Adam Michnik?" I knew I had to make this journey, but I had no idea what it would bring.

In New York a visiting Polish scholar, Aldona Jawłowska, had made arrangements with Janka Jankowska to pick me up at the Warsaw airport. Jankowska, who produced underground audio tapes for Solidarity, briefed me at her apartment and then arranged for her husband to take me to Warsaw's Central Station for a train to Gdańsk. Since seat reservations were necessary, though nonexistent, I sat in a compartment reserved for the military but occupied by people who, like me, had tipped the conductor. There was some uncertainty about whether we would be kicked off the train midway to Gdańsk. Our conversation was limited to speculation about that possibility, and marvelings about my Polish linguistic ability. (My Polish, actually, was quite rusty, but whenever a foreigner without Polish ancestry speaks even rudimentary Polish, it is cause for wonder.) I learned later that one of my fellow passengers knew exactly who I was and what I was doing; but, as an activist in the Solidarity underground, she did not reveal herself to me.

We got to Gdańsk at night, in the rain. Jankowska had given me an address in the Old City, the apartment of Joanna Wojciechowicz, and after leaving the railroad station I searched for it on foot. The streets seemed deserted, and I hadn't packed an umbrella. When I finally arrived at my destination, cold and wet, I found to my surprise that Wojciechowicz was having a birthday party. The most distinguished guest was Andrzej Gwiazda, one of Lech Wałęsa's major opponents for union leadership in 1980 and 1981.

Ten minutes after my arrival, the phone rang. The call was from a group of Solidarity activists who were monitoring police activity. "Whoever just walked into the apartment is being followed by the police." I realized that both the Polish authorities and my friends were expecting my visit.

Five minutes after that, Michnik's fiancée, Basia Szwedowska, called, insisting that I, as Adam's close friend, stay with her in the neighboring city of Sopot. I agreed at once. Andrzej Gwiazda went out with me onto the rainy street and helped me to find a taxi for the short trip to Sopot, where I stayed with Basia for the duration of my ten-day visit.

Adam's trial was scheduled to begin the day I arrived. I attempted to observe the trial but was denied entrance, met Adam's and Basia's friends and supporters, corresponded with Adam, and spent time with his lawyers. I was overwhelmed by the complexity of the social relationships that fortified the activities of Poland's "natural political authorities." These extended from the shipyard workers on the street who carefully watched the goings-on outside the courthouse to the workers who kept up and protected the Solidarity monument commemorating the martyrdom of workers who died during the first shipyard strike in December 1970, to the lawyers who not only defended Adam in the way he required—by providing him a platform from which to accuse the regime—but also tended to his primary concern, bringing him the books and papers he needed for his writings. There were renowned Catholic priests like Father Henryk Jankowski who publicly ministered to the needs of Lech Wałęsa and his comrades, as well as lay Catholic congregants who carefully documented the case of each political prisoner and distributed food, clothing, and medicine to the families of the politically persecuted. All were essential, in what amounted to the support of civil society for its "natural political authorities." Ordinary steelworkers and architects, university professors and businessmen, teachers and students, I observed making their own contributions, maintaining an independent network of information and support.

During this visit, when I was forced to observe Michnik from the distance created by his incarceration, I came face to face with his bravery; but what I found most remarkable was the way his heroism was repeated by many less visible people, who had turned the "as if" civil society into a fully self-constituted civil order. This was a period of Solidarity's lowest ebb, with the movement in great danger of succumbing to pessimism, but it was also a time of the great promise and import of an independent civil society. My Polish friends and acquaintances had created a network of interaction that was functioning amazingly well, despite the overwhelming power and resources of a modern tyrannical state. Here, certainly, was a social force to be reckoned with. A well-developed and extensive independent civil society was flourishing right under the noses of the martial-law authorities.

Then and there I became convinced that the days of Marxist totalitarianism were numbered, both in Poland and in the entire Soviet bloc. I didn't realize, of course, how suddenly the fall would come.

But it was in May 1985 that I began to understand what in retrospect should have been obvious: the unpopular and illegitimate political orders of Eastern Europe would some day come to an end.

Michnik's trial was postponed and rescheduled. I stayed around until it resumed and tried again to get in, but without success. I finally left for Warsaw, where I came to an agreement with Geremek about the continuation of the democracy seminars in Adam's absence. Although Adam sat in jail for a few more years, his notion that a civil society should function apart from the state continued to flourish; and in the end, society won the battle against the party-state, not only in Poland but throughout the region.

In the West, we observed the rapidity of the victory with amazement. Eastern and Central Europeans experienced the change with amazement as well, but for them, especially after the fact, it may not have seemed so rapid. Generations were lost. The "God that failed" destroyed human life and natural resources to a degree that is only now becoming apparent to them and to us. The worldwide euphoria of the fall of 1989 has been followed by a pessimistic malaise; to my mind, overly pessimistic. I recall that the worst of times, the mid-1980s, was a prelude to the best of times, the fall of '89. While there were and are many problems in postcommunist Europe, the sometimes half-hidden resources for democratic change should not be overlooked. The most independent of these is the same sort of autonomous social action that provided the grounds for the fall of communism in the first place.

As in the totalitarian period, in the postcommunist era, the central issue is coming together and articulating difference. The people who supported Michnik, and for whom he attempted to speak, were not of one mind. They were secularists and devout Catholics, socialists and laissez-faire liberals, from different factions of the Solidarity movement. Yet, they formed an independent social movement in common, without suppressing or denying their differences. This they must continue to do, and it is a problem both for them and for us. Serious political reflection is in order. Many experts—some instant, some long seasoned—explain why democracy can't be established in the "other Europe." Nationalist ghosts haunt the region. Tolerance and liberalism are little known. Economic breakdown and impoverishment provide little room for political experimentation or mistakes. Yet, I believe, such diagnoses can work as self-fulfilling prophecies. Just as acting as if one lived in a free civil society helped constitute a free civil order, if we define democratic prospects as impossible, they in fact may become an impossibility. I am convinced that we need to judge the post-totalitarian situation with a careful consideration of its political promise. To this we now turn.

CHAPTER 2

Post-Totalitarian Politics

W
e are experiencing major changes in global and everyday politics. The Soviet bloc is disintegrating, while a broader Europe is reemerging and integrating, apparently with only economic weakness distinguishing, for example, Hungary and Poland from their Western European neighbors. But the fall of communism, and of anticommunism as well, has even more profound implications. We are also experiencing frontal challenges to our conventional understandings of political and societal life, and these challenges must be recognized and addressed. In Eastern and Central Europe, the intellectual oppositionists had to break with intellectual convention in order to get on with their political activities. Now, with their victory, their course of action presents a series of broad challenges. Are there any longer significant differences between left and right, and between socialism and capitalism? Is Marxism just another intellectual tradition—properly alive in the academy and even more

properly dying in the political realm? Recent events force them—and us as well—to face such questions. We will not and should not agree on the answers, but we must discuss our differences. They constitute a new political culture that doesn't fit into the easy categories that seemed viable to most people just a few years ago.

Consider a Polish joke, not of the ethnic American kind, but of the political Polish kind, really more aphorism than joke:

> *Question:* How can you now tell the difference between a leftist and a rightist? *Answer:* The leftist will maintain that the distinctions between left and right no longer make sense, whereas the rightist will maintain that they do.

We can interpret this joke in at least two ways. First, it suggests a rightist center of gravity in Polish political life. The left hides its true political colors, while those on the right proudly display theirs. Yet the joke was told to me by Kostek Gebert who, under the pseudonym of Dawid Warszawski, published clearly leftist commentaries in the post-Solidarity martial-law period. His is a respected voice of the beleaguered Polish democratic left. Why was he telling this joke? It suggests a second post-totalitarian interpretation, pointing to self-deprecation as a prelude to empowerment.

Gebert told me the joke to underscore that, contrary to prevailing wisdom, the political project of the left is very much alive (or soon will be) in Poland. He pointed out that the right openly identifies the nation with the church and emphasizes national independence as the primary political good; while the left, which seeks to minimize the value of the left-right opposition, is more minimalist. Its major goal has been negative, in other words, anti-totalitarian. It has renounced much of its political legacy—communism, statist economics, and Marxism.

In the 1960s in Poland and throughout Eastern Europe, the still vibrant critical left attempted to formulate a revitalized theory, Marxist humanism, and practice "socialism with a human face." Both the theory, in its varieties, and the practice, attempted to address (within the fundamental contours of the existing system) the problems of stagnating economies and societies. Attempts were made to introduce market mechanisms into the economy, to disengage and support socialist ideals within the context of the prevailing communist (more precisely, Stalinist) order, and to use Marxism as a critical guide. Escalating repression put an end to this effort. In Poland sucessive waves of political repression and social, cultural, and economic ineffectiveness extinguished any semblance of a loyal opposition. In 1968, the Party crackdown on student politics, which led to an antiliberal, anti-Semitic campaign, promoted an identification of communism with reactionary views. In 1970, 1976, and 1980, aggressive workers' strikes starkly revealed that the workers themselves were very much against the proletarian state. The developing cooperation between secular and religious forces, and between workers and often privileged intellectuals, suggested that class analysis concealed more than it revealed about the prevailing situation and about what was to be done. Therefore the left, led by Michnik, has identified its concern for democracy and political independence with rightist anticommunism, declaring that the diverse groups of the noncommunist polity have more things in common than they do differences.

The right appropriately derides this view, as does, generally, the Western left. The position, although it has historical grounding, seems to have little substance beyond the fact that the groups share a stance of opposition. It provides little guidance, let alone a blueprint for future action. It does not address the significant issues of the post-totalitarian era concerning economic reforms along with political, social, and cultural values. The right takes positions. Those on the left do not.

Or, more precisely, they *did* not. For Gebert's joke, told in 1988— before the fall of 1989, before the round table, before the elections and the rapid disintegration of the communist regime in Poland and then throughout Eastern and Central Europe—clearly points to new political realities. The competing claims of democracy and nationalism must be mediated. The concerns for economic efficiency and social justice must be balanced. The opposing sensibilities of religious revelation and secular ethics must be made compatible. On these, as on many other issues, there are responsible leftist and rightist positions.

But what has this to do with socialism and capitalism? On this question the European post-totalitarian polities (previously known as the satellite nations, or existing socialist or Soviet-type societies) reveal striking differences. In Poland and, I believe, to a lesser extent in

Hungary, positive talk about socialism seems silly. Socialism as a political-economic system is discredited. What people want is "not socialism." There is a robust romance with the free market, a true love for the market of the purest kind—the Thatcherite variety. People imagine that market rationality will ultimately solve all significant social problems, from urban decay to consumer shortages. The major concern, for those with liberal, laissez-faire economic convictions, is how can the populace—who will certainly suffer during a period of transformation from plan to market—come to accept the changes?

Some propose apocalyptic scenarios. They argue that the nation must accept market rationalization or descend to disaster. Others, with the same script in mind, ominously speak of a need for a strong authority to impose market discipline on a possibly resistant population. (In the Soviet Union, reforming authoritarians have supported Gorbachev for this role.) But still others move away from such extremist visions of market economics and try to reconcile their commitments to market rationality with democratic principles. One of the prominent proponents of this view, Jacek Kuroń, Solidarity's first minister of labor, argues that the way to get public support for the necessary changes is to disassociate the delivery of social services from the workplace. (In the People's Republics, subsidized housing, meals, vacations, medical care, and so forth, emanated from the place of employment.) A viable economic system must not be developed without an adequate system of social welfare.

This is not only the way to achieve worker discipline; it is, as well, the way to maintain democratic commitment along with economic reform. Workers must have a sense that they have a stake in a sound economic future. If they lose their subsidized, though mediocre, housing and food, free medical and child care, and higher education; and if they risk unemployment in order to contribute to a more robust gross national product and a better balance of payments without any foreseeable personal benefits, they will resist, as they can do so well. Their resistance could slow down recovery or kill economic reforms. And if the economic reformers and democratic politicians insist that the only future is one that links democracy with the suffering of workers, then the very social movement that brought democracy into being may bring it down.

But this dénouement is not inevitable. There is a good chance that the normal political contestation now emerging will lead to significant and necessary controls on market activity, which will promote a social-democratic transition. The free-market liberals, of course, retort that such a system will overwhelm the economy and prevent change.

It is difficult if not impossible to appraise the economic cogency of each position, though on political grounds I have a clear preference. What most intrigues me as a sociologist of political culture is that in this debate a distinction between left and right is again beginning to emerge in the "other Europe." The left places special emphasis on social justice and democracy, the right on nation, social discipline, and efficiency. There are hopeful and unhopeful varieties of both leftist and rightist positions: both sides have authoritarian and democratic wings. The authoritarian liberals follow what might be called the Chilean model, in which it is understood that the nation is not yet ready for the responsibilities of democracy. It must first be disciplined. In the name of efficiency, national pride, and survival, the people must be quieted and schooled (especially in Poland, where they have developed such impressive instruments of resistance). On the other end of the political spectrum, there is an authoritarian populism. In Poland, Alfred Miodowicz, the leader of the union established to replace Solidarity by Jaruzelski's junta, promised militancy in the face of economic reforms. Reason was not part of his repertoire, only impossible promises and demands. Aligned as he was with Party hardliners, this former Politburo member's project seemed to resemble a leftist Peronism, with authoritarian appeals made in the name of the masses. It should be emphasized that his chances of success were always slim.

The distinction between left and right appears in a variety of constantly shifting forms all around the Eastern bloc. In Czechoslovakia and East Germany, just after their transformations, an open espousal of socialist convictions apparently still had meaning for the population. Yet things changed rapidly. In Germany, because of official corruption, a process of radical disillusionment led to the widespread support for integration into West Germany. In Czechoslovakia, in contrast to Poland, only a small proportion of the population at first sought a privatization of the economy. More than 90 percent wanted either a mixed or a planned economy just after the Velvet Revolution.

While support for the free market then increased, it was consciously balanced with concern for social welfare.

It seems to me that both the Western left and social scientists in general must ask: What is socialism in all this? Is it a project of a planned economy, or a mixed economy, or, following Kuroń's suggestions, a privatized economy in a system of government that attempts to address democracy as a balance of self-rule, economic rationality, and social justice? As an aspiration, with the diverse experience of Eastern and Central Europe in mind, socialism may be any of these. Does it, then, mean anything in particular? And, even if so, how is it distinguished from this thing we call capitalism?

There are two ways to answer these questions. One would be to roll up our theoretical sleeves, perhaps with *Das Kapital* in hand, and carefully arrive at new theoretical distinctions. We could posit new ways of understanding social relations, not only concerning the practical and empirical relations between market and plan, the economy and the state, but also concerning the normative dimensions of these relationships, for example, between the ideals of socialism and perhaps even those of capitalism. Alternatively, we can—and they do—move against ideology. Put frankly, we can resign from "isms," welcome and support a new end to ideology of all kinds.

On this issue, I believe, there is a consensus in the post-totalitarian orders of Central Europe (at least among those who are gaining authority and power). A totalitarian culture—with ideological politics, scientistic utopias, and complete resolutions to complex societal problems—is rejected. Václav Havel, the Czech dramatist, political theorist, former leader of the democratic opposition, and president of Czechoslovakia, most poetically characterized this rejection and its implications when in the context of totalitarian control it was still only a dream. In his classic essay "The Power of the Powerless," written in 1978, Havel told the story of the manager of a fruit and vegetable store who placed in his window the slogan "Workers of the World, Unite!" By analyzing why the greengrocer put the slogan in his window, and what would happen to him if he took it down, Havel phenomenologically revealed the complex basis of totalitarian control. He showed how the official language and its ideology penetrated everyday life, and how the subjects of totalitarian repression constituted that repression. He argued that ordinary citizens, by complying with the totalitarian system and playing the roles the authorities demanded, not only survived the system but produced it. As Havel put it,

> Individuals need not believe all these mystifications, but they must behave as though they did, or they must at least tolerate them in silence, or get along well with those who work with them. For this reason, however, they must *live within a lie*. They need not accept the lie. It is enough for them to have accepted their life with it and in it. For by this very fact, individuals confirm the system, fulfill the system, make the system, *are* the system.

With such insights in mind, Havel called upon people to "live in truth," independent of the official lies. When geopolitics made such action possible, the world changed.

The rapid disintegration of the communist regimes and parties and the collapse of totalitarian control are understandable from this perspective. Ordinary people knew they were living a lie and would have sought an alternative, but they deemed the effort so unlikely to succeed that they didn't try. The active search for alternatives was reserved for those at the political and cultural fringes. But when alternatives presented themselves, a broad cross-section of the population acted "in truth," that is, without resort to the official ideological script. The cynical articulation of official culture, backed by force, was a kind of legitimation of disbelief. People pretended to believe the lie, and this pretense was politically consequential. Such a political culture, with force defining reason, was at the very center of totalitarianism and its reproduction. Now different political cultures, democratic and otherwise, are emerging while old slogans, phrases, and key words are rejected, including socialism. During the course of the events of 1989, Havel wrote,

> Gorbachev wants to save Socialism with the market and free speech. . . . Li Peng saves Socialism by massacring students and Ceaucescu by rolling a bulldozer across his country. It is always worthwhile to mistrust words. . . . You spoil less than by giving them excessive confidence.

In the matter of the dilemma concerning capitalism and socialism, Havel's position suggests to me (though not I suspect to all partisans of socialism or capitalism) a clear course of action. The empirical and historical problems of understanding the distinctive relations between market and plan, economy and state, may be named "capitalist" and "socialist" perhaps as ideal types in the Weberian sense, but certainly not as ideals in the political-normative sense. As the latter sort of ideals, they are too intimately implicated in modern horror, and too remotely or ambiguously related to that which still does distinguish the political left from the political right. If the rise and the fall of communism tell us anything, it is that socialism is not the magic wand that solves the problems of social injustice, human indignity, environmental destruction, and so forth. Indeed, it has in many instances made matters much worse. And Marxism, especially of the Leninist variety, has been a political abomination.

This is the starting point of a post-totalitarian politics, but what follows is quite uncertain. The politics of civil society began with a vision of society against the state. This vision necessarily involved a conscious distancing from the legacies of the Manichaean battles that dominated twentieth-century politics: the free versus the totalitarian world; the progressive forces against the reactionary forces. In the democratic oppositions in Poland, Czechoslovakia, and Hungary, people like Michnik, Havel, and György Bence (the three people Michnik and I agreed would initiate the democracy seminar of 1984) saw as their major task the separation of social and cultural life from totalitarian definitions. In this sense, they sought a normal civilized society.

To listeners in the West with critical sensibilities, such declarations sounded naïve. What was normal about Western capitalism? Why was this particular historical configuration, in which the pursuit of the good society seemed to have been reduced to the pursuit of consumer goods, granted universality? Clearly, from the point of view of such questioners, the Eastern and Central European writers and activists were confusing their own noble anti-totalitarian struggle with a more generalized anti-ideological struggle. But because a key aspect of totalitarianism was and is ideology, the retreat of totalitarianism demanded a more general reconsideration of the place of ideology in contemporary social and political life.

In my view, it is not that capitalism has buried socialism (to echo Khrushchev's famous boast that they would "bury" us). Rather, the ideological contrast between capitalism and socialism as totally opposed systems must be abandoned, no matter which side one is on. We may try to force the emerging left and right in post-totalitarian politics into the ideologically constructed boxes of socialism and capitalism, only to discover that in the end, in Eastern Europe, they are *all* capitalists—to the dismay of the Western left and the joy of the right. But this view overlooks the most important implication of the fall of 1989, the chance to avoid ideological politics.

What does the term "capitalism" mean? Some use it to identify all modern political economies of Western Europe, including Sweden, Germany, and England. Others want to reserve the term "socialism" for Sweden, or Sweden and Germany, or (in contrast with the U.S. economic system) Sweden, Germany, and England (with its socialized medicine and much more extensive welfare system). But if we take the fall of communism seriously, we cast Marxist teleology into strong doubt. We realize that political-economic debates concern the exchange of views about the way to order modern economic life so as best to implement various conceptions of economic and social efficiency and justice. The telling problem is how to assess the relative roles of the state, the market, and the civil society (which is not identical to the "state" in totalitarian practice, or the "market" as conceived by capitalist ideologues).

The democratic oppositionists in Central Europe revealed the theoretical and practical import of civil nonstate and noneconomic life in contemporary affairs. In doing so, they highlighted themes that have long been central in political and sociological inquiry, themes most elegantly addressed by Alexis de Tocqueville in the nineteenth century and Hannah Arendt in our own times. Michnik and Havel continue this great tradition. They have significantly helped to reawaken interest in this intellectual tradition not only among their own compatriots but also among Western observers. Here, too, escape from ideological certitudes is a pressing matter. For us, democratic critique then becomes a possibility. For them, a clear view of the importance of autonomous civil society is necessary for the formation of a democracy. Ideology must be overcome.

CHAPTER 3

Ideology Ends Again

I n November 1988, I was a courier of sorts between Adam Michnik and Václav Havel. After spending a few days in Warsaw, which included observing Adam's presentation of a paper to the democracy seminar on the relations between the Polish secular and religious traditions, I traveled to Czechoslovakia with Jonathan Fanton, president of The New School for Social Research, and Ira Katznelson, the distinguished political scientist and dean of its Graduate Faculty. We hoped to establish a firm relationship with the Czechoslovak opposition and initiate a democracy seminar in Prague. Following Michnik's original vision, I hoped to talk about it directly with Havel.

Since the Polish independent press had recently published a collection of Havel's essays, Michnik inscribed a copy for Havel, suggesting that presenting this volume would be a fitting way for me to introduce myself. With the same purpose in mind, I also carried page proofs of my own *Beyond Glasnost* to give to him. Remember that at the time Havel was not a head of state, but a freewheeling and courageous oppositionist. He was also a serious (absurdist) playwright.

Armed with these gifts, we arrived in Prague and were met there by Steven Lukes, the English social philosopher, and his old and close friend Alena Hromádková. In the 1970s and 1980s, this couple had helped bridge Czech and English scholarship. Hromádková is a conservative Catholic, basing her intense dissident activities on the traditions of her family and her church. Lukes is a social democrat, a neo-Marxist of sorts, who had engaged himself in Czech dissident affairs without abandoning his leftist orientation.

As it happened, when we got to Prague Havel was at his country house writing a new play, so Hromádková took it upon herself to introduce us to the workings of the Czechoslovak democratic opposition. We met a number of embattled oppositionists. I found their situation to be remarkably different from that of my Polish friends, who enjoyed broad-based and open societal support. The Czechs, in contrast, were a close-knit group feared by and closely watched by the authorities and isolated from the majority of the atomized general population. Nonetheless, they had created a miniature "as if" civil society. Now Havel is president, and his associates, such as Petr Pithart and Radim Palous, hold positions of considerable authority (prime minister of the Czech Republic, rector of Charles University)—but in 1988, they were maintaining an impressive and vibrant intellectual life. They were "living in truth," like Havel's greengrocer.

I had an opportunity to observe the implications of this kind of life in action and, to my surprise, briefly become a part of it. The day after our arrival, we attended one of Prague's famous "apartment seminars." It was conducted by Pavel Bratinka, a conservative political thinker as well as an old friend of Lukes, who had organized a public discussion on Lukes' writings on politics and ethics. Lukes himself had just published a book on *Marxism and Morality*, so the seminar discussion was centered on the possibility of resistance to a tyrannical order and the resulting moral issues. The chief question was a classic utilitarian one: because the price of resistance of any visible sort was not only the loss of career and livelihood but dimmed future prospects for family and relatives, no rational person should engage in such activity, even if the result was highly desirable.

In the language of contemporary theories of rational choice, this was a variation of the so-called "free rider question." The theory suggests that it is not rational to vote, for instance, because one vote will not decide an election. It is unnecessary and irrational to join a social movement, trade union, or political party if it has costs, because ultimately one person's participation will not change results. It is better to benefit without costs. Many of the seminar participants enthusiastically endorsed this sort of view with its strong individualistic bias, even though it didn't apply to themselves. They didn't want to have overly high expectations of ordinary people. They felt that it was dangerous to impose their own moral vision upon others, and demanding sacrifices from the masses was something they particularly wanted to avoid. They even chose to explain their participation in oppositionist intellectual life in highly individualistic terms.

Most of the participants in the seminar were frustrated students at the university, who came to the illegal gatherings to get a real education. They chose to interpret their activities as motivated by individual need rather than as the collective constitution of an alternative cultural and social world. I argued that such activity should be interpreted as mediating between individual and political needs, and that this view of "dissent" explained the infectiousness of a personal pursuit of life in truth and the emergence of Solidarity in Poland. They responded, simply, "Czechs are not Poles."

And of course they were right. But they were not as dissimilar as they imagined, which became evident in the fall of 1989. In Czechoslovakia, as in Hungary, Bulgaria, Romania, Croatia, and Slovenia (as well as in Russia and many of the other nations of the Soviet Union), the move toward the constitution of a civil society as the basis for democracy has become a common experience. It is tied to a decisive turn against ideology—but not against shared political principles and ideas. On that evening in Prague at Bratinka's apartment, I had the feeling that the students feared ideological politics so greatly they were reluctant to express any political principles.

That feeling was reinforced the next day. Alena Hromádková, who had volunteered to deliver my presents to Havel, had spent the whole night reading my book before sending it on. She told me that she liked it, with one major reservation concerning Milan Kundera. In the book I use Kundera's writing as a springboard for outlining post-totalitarian culture and politics. Hromádková regarded this as highly inappropriate. In her mind, he was little more than a mediocre opportunist. Nonetheless, she thought my book of sufficient interest to propose to Ladislav Hejdánek, a distinguished philosopher expelled from the university in 1969, that it be the subject for his seminar that evening. He agreed, and I was honored. This seminar, held weekly in Hejdánek's modest apartment, was one of Prague's most famous. Over the years, guest speakers had included many world-renowned scholars.

I agreed to make a few introductory remarks and then publicly talk about the book with Alena. But when I arrived at 8:00 P.M., Alena's plans had been changed; she had to leave at 8:15 and would return at 9:30. So I was forced to give an impromptu lecture. I decided to provide an overview of the book by recounting how I came to write it, from the conversation with Michnik that forced me to reconsider the notion of totalitarianism, to a concern with the special language that seems to distinguish political and cultural alternatives to totalitarian practice. It led me to close with a question: What about Milan Kundera?

My talk stimulated intense discussion, providing me with a window on the diversity of independent Czech opinion. Most dramatic was Hejdánek's comment. He took issue with my contention that contemporary communist societies were totalitarian, saying that the current regimes could not be compared with the Nazi domination.

I was taken aback. I would have expected such a comment in an American university, where the theory of totalitarianism had long been abandoned in favor of more neutral and euphemistic phrases like "existing socialist bureaucratic authoritarianism." But my experience in Eastern Europe told me that among the critically inclined and active, the term was still widely accepted. Indeed, until the mid-1980s I had shied away from the term because it seemed to have two primary problems in explaining societal life. First, most broadly, it did not make sociological sense. The totalitarian model of society suggested complete domination from above by an ideologically inspired elite. A complex society, I reasoned, could not function under such conditions. Second, the theory couldn't account for systemic resistance. I had studied the recurrent emergence of opposition within the structure of bureaucratic authority in communist societies. The indigenous critics who often used the term "totalitarian" to explain their societies couldn't explain their own existence.

Yet my friends, particularly in Poland, had impressed upon me that there was something special about the oppression they were experiencing. Unlike traditional forms of oppression, there was something uniquely modern about the communist dictatorship. According to Hannah Arendt, terror and ideology are the two essential components of totalitarianism. Truth and coercion become indistinguishable. There is an official truth and syntax, tied into a complete understanding of history, past, present, and future. The understanding comes from the powers that be, and when the powers change, so does the complete understanding. Even without terror, this ideological existence constituted the world of existing socialism.

This was my argument. But I hesitated to make it. I began my response tentatively. "It would be ethically unacceptable for me to try to convince you that you live in a totalitarian order." I then conceded that present-day Czechoslovakia should not be equated with Nazi horrors. But I suggested that the same kind of culture—a totalitarian one, with truth conflated with coercion—was dominant in both cases.

These words successfully defused a tense moment. There ensued a discussion about the nature of everyday Czech life, which led to a discussion of Kundera's work, the possible bases of resistance, and the relation between religion and political progress. Hromádková and Hejdánek argued about religion. She underscored that the most forthright anticommunists were emerging from the church, which provided moral resources in an amoral world, and sanctuary for those who dared to think differently. Hejdánek warned of the dangers of superstition and fundamentalism. He sought a secular ethical basis for political opposition.

An animated discussion followed. Since the "Velvet Revolution," the different positions voiced that night have become important principles for political conflict. Yet that night, consensus was reached on the topic of Kundera. He was denounced ethically as an opportunist: he had managed to live well as a communist and a liberal in the sixties, when to do so was both fashionable and possible. Then, when things got tough, he fled, managing to live well in the West by again being fashionable, presenting to Westerners what they wanted to see of the East. Politically, he was criticized for his cynicism. His ridicule of dissent was controversial in Czechoslovakia in the late sixties and early seventies. He had engaged in a heated debate with Havel concerning the political astuteness of open letters of protest against the Soviet-backed crackdown. He had denounced the protesters as exhibitionists. Then, in the West, he had turned his questionable political position into art through the story of Tomas, a character in his international best-seller *The Unbearable Lightness of Being*.

These points made people angry. Clearly, among dissidents Kundera had touched raw nerves. The most telling criticism, though, came from a young philosophy student who approached me after the public discussion. He tried to explain that Americans have a writer very much like Kundera, one who deals with serious issues in artful ways, and at first glance appears to offer more than he actually delivers — Kurt Vonnegut. The other criticisms did not strike me as very convincing, but this observation got me thinking. Yet Kundera points to ambiguity and questions, not benign resignation. He explores human dilemmas by challenging the reader — at least this reader — in ways that Vonnegut does not. Even his political unreliability (from an oppositionist point of view) illuminates, raising ethical issues, working against sentimental oppositionism.

There were important differences of opinion expressed in those two seminars in Prague. The first night, people were most concerned about imposing their values and commitments on others. The second night, the discussion of Kundera clearly indicated a general commitment to political and ethical principles, suggesting a desire to avoid ideology without avoiding a principled politics.

The weakness of ideological thinking is no more evident than in the immediate Western reaction to the communist collapse. Among conservatives, two opposite reactions were forthcoming. On the one hand, there was celebration. The Cold War was over; the West had won. Capitalism, democracy, and freedom were forever to be identified. On the other hand, there was suspicion. Gorbachev, the most cunning of communist tyrants, was fooling the West, using its own slogans to strengthen his tyranny. Military preparedness and escalation were understood to be more necessary than ever in this new and more dangerous phase of the Cold War, in which it appeared to be over but really was not.

Among American liberals, the changes were viewed differently. Celebration was the rule, but it tended to be mixed with concern for supporting the solidification of the changes, and for using the geo-political opportunities to demilitarize and address pressing domestic problems. Liberals understood that the changes were real, but they did not understand exactly what was different, how deep the changes were. They primarily focused on the new enlightened Soviet leader-ship, specifically Gorbachev, and less on political, economic, and cul-tural transformations. These, in my judgment, were less the direct results of Gorbachev's politics and more the results of social forces that made his policies (or policies very much like his) virtually inevitable (at least as long as a full-fledged revival of Stalinism—the "Chinese solution"—was not the chosen road). By focusing on Gorbachev and other political leaders, liberals hoped to get on with their preexisting political agendas: increased international understand-ing, demilitarization, and, at home, social justice and welfare.

Such business as usual was not a realistic option for radicals of the left, though of course ideological denial is always a possibility for some. The failure of "actually existing socialism" (as it has been called by those who wish to distinguish between realities and their dreams) has been so thoroughgoing that the connection between dreams and realities could no longer be denied. The bankruptcy of class analysis as an adequate explanation for social life and political policy is now clear. Abolishing capitalist social relations has not solved all societal ills. Racial and ethnic conflict, environmental degradation, inadequate education and medical care, and even gross economic inequities out-lived capitalism. In some cases things got much worse.

The Western communist left now seems ridiculous. But even the noncommunist left is having its problems. It must come to terms with the striking evidence that socialism is not a higher stage of human development. Some on the left ignore the implications of recent events, trying to explain away the significance of the changes.

According to Paul Sweezy, for example, it took centuries of twists and turns for capitalism to emerge and solidify. How can we expect more of socialism?

But those on the left who are more specifically and concretely concerned with social justice, democracy, and the dignity of common men and women, those who don't think in terms of millennia, applaud the changes in the East and now must explore the implications for the West. The fall of 1989 is a mandate to explore how the principles and traditions of the left can be realized without depending on ideological certitudes.

Conservatives and liberals who celebrated "our" victory in the Cold War overlooked the fact that Mikhail Gorbachev was, as he so often declared, a communist, who had no intention of dismantling the Soviet Union or communism. Conservatives, by contrast, who realistically emphasized this fact and therefore called for vigilance, minimized the significance of immense changes. Nonetheless, the "celebrants" and the "vigilants" still had Cold War ideological dichotomies in common. The celebrants cited the liberation of practically all political prisoners, the emergence of a strikingly free press, the honest accounting of historical distortions and atrocities, the development of free literary and artistic life, and a fundamental search for economic and democratic reforms, and they perceived in it all the development of a free, democratic, and capitalist order, just like our own. They maintained a bipolar ideological map. A country is either free or totalitarian; it is either a democracy or a dictatorship; it is either capitalist or socialist (or "communistic"). The vigilants used the same map, but they were positive purists. They knew that capitalism, democracy, and freedom, as they understand them, had not been firmly institutionalized in the former satellite countries, let alone the Soviet Union, so they knew that the communist threat still persists. We may have been winning the war, but it had not yet been won.

Viewed from the left, such Cold War thought exercises can be rejected; their ideological bias is evident. Democracy does not capitalism make. Capitalism, supposedly the natural end of economic reform, exists not only in Western Europe, North America, and Japan; it is also found in Brazil, Chile, and South Africa. Its touted economic efficiency generates not only "the pursuit of happiness" but also human degradation. If capitalism and free enterprise are all their Cold War advocates claim, why the broad appeal of socialism and Marxism in the first place? Further, what sort of democracy is it that seems to make wealth, or significant support by the wealthy, a prerequisite for holding political office and effectiveness? How many people of modest means are there in the American Senate or House of Representatives? What influence does an ordinary citizen have in comparison with a large-scale corporation and its lobbyists? Is a society free when it cannot distinguish and willingly support cultural value in artistic and intellectual works, apart from their market value? In fact, in "free" American society, many responsible intellectuals, such as Edward Banfield, argue against such support in the name of "freedom." The basis of this view is that all freedoms are grounded in freedom of property for the propertied—which reveals, from the point of view of the left, its ideological stance.

This kind of observation is the starting point of leftist ideological critique. Marx maintained that the young Hegelians actually supported the existing social order, even as they appeared to criticize it. But after Marx, something curious happened along the ideological road. A critical practice became a positive enterprise. Lenin knew not only that the capitalists and their hired intellectual hands distorted reality; he also knew that the working class, left to its own devices, accepted the distortions and amplified them (in labor-union consciousness). Therefore they needed to be led by professional revolutionaries, who could provide the masses with the correct ideological positions and interpretations. Thus the party ideologist is a major political figure.

Other ideologies and ideologized critiques were then forthcoming. Marxism became Stalin's Marxist-Leninism. Mussolini gave the world fascism, and Hitler, national socialism. These totalitarian ideologies defined and produced twentieth-century barbarism. They told the complete truth about the world, past, present, and future, on the basis of a crucial key (class, race, or nation) to all human endeavors. They enforced their truths in brutal fashion. Force defined reason. Their absolute truths destroyed critical reason. The totalitarian idea of progress, for those outside their megalomania, belied the central modern political principles dating from the Enlightenment.

But ideology did more than directly corrode the Enlightenment's dreams of reason and progress. Ideological definitions of politics and culture became more widespread. In practical politics, all political ideas and principles, or sets of ideas and principles, came to be identified as ideologies. Recall the debate between Michael Dukakis and George Bush. Dukakis maintained that the presidential campaign was not about ideologies but about competence, while Bush argued on the basis of ideology. Neither came to grips with political ideas and principles.

At a more refined level, political scientists and sociologists also identify ideas with ideology. They interpret articulated political principles and ideas as rationalizations for competing interests. Social force lies behind political expression. Political ideas are but instruments for the realization of particular interests. Interests are real; ideas are ideologies. Thus, although Daniel Bell maintained in the late 1950s, as I am arguing here, that ideology had come or should come to its end, critical social scientists of the 1960s "knew better." They analyzed the "end of ideology" ideology by showing that it was a rationalization of the prevailing social order, serving the interests of the dominant social classes.

There is confusion in this way of thinking, both for the politics of daily life and for the academy. Politicians and academics do not appreciate the difference between political ideas and ideologies, and thus do not understand how ideology might end. The mistake, from Marx onward, of ideological critique, and of a great deal of the sociology of knowledge, is to view the link between interests and ideas as one of determination, with the former producing the latter. The mistake of our politicians is to treat all ideas as material for campaign slogans. Political ideas, then—because they are so often not taken seriously, either in the political arena or in the academy—cannot be distinguished from ideologies. But they must be so distinguished; or else, just as ideology ends, it may start up again—perhaps in a postmodern package.

While the most forceful and reprehensible ideological response to Marxist-Leninism was interwar fascism in its various forms, in the postwar period, during the Cold War, fascism was replaced by odd ideological hybrids—liberal and conservative anticommunism. The underlying truth of anticommunism was the deep structure of politics. Politics revolved around the big battle between the free world and communism. The good anticommunist battle (American kitsch, according to Milan Kundera) was the basis of a broad political consensus in America, at least until the Vietnam War. Even when that war escalated and then ended, attempts to develop national domestic and foreign policies without regard for the anticommunist struggle failed. George McGovern was defeated decisively at the polls; and Jimmy Carter's attempts to pursue a foreign policy centered on a concern for human rights (erasing the traditional distinction between unpleasant friends—that is, authoritarians—and communist enemies), and a domestic polity focused on a concern for social justice and economic productivity, were ineffective. Thus a broad range of social and political policies revolved around anticommunism during the period of Cold War consensus (about 1948–1968), and in domestic Cold War contestation (1968–1988). Arguments for and policies supporting free enterprise, social-welfare reforms, education, and highway construction, among many others, were part of and in effect constituted the anticommunist struggle.

This is why the reaction of conservatives and liberals to the fall of Marxist-Leninist regimes is so muddled. Anticommunists and communists, leftists, centrists, and rightists, all need the specter of communism. Without it, politics makes no ideological sense. That it still can and must make sense, as the second seminar in Prague graphically illustrated, invites us to reintroduce serious political ideas and pressing human concerns into our political life, which suggests a new post-totalitarian politics.

But what is Central European post-totalitarian politics? Many in the West, both on the left and on the right, would have us believe that it is no more than bourgeois liberal democracy. Perhaps, for some, I've even inadvertently confirmed this view. But to reject ideology, or the priority of a particular intellectual model for interpreting politics (such as Marxism or anti-Marxism), or an economic typology (capitalism or socialism) as a guide to political action, in our present political situation suggests not the victory of capitalism over socialism, or some form of anti-Marxism over Marxism, but instead the constitution of a new political terrain, where democracy is a revitalized political ideal under very significant economic, political, and cultural constraints. Let's think about them, and then about ourselves.

If "not socialism," the starting point for Polish economic reform, is considered outside the framework of the socialist-capitalist dichotomy, then the Polish political and economic actors must address a series of practical problems, none of which has easy or self-evident solutions. Jeffrey Sachs of Harvard, a whiz kid of economic reform—and economic adviser to the Polish government—wants to bring them the magic of the market. With considerable ignorance about how the present Polish economy works (or doesn't work), what existing resources the Poles have, and what their most immediate needs are, Sachs proposes radical solutions for complex problems based on simple propositions. From my point of view, he represents for Poland a new totalitarian temptation of the laissez-faire kind. Sachs trusts that existing political bureaucracy can be disciplined by the market, instead of subverting it, when the market shows what's efficient. Managerial expertise will appear when needed, as will housing. (Not only is there a severe housing shortage, but even among those who have adequate shelter, often it is located near inefficient economic enterprise, not in areas with economic potential.) Further, he doesn't consider seriously that newly organized and powerful citizens, especially of Solidarity, are simply not going to accept a definition of themselves as an element of production to be controlled. Neither socialism nor capitalism, either as model economies or societies, will address such complexities. Rather, the situation will require pragmatic political and economic action formulated through democratic deliberations.

In Czechoslovakia, they may want to call such action democratic socialism or social democracy. In Hungary, they may call it "neither socialism nor capitalism." Perhaps, in Poland, they'll call it capitalism. But the types of economic reforms are likely to be the same. Of course, because the German Democratic Republic could not maintain the socialist label, it disappeared, and in the Soviet Union, where distrust of capitalism and capitalists seems to be still alive, and where the idea of socialism and the unity of its republics is apparently all that stands between order and the collapse of a nineteenth-century political structure, the socialist myth may be kept alive. But this is socialism in Havel's negative sense.

The real challenge is whether a pragmatic economics, along with a principled democratic politics with cultural, religious, and individual freedoms, can be sustained against less desirable alternatives to crumbling totalitarianism, specifically, authoritarian nationalism and technocracy. The unpleasant nationalisms are visible everywhere, from the Balkans to the Baltic to Baku. Technocracy can be perceived on the not-too-distant horizon in the form of so-called benevolent dictatorships.

For a long time, democrats and nationalists, Solzhenitsyn and Sakharov could fight the good fight together against the totalitarians; but now the tensions between them are probably more significant than those between them and the crumbling totalitarian parties. Yugoslavia is proving to be a mythic political entity. Civil war effectively rages on the Soviet Union's southern rim. Those in Estonia, Latvia, and Lithuania call for sovereignty and, in effect, the dismantling of the Russian empire, something the Soviet power elite may refuse to do. In Poland and Hungary, a major—if not the major—political fissure is between xenophobic nationalists and European-oriented democrats, and in Poland, a sacralized politics is thrown in. All over the former bloc, nationalist forces of conflict and disintegration are evident, which clearly draw upon long-standing but also long dormant traditions.

There seems to be good reason to view the events after the revolutions of 1989 primarily with dismay, or with cynical calculation. The cynically inclined may dismiss the fortunes of Eastern and Central Europeans and the oppressed nations of the Soviet Union as hopeless, and view the weakening of the Soviet Union as the most significant positive end of the Evil Empire: we've won the Cold War and that's the end of it. The old anticommunist lens, then, is still being used, even when communism is no longer a real threat. The practical problem with this position is that it overlooks the real dangers of geopolitical chaos in the nuclear age. The more humane problem with such neo-anticommunism (or anti-Sovietism) is that it ignores substantial human suffering and the false hopes we have inspired. If the Cold War really had something to do with a struggle between freedom and totalitarianism, it is only after the fall of totalitarianism that the most significant political struggle begins. The real force limiting free politics now is not the Soviet Big Brother, but one's own relatives and neighbors.

The most sober view of democratic prospects in the old bloc must rate them as unlikely. Nonetheless, there is some reason for hope. Between the fairly distant past and an authoritarian nationalist future lies the rejection of ideology; the sensibilities of such political activists, theorists, and writers as Václav Havel, Adam Michnik, and George Konrád; the constitution and experience of civil society. A democratic culture of opposition emerged, a post-totalitarian mind that cuts across nationalist particularisms. The Eastern and Central European democrats may not succeed in their struggle, but their consensus is significant, as are their early victories.

And contrary to the laissez-faire liberals, who fear democracy in Eastern Europe as they have in Latin America and elsewhere, democracy is not only possible, it may very well be necessary for economic modernization. The changes require popular support, and because of the long and sorry experience with communism as a benevolent dictatorship, a new liberal or technocratic dictatorship would not generate that support. Attempts to bring together economic reform, democracy, and social justice will involve a great deal of confrontation, but I am convinced that positive change cannot be achieved in any other fashion.

So how should we act and react in the West? First and foremost, we should not concentrate overmuch on the problems of order and disorder. We live in a new political era, and it is disorienting. Old distinctions sometimes do not hold (capitalism versus socialism), or at least not in the accustomed way (right versus left). Some Cold Warriors are already waxing nostalgic for the good old days when they knew where they were. They had their Evil Empire, and they knew what to do. But disorder in the context of epochal transformation is necessary, as conflicting opinions are essential for an ongoing democracy. We should not be too anxious about the disruptions of the reform process, because reform is inherently disruptive. Unpleasant views will be expressed, submerged conflicts will come out in the open. It is not a wise course to support too quickly those who promise to control events politically, whether they are the rigid old men of Beijing or the master politician in the Kremlin.

During and after the fall of 1989, too many people from the left, right, and center expressed unqualified support of Mikhail Gorbachev.

He was too quickly given credit for too much, and he was seen as essential for a happy future. In the daily press, the only expressed exceptions to this judgment seemed to come from old Cold Warriors who insisted on fighting the battles of the last war. Yet, if we had kept in mind that Gorbachev was as much reacting to the major transformations as he was creating them, we would have understood that a much more nuanced approach was necessary. The changes in the Soviet bloc and in the Soviet Union itself clearly would not have been possible without Gorbachev's policies of *perestroika* and *glasnost*. But Gorbachev would not have moved beyond his initial neo-Stalinist ideas of societal reform if he hadn't been pushed by genuine post-totalitarian democratic forces. Gorbachev started with calls for increased discipline and an anti-alcoholism campaign. When this didn't work, he advocated openness and democratization (of a limited sort) as a way to instigate economic reform and increased productivity. Since then, things have gotten out of his control, and this is for the good.

Real democratic forces, with political connections to the journalists at the Lublin Festival of Youth Theaters and the seminar participants in Prague, are now creating new political orders. Personally, I am gratified to see once obscure old friends and colleagues emerging as political leaders, even though they don't always get along. We and they must appreciate that their disagreements, while not always pleasant, are not necessarily signs of failure. Both their earlier anti-ideological agreements and their new political differences constitute a new post-totalitarian politics.

But the exact nature of the new political constitution is difficult to identify. The post-totalitarian terrain is filled with dilemmas, confusions, and ironies. Central among them, in my judgment, is that in place of those previously totalitarian social orders, which were completely politicized, the first order of the day is to reconstitute a truly political domain. These societies need to be adequately and democratically politicized. They need to open central issues to debate, and to decide them democratically; they need to civilize the articulation of political difference so that it is both meaningful and consequential.

CHAPTER 4

What's Left? What's Right?

On November 9, 1990, through a series of accidents, I found myself having a philosophical discussion with the Czechoslovak minister of the interior, Jan Langoš. The circumstances leading to our meeting, and the substance of this discussion, nicely represent the complex and ironic framework of the post-totalitarian political situation.

I went to Czechoslovakia one year after the "Velvet Revolution" (so named by Václav Havel) for three reasons: to help my Slovak colleagues initiate a branch of the democracy seminar in Bratislava; to give lectures in Bratislava and Prague on recent developments in the sociology of politics and culture as part of a New School initiative to reconstitute the social sciences in Eastern and Central Europe; and to take a look at Slovak nationalism and its impact on the formation of Czechoslovakia's new democracy. The arrangements for my visit proved to be quite faulty. The person who was supposed to meet me

52

at the airport never showed up. My social-science colleagues had only the vaguest information that I was coming, and no idea why. And Fedor Gal, the head of Slovakia's most important democratic movement, The Public Against Violence—who had earlier expressed interest in working with me on setting up a democracy seminar in Bratislava—didn't even know I was in the country.

It was seven hours before I met my contact, Jiřina Šiklova, and found a place to stay. When I finally got settled, I realized that I was on my own in achieving my goals. Instead of presenting my paper and inaugurating the New School's social-science curriculum center in Prague and Bratislava, I would have to lay the groundwork for a smooth reception for the next Western visitors. But after all, that task turned out to be relatively easy. Making my way to Slovakia was another matter. Of the people I needed to contact there, I couldn't reach anyone by telephone either at home or at the office. Some people didn't have phones, and the others all seemed to be out of town or in meetings where they couldn't be reached. My only lead was a memorial service to be held at the Palace Hotel in Prague for Milan Šimečka, the late Slovak journalist, political activist, and theorist. Šiklova told me that of the many Czech and Slovak activists and former dissidents who would attend, someone would surely be able to help me.

I went to the Palace Hotel (Prague's finest) expecting a large public meeting. Instead, I found a small gathering of the Czechoslovak political and cultural elite, including Jiři Dienstbier, the foreign minister, and Šimečka's widow, who was accepting her husband's posthumous award for journalistic excellence from a Dutch-based international press association. Without any real grasp of the nature of the meeting, I was introduced by Šiklova to Mrs. Šimečka and her son. I didn't quite understand whether I should express my condolences or congratulations. (Šimečka had died two months earlier, but at the time I didn't know that.) So I expressed both, and awkwardly asked my groping questions: who might I meet the next day in Bratislava to talk about the current political situation, and how might I meet them? I felt I was intruding, but they didn't seem to mind, and did try to help, knowing that I had written with some intelligence about the old Soviet bloc and its transformation, and that I had good contacts in and information about Prague—but not Bratislava.

After speaking to a number of well-placed Czech and Slovak citizens, along with a few Western journalists, I was introduced to Gabriela Langoš, who told me she might be able to help. Her husband, the minister of the interior, would be going to a special retreat called Harmonia, just outside Bratislava, where officials of the Czech and Slovak national governments and the federal government would be meeting at the invitation of The Public Against Violence. Gal, as well as the other people I wanted to meet, would most likely be attending. She suggested that I come to her Prague apartment that evening to meet her husband.

The Langošes lived in a very comfortable, modern apartment building outside the center of the city—a rarity in the former Soviet bloc. This, along with the fact that my taxi driver had a lot of trouble finding the address, suggested to me that I was entering what had apparently been a housing complex for high-level communist officials, discreetly hidden away from broad public view. Langoš was living among them, but was not one of them. Before his recent appointment to the ministry, he had been a person living on the margins, working openly as a computer scientist and clandestinely as a conduit in dissident circles. A native Slovak with his own apartment in Bratislava, he had evidently been given this apartment by the new government upon appointment to his post.

His is a job of incredible difficulty. The transition to democratic normality is a wrenching operation, and some of the dirtiest aspects fall on the shoulders of the interior minister. Czechoslovakia had been a training center for international terrorists, and the terrorists and their trainers had to be brought under control. According to the minister, they still existed, though not out in the open. Also the secret police, under the control of the previous minister of the interior, had penetrated broadly and deeply into Czech and Slovak societies, and now it was Langoš's task to remove the most compromised from public life and high-level positions of responsibility. It is likely that among them were some of his neighbors.

He does not look the part for this role. He looks more like an aging rock musician, with a scraggly beard, shoulder-length hair, and informal clothes. When I was introduced to him in his apartment, I suddenly remembered that Langoš was the high-level Czechoslovak official in Havel's entourage who had been strip-searched on the Canada–United States border by Canadian border authorities in early 1990. The incident had caused a minor international scandal. Now, seeing him in person, I could guess why the search might have happened. His appearance was an open challenge to the police mentality and demanded a reaction.

The severe challenge presented to this minister by one of the most repressive police apparatuses in Eastern Europe—equal to that of East Germany, Bulgaria, or Romania—could not be overestimated. This was a man with a dangerous job. He was symbolically and actually challenging those with the greatest investment in the old order. In fact, he was the second democratic minister of the interior. The first, Jan Ruml, had had to resign when one of the people he was attempting to ease out of public life fought back, causing a significant political uproar.

This kind of problem is delicate. Hundreds of thousands of people, if not millions, had collaborated with the secret police. Their activities ranged from full-time undercover work and espionage to coerced signed agreements to cooperate with state security when traveling abroad. Such agreements amounted to little more than an acknowledgment on the part of the signatory that he or she was being watched. Thus, a purge of all who cooperated would lead to a widespread witch-hunt, but would not identify those who were direct agents of repression.

Nevertheless, permitting them to hold positions of authority was understood to be both immoral and impractical. If those who were involved in the repressive apparatus continued to flourish, it would indicate to many people that no real change had occurred. There exists, then, in Czechoslovakia, and throughout the old Soviet bloc, a political struggle over the legacies of the police state. There are those who fear a new purge, which they think would show the new authorities to be no better than those they replaced; and there are those who are concerned that the new authorities are shielding the oppressors of the old order, also demonstrating the shared identity of the old and new authorities. Significantly, at its demagogic worst, this political debate sees both sides labeling their opponents Bolsheviks.

These issues were an important part of the dramatic political conflicts in Romania and Poland, countries I had recently visited. In Romania, for instance, an atmosphere of mistrust and suspicion seemed to make it impossible for both the new authorities and the opposition to function. Effectiveness required the participation of former communists in both official and unofficial activities. Yet the predominance of high-level communists in the government was leading many to the natural conclusion that the only thing "new" about the new government was its innovative political form—neocommunism. Many students and highly respected urban intellectuals held this conviction, and therefore they opposed the government with strenuous force in a variety of ways. But they themselves were severely divided on this especially controversial issue of retribution and tolerance. To some, for instance, Silviu Brucan was one of the new government's most telling critics: a disaffected founder of the National Salvation Front, a self-described leading dissident during the Ceaucescu period. For others he was simply a Soviet agent; they felt that the dominance of former communists in the new government was proof that it represented just "more of the same," and they condemned the noncommunist participants in the government as collaborators. For them, the only acceptable course was an absolute ban on communists in political life. At the same time, some of the most seasoned democratic oppositionists viewed these attitudes with dismay. They saw unrestrained purges on the horizon.

This issue was also central in the Polish presidential elections. The anticommunist labor leader Lech Wałęsa called for a clean sweep of those communist riffraff, the *nomenklatura*; Prime Minister Tadeusz Mazowiecki called for a sober and, in the final analysis, passionless tolerance; and Stanisław Tymiński, the Canadian emigré with a shadowy past and no real program, upped the stakes, labeling the prime minister a traitor and the union leader a secret agent. The legacies of the police state loomed large in Polish politics, underscored by Tymiński's meteoric rise, though they did not prevail.

I wanted to discuss these matters with Langoš. After he interviewed a potential press spokesman, his wife introduced me to the assembled people: the job candidate, a Czech friend, a Czech-American journalist, and her husband. She explained who I was and what I was doing in Prague. And now Langoš, I hoped, would explain to me the process of the detotalitarianization of politics as it was practiced not in public but backstage. Yet Langoš turned our conversation in another direction. Upon hearing about my interest in post-totalitarian political culture, he wanted to talk about one of the main issues: what's left? what's right?

We agreed about a great many things: that we lived in a new political world, where the old categories and guideposts no longer functioned; that Marxism as a theoretical system should be understood as a beguiling temptation, worthy of academic study, but worthless as a guide to politics; and that religion, nationalism, and politics should be mixed only with extreme caution, otherwise the results could be disastrous. Now was the time for a principled but pragmatic politics, open to compromise, with dialogue as its first principle.

But about labels and their implications we had disagreements. I told him that while I believed that the categories of left and right needed to be rethought, they still had relevance. Their continued meaning for our inherited political traditions presented puzzles, but still helped us to make sense of our world. Langoš didn't think things were so puzzling. He said that the left and the right presented clear alternatives, and he chose the right. Why? Because, according to the minister, the left dreamed, and based politics on illusions and wishes, which led to catastrophe; the right was more sober and realistic.

We were sitting around a coffee table. Our conversation was in Slovak, Czech, Polish, and English. The Czech-American journalist translated Langoš's Slovak into English and my English into Czech (which of course Langoš understood). Czech and Slovak are very close, but so are Slovak and Polish. I found myself understanding a great deal of what the minister was saying without the benefit of the translation. On occasion I moved from English into Polish so I could speak with him more directly. In this polylingual Central European atmosphere, aided by vodka and slivovitz, Langoš tried to clarify his position with a concrete image—the round coffee table.

"The left sees this coffee table and dreams of what it might be: a desk for writing great books, a dinner table for a sumptuous meal, or something of a completely different order. The right views the table clearly, will use it, and will not try to turn it into something it is not.

The left is never satisfied, just a table is not enough, something grand must be constructed. The right knows the coffee table is just so, a coffee table, to be appreciated for what it is. When the left gets down to its work, not only are the dreams not realized, but the realities are lost. No great desk or dinner table appears, and no coffee table remains. At least with the right, there is a coffee table."

I understood Langoš, even agreed with him to a point, but I felt (and feel) that his arguments needed to be qualified, both from the point of view of the left and from the point of view of the right. It seemed to me that he was confusing a critique of ideology and ideological politics with a critique of the left. A politics based on ideological conviction revolves around a single idea, which provides the "key" for understanding and acting in the political world. All of human existence, to this way of thinking, can be understood as a series of deductions drawn from the simplistic key idea. The complexity of the human condition is thus easily understood, and when there exists a gap between the empirical world and the ideologues' simplifications, two alternatives are available. One is denial, and the other is theoretical deduction based on critique and political action based on that deduction. Thus, for example, according to a Marxist ideological script, since all history can be understood through the process of class struggle, and since the working class is the historical subject who will overthrow the capitalist order, the failure of the workers to overthrow the capitalists using parliamentary means indicates that parliamentary democracy is a mere instrument of the capitalists. It is an instrument of bourgeois liberalism, not to be appreciated as having any value apart from its class basis. If it is shown that workers vote for bourgeois parties, or that worker representatives support liberal parliamentary institutions, ideology observes that they are not really workers (denial), or that they are workers suffering from "false consciousness" (deduction), because they do not hold the same position as the ideologue. Their opinions and judgments must be the product of class domination.

Missing from this reasoning is an appreciation of parliamentary institutions and their necessary functions in modern democracy. The ideologue, focused on the key idea, does not really consider the political world as it exists, but sees it as a means to realize his or her more profound dreams. Contrary to Langoš's feelings, however, such thinking is not a monopoly of the left. In the name of the nation and the folk, the right has also ignored the resources and problems of the political world as we inherit them. Real, pressing problems of human diversity have been explained away in the name of national strength and resolve; the complexities of modern economics, with their serious problems, have been denounced as manipulations of one foreign or international conspiracy or another. In fact, such an ideology seems to be flourishing among Langoš's native Slovaks.

I later came face to face with Slovak neofascism, but the conversation with Langoš remained metaphoric and abstract. I agreed that a denial of political reality was a problem of the Western left, and had been a problem of the Eastern left, but I pointed out that the ideological right too had a history (and perhaps a future) of such denial in Central Europe, with barbaric consequences. The reputable approaches of the left and the right constituted normal political reality. "We should not try to transform a small, round coffee table into something completely different, but it can be used for different purposes; and on occasion it may need repair."

We were both delighted with the metaphor of the round table, because power transfers throughout the region had been negotiated around such tables. The issue was how such round tables managed to stand, and what transpired around them. "The democratic left understands that this round table is a coffee table. But it also knows that the table has legs, which must support it. If they are poorly designed or made with weak materials, the table may only hold tea and coffee. If the materials are better, the table may hold not only the tea but also pastries. Improve the design and the feast in front of us proliferates: tea, coffee, sandwiches, pastry, wine, vodka, and brandy. The democratic left tends to observe the table critically and look for ways it can be improved. The right tends to be satisfied with the way it is."

Trying to sum up the metaphor in order to move away from it, I suggested that each of the legs might be viewed symbolically by considering the table as a sound democratic polity. "One leg is the nation, another is the economy, the third religion, and the fourth the political culture of tolerance. The right tends to be concerned about the nation and religion more than the left, and to have a different approach

to the economy and liberal culture. Where the right sees healthy patriotism, the left may see a nationalistic danger; and where the right sees
the moral basis of a community in religious life, the left may see the
threat of dogmatism and sacralized politics—what Adam Michnik
calls the 'Iranization of politics.'"

I didn't develop this extension of the metaphor systematically
because I well knew that matters get confusing. For instance, where
should we locate advocates of free markets? In Poland and Hungary
they tended to be those who understood the pressing need to make
their national economies like Western Europe's, and because these
same people were associated with the democratic left, free-market partisans tended to be labeled leftists. In Czechoslovakia, however, as in
the West, they were labeled rightists. And as far as a liberal political
culture of democracy was concerned, the question was whether the
claims of nation, religion, and the free market could be modified, in
order that such a culture might flourish. At this point the left-right
distinction seemed to collapse.

Langoš agreed that right-wing ideology was as bad as that of the
left. He agreed that the body politic stood on a number of different
legs, and in a democracy there had to be room for competing judgments concerning their relative importance. But, basing his contention primarily on his personal experience, he maintained that the
left today was more likely to overlook existing complexities in pursuit
of utopian dreams. A simplistic leftist view of progress—which
Kundera calls the Grand March—ignores the importance of a civilized ordering of political contest. Thinking of the situation back in
the West, I had to admit that he had a point. Our conversation then
shifted from theory to a personal exchange about mutual friends and
interests, and we agreed to meet the next day and go together to
Bratislava.

I left the Langoš apartment with the sense that I was about to
come face to face with the complex problems of the relations between
democracy and nation, and a conviction that the political culture of
democracy was in its infancy in Czechoslovakia and its neighbors.
Langoš spoke intelligently and with wisdom about the dangers of ideological theory and action, but he didn't seem to understand how
principled agreement and disagreement had to become a routine part

of democratic politics, and how consensus and dissent could be ordered.

For Langoš, the left was discredited, and therefore the right had political wisdom. But it was unclear what Langoš meant by the right, and all too clear and inclusive what he meant by the left. Like many throughout the old Soviet bloc, he has lost a sense that there is a spectrum of respectable political opinion. Such people view the left as identical with communism, and therefore everything associated with the left is quickly dismissed as communist. The right, by contrast, is identified with anticommunism; therefore it is fundamentally correct in its political orientations and positions. Differences of opinion, then, too easily degenerate into mutual accusations of leftism.

Langoš seemed to think that the central characteristic of the right was its respect for the wisdom of tradition and well-established procedures. Democratic change should work outward from conventional ways of doing things democratically. Therefore, he is a strong supporter of parliamentary democracy as it has developed in the West. But for others who identify with the right, especially those who want to underscore the importance of national or religious traditions, positions like his appear to be clearly leftist. In Poland, I read of a Polish Catholic who heatedly condemned the communist notion of separation of church and state.

Yet all this concern with tradition and established ways, of clear rightist commitments, presents fundamental problems. It overlooks the indigenous roots of democratic developments in Central Europe. Talk about the democratic innovations of civil society as developed by the Czechs, Poles, and Hungarians, from Langoš's and his rightist opponents' point of view, may seem utopian and leftist—both derogatory adjectives. Such talk seems to involve a suggestion that there may still be some magical "third way"—neither capitalist nor socialist.

But overlooking the civil developments may be a guarantee of political failure. Something significant was created in the antitotalitarian opposition, and it is an important resource for democratization. If it is condemned as a new ideological leftism, democratic prospects are dismal. Insisting that the left is totally discredited so constrains political discourse that real political problems, from nationalism to the economy, will not be addressed.

One year is a short time for the development of a democratic political culture, as my conversation with Minister Langoš revealed. Some countries had a head start. Hungary, and especially Poland, had had well-developed and extensive political oppositions for more than a decade. Other nations, such as Bulgaria, Romania, and much of the Soviet Union, had faced the most intense political repression with little experience of political opposition. Although all of the countries in the old socialist bloc shared the experience of Stalinism, and although their organization of the ruling Communist Party and its relationships with government, industry, trade unions, cultural and educational institutions, and much else were quite similar, they were freeing themselves from totalitarian practices in different ways. Czechoslovakia was a most ambiguous case. It had a well-developed and extremely talented democratic opposition—particularly Charter 77—which did not penetrate deeply into the lives of most Czechs and Slovaks. The implications of this situation were most apparent just after the Velvet Revolution. A way to balance the need for unity and the need to articulate differences systematically (summarized by the left-right dichotomy) was far from evident. It would require sensitive political leadership, capable of resolving immensely complex political problems.

II

LEADERSHIP

CHAPTER 5

Havel to the Castle

I mmediately after the fall of 1989, while walking around the streets of Prague, I was struck by a remarkable irony. Plastered on building walls, in subway corridors, in car and store windows, on all available spaces, I saw the smiling, benign image of Václav Havel. He was not only the president of the new Czechoslovak polity, nor was he simply the major opponent of the previous communist order; he and his image represented Czechoslovak unity and democracy, the symbol of a civil society. The very existence of the Velvet Revolution was personified by this professional playwright and purportedly amateur politician. The ubiquity of Havel's name and image was overwhelming. Before, wherever one looked in socialist Czechoslovakia, one discovered the banal slogans and jargon of the communist overseers: "Workers of the World,

Unite!" Now, instead, there was "Havel to the Castle!" The irony, of course, was that Havel had made his name as a critic of such political jargon and as a deep skeptic of political mystification.

But political symbols are important for the unity of democracies as well as for the unity of tyrannies. George Washington's heroism was celebrated before he even once engaged the enemy. Early tales of his prowess included the way he sent and received letters. He was deified before, during, and after his presidency. A monarch personifies the unity of a hierarchical order; Washington represented a democratic one; and Havel, clearly, was fulfilling the same role in Czechoslovakia. But of course, as with Washington, the process is not without problems. Washington and some of his closest associates and promoters were condemned for monarchical tendencies and ambitions. Some have seen in Havel the makings of a neototalitarian tyrant. But—again as with Washington—in the period immediately following the revolution, when changes were vulnerable and far from fully realized, public criticism of Havel at first was rare.

Three sorts of public criticism or opposition could be discerned. Among a small group, those who directly benefited from the communist order and who would have great difficulty in transferring their advantages to the new order, there was frontal (though necessarily clandestine) opposition. Thousands in the military, police, and Party, among them political generals and foot soldiers, Party leaders and political informants, were completely compromised. After the revolution, they attempted to hide, and on occasion attacked, trying to make change impossible in specific social settings.

Much more numerous were those who had survived and even flourished during the repressive years. They had placated the communist political princes as minimally as possible, some thinking of themselves as a hidden political opposition. When they were able to come out in the open, they feared that their new leaders did not fully appreciate what they had accomplished by their former activity, and they were critical of this supposed neglect.

Last, there were those who had forthrightly fought the difficult antitotalitarian battle, or at least imagined that they had done so. Seeing compromised people still holding significant positions of authority, they demanded more forceful and complete change.

The modes of criticism and opposition mirrored the modes of adaptation to the previous order: support and collaboration; survival and clandestine opposition; or steadfast opposition. But there was not a one-to-one correspondence between former political position and present political tendency. Few people had been so visible in their support of the old order that they were now forced to resist change at all costs. Most who had supported or collaborated with the *ancien régime* could at least pretend that they had merely been surviving. Adaptive survival had been the situation for the vast majority of the population. So people were free to criticize the new order on the grounds that it was moving either too rapidly or too slowly, or that it was ignoring the accomplishments of the "hidden opposition," or that it was not thoroughly cleaning up the overpoliticized house. There was passion in this, but little coherence.

Students of sociology at Charles University remembered the actions of one of their professors. Throughout the 1970s and 1980s, this man had boasted about his active support of the Russian-led Warsaw Pact invasion of Czechoslovakia in 1968. He told his students about the troubles faced by him and his family because of his immediate support of the invasion. He had been ostracized by his neighbors. Local merchants would not sell food to his family, and the family had had to buy supplies in a neighboring town. His storytelling had clear significance. It was not just an inappropriate personal digression; he was a terrorist as raconteur. He knew his political position had been unpopular, both immediately after and throughout the twenty-one-year post-invasion period. But he was in power, telling his story, in Czechoslovakia's most venerated university. He was enforcing silence, demonstrating the relation between force and reason in the so-called Socialist Republic. His storytelling encapsulated totalitarian culture, and the only response available to the students was compliance. For those students, his continued presence at the unversity suggested the limits of the Velvet Revolution.

Professor Ladislav Hejdánek presented a strong argument for the same position in a speech at the first public meeting of Charter 77 on March 18, 1990. For him, the softness of the Velvet Revolution implied a reluctance to make necessary radical decisions and enforce them. This distinguished professor of philosophy—student if not philosophical disciple of Jan Patočka—maintained that this situation was unacceptable. Although he would not advocate violence or a mindless purge, he did maintain that democratic dialogue based on reason and conscience should yield decisive action.

The professor was speaking to an assembly of the charter's members and supporters. In the late 1970s, Charter 77 was the major autonomous societal institution in Czechoslovakia. It presented a sustained challenge to the communist authorities. Distinguished apolitical academics and former communist officials, religious traditionalists and counterculturists, Marxist humanists and committed anti-Marxists—all signed the charter demanding the recognition of human rights and promising to monitor and report on the condition of the human rights situation in Czechoslovakia. By the late 1980s, about twelve hundred people had signed the charter. These "charterists" were among the few in revolutionary Czechoslovakia with unambiguous antitotalitarian credentials, and they displayed a sense of vindication. Along with their president, they, as once-isolated idealists, had proved to be the realists. Toward those who had chosen what seemed to be a more realistic path, who had accommodated to harsh realities, who in their own minds had opted for an ethics of effectiveness rather than an ethics of ultimate ends, and who had proved to be fundamentally mistaken, the Velvet Revolution, especially Havel or his leadership, could show its harshness.

This position appeared to some to have quasi-totalitarian qualities. Two people with such fears explained to me that Civic Forum, the Czech organizational structure of the social movement for democratic transition, along with its Slovak equivalent, The Public Against Violence, had only a vague program, despite their mass support. This support could yield mass disillusionment. Civic Forum was acting both as a broad-based societal movement and as a particular party competing with others. It was identifying its view with the interests of society as a whole. The contradiction was clear: the inexpert and closed quality of Civic Forum and Havel's government could lead to doubts. Havel had not sufficiently included the "invisible" or "quiet" oppositionalists, in other words, the bulk of the population, those who had supported the changes in the leadership of their institutions in votes of confidence organized by Civic Forum. The old guard had been expelled when clerks, workers, farmers, experts, and intellectuals had organized against them, just as the students and workers had organized against the national leadership in November and December 1989. But Havel, for the most part, had chosen as leaders those closest to him in the charterist movement and dissident artistic circles. According to the two formerly hidden oppositionists, he had shut out of the government a broad cross-section of society: those who, like themselves, had conformed outwardly to the old regime, but had finally grown disgusted and participated in demonstrations for change and local votes of no-confidence. To people like themselves, with misgivings, the new government and Civic Forum seemed to share unfortunate formal similarities with the old order—essentially, it was another closed leadership, distrustful of the population.

But the previous circumstances made trust after the fall very hard to build, even with goodwill. As an oppositionist, Havel had explored this situation in his plays and essays. He had shown how the official order had been constituted by cynical cooperation with the existing powers on the part of those who were now referring to themselves as the hidden opposition. People might not have believed what they were forced to say or do, but because they had said and done it, the system had functioned. Now, how could one discern who had lived in good faith, and who had lived in bad faith? Who had been a simple functionary, and who had been a member of the secret opposition? Who had made things worse because he or she had zealously fulfilled the expectations of tyrants, and who had made things better because he or she had clandestinely subverted the system by fostering the unusual, or at least by not acting as repressively as was expected? Those who had sacrificed everything often viewed such nuances as morally suspect.

Havel recognized these issues even before they appeared as open political problems. In his 1990 New Year's speech to the nation, he applied his oppositional wisdom. Since living the lie—that is, following official expectations—had produced and reproduced the system, those who had acted according to the expectations of the prevailing order (just about everyone) had constituted the totalitarian system and in their actions had been shaped by the system. Therefore, the society would not be reformed by simply replacing its leaders. It would be reformed only when people themselves changed. Democracy must be learned. A civil society must be created.

• • •

Although the symbols of Havel himself and of Havel in his actions provide the common ground necessary for both civility and democracy, important differences concerning national identities, economic interests, and opposing political judgments also must be articulated. A responsible left and right must be formed. Here Havel's high moral ground is endangered. The situation in Czechoslovakia is especially raw because open opposition and the culture of dialogue of post-totalitarian politics were not broadly developed before the fall. Even among the charterists the open exchange of opposing views and respect for those holding different political positions were rare. Such experience is badly needed. This is a democratic challenge.

In the city of Brno in Moravia, two signers of Charter 77 have engaged in brutal conflict. Jaroslav Šabata was one of the most heroic dissidents. Imprisoned for eight years, this sixty-two-year-old psychologist was appointed by Civic Forum to the Parliament and was named chair of its Foreign Affairs Committee. Because of his generally recognized reputation, he had become the leader of Civic Forum in Brno and Moravia when the movement was founded. His leadership was as much viewed as a foregone conclusion as Havel's. Nevertheless, like 140 of the original 242 signers of Charter 77, Šabata is not only a former dissident but also a former communist, which led to a campaign against him almost as soon as free speech and politics were reborn. Petr Cibulka, formerly an underground producer of songs and books, led the campaign.

The forty-year-old Cibulka served in prison for fourteen months. The Velvet Revolution set him free. He controlled Civic Forum's press and information center even after becoming a candidate of the Movement for Civil Liberty, which opposed Civic Forum's slate. He is a radical anticommunist. When Šabata supported retaining the communist mayor of Brno until free elections could be held, Cibulka led an anticommunist campaign, denouncing Šabata and the mayor as Red Barons.

Mediation between the two sides was attempted. Jan Urban, the head of Civic Forum in Prague, arranged for Šabata and Cibulka to air their differences publicly on television, and then, in order to prepare for elections, to confirm that their shared principles were more important than their differences. But during the broadcast on March 13,

1990, Cibulka broke the agreement and used the occasion to denounce communist domination and Šabata's failure to oppose it. According to Cibulka's partisans, Šabata, with his communist-trained demeanor, purposely provoked and enraged Cibulka. Those who were prone to sympathize with Šabata, or who sought unity with expressed differences in Civic Forum, viewed Cibulka as self-centered, unstable, and unable to make political compromises.

The conflict has been politically consequential. Wild anticommunist demonstrations have occurred in Brno, with calls to send the communist mayor to the stake and to oust Šabata. The local government has been disrupted. Czech-Moravian tensions have increased (alongside the more inflamed Czech-Slovak tensions), with the central coordinating council of Civic Forum denouncing Cibulka, as he became a populist, anticommunist hero in Moravia. The citizens of Czechoslovakia must grope for ways to deal with differences of opinion, for ways to break with the Communist Party's domination of the past, and to accommodate psychological weaknesses, pecularities, and subterfuge.

Unity and morality alone are not enough. When Havel did not intervene in the Brno conflict, criticisms were quietly voiced by those who feared that an irrational anticommunist hysteria threatened to overwhelm the fledgling democracy. Havel, they maintained, should have taken sides; but, like the first American president two centuries before him, he was reluctant to do so. The Czechoslovak president wanted to transcend the sides.

On political grounds, within the context of daily struggle, the problems with Havel's position were evident. From the point of view of the radical anticommunist, he was not being sufficiently vigilant. From the point of view of the anti-anticommunist, he was not facing down a mass hysteria that could lead to a witch-hunt. But Havel's position becomes more understandable when interpreted outside the immediate context, without recourse to outmoded ideological thinking (and the ideologue's tendency to view disagreements in bipolar terms). By avoiding a partisan position, he was attempting to support the common ground where people with differences could meet. In each of the developing European democracies, this ground must be staked out and defended, as must be the differences expressed there.

In Czechoslovakia, an elegant strategy was apparently in place to realize this dualistic good. By calling for free elections in June 1990, rather than at the beginning of the year, Jan Urban and his colleagues attempted to transform the election from what would have been a referendum against communism into a real political contest. They understood that, if given time, in the countryside, especially in Slovakia, widespread support would develop for Christian Democratic politics, and that the interests and views of Civic Forum and The Public Against Violence, though clearly closely related, would at times conflict. The leaders apparently hoped to have a real election, which would avoid the problems of rushing into an artificial and momentary unity. They sought a coalition government (in the interwar Czechoslovakian tradition) in which not only would a consensus be reached to condemn the older order but also the healthy and normal differences of opinion that occur in a democratic society could develop. In Havel they had a symbol of unity; in the parliamentary elections, the symbol and reality of democratic pluralism.

I am not at all sure that such a strategy was broadly understood. Conversations with people in and outside the Forum suggested an appreciation of this possible outcome, but there were people, quite visible in Civic Forum's leadership, who did not appear to be informed about such a grand strategy, and spoke with alarm of the slippage in the Forum's popularity and the possible need to take extreme actions and return to demonstrations and strikes, to rally mass support. In a circumstance where people lack experience in the tensions of democratic process, misunderstanding and phobias may prevail.

The difficulties of the situation should not lead to a premature despair. The people of Czechoslovakia have engaged in exactly the sorts of conflicts appropriate to their situation. Denying the articulation of the conflicts or attempting to control their outcomes would have constituted a problem. They had to be brought into the open. Working out a means to express differences of opinion within a democratic consensus was also crucial. Although new ideologies in the name of democracy are first-order problems, arguing about the proper democratic balance is an important way to address them.

The difference is subtle; the implications are immense. If Havel or his supporters or advisers should decide that national unity as represented by Havel himself is the democratic manifestation of the national will, and that any opposition to this manifestation is both antidemocratic and treasonous, democratic promise will fade. Likewise, democracy will be lost if anticommunists decide that any connection with the Communist Party past or present must disqualify people from full citizenship, including the possibility of political leadership. In the context of the past domination of the Party and the different ways people disassociated themselves from that domination, one circle of true believers would simply be replacing another. Pluralism would then be able to exist only as a ruling myth. But to insist on a fully articulated pluralism before the repressive apparatus of the totalitarian order has been controlled through consensus, and before people have learned together how to deal with each other with democratic mutual respect, could lead to political chaos instead of political deliberation. Either path would stifle democracy. Instead, the fundamental requirement for a democratic polity is a constituted system in which these and other viewpoints can be openly articulated without any one overwhelming the others. Thus, current splits in Civic Forum, like the differences of opinion in Solidarity, are not in themselves a bad thing if they promote the clear articulation of opposing points of view and interests within a context of mutual respect. False unities must be avoided, and people with differences of opinion should face each other as opponents, not enemies. But the change must take place not only at the heights of the state but also in the discourse of everyday social and cultural life.

CHAPTER 6

Democratic Dialogue

Michnik, who is in a sense the Thomas Jefferson of the revolutions of 1989, has dedicated his life to drawing the distinction between enemies and opponents as a way of making possible the development of a democratic culture of politics. He was Poland's premier democratic theorist before the fall, author of many crucial essays that formulated the strategy and ethos of Poland's self-limiting revolution. In "The New Evolutionism," he rejected the notion that communism could be reformed from above or revolutionized from below. Instead, he proposed gradual reform from below, built upon his idea that if people acted as if they were free, they would in fact establish a free civil society and force a transformation of the system. This work was, in effect, Polish society's Declaration of Independence. The same principle was then applied throughout the bloc. In *The Church, The Left: A Dialogue*, Michnik further defined his ideas about independence. As in other societies with a strong church, there was a deep anticlerical tradition among Polish intellectuals. Michnik's book argues that those who come out of this secular tradition (the left), and those who are more deeply embedded within the Catholic tradition (the church), when true to the ideals of their positions, have a common antitotalitarian ground that is more important than their differences. He did not advocate that people abandon their principles, but showed how they were compatible. He advocated diversity within a democratic unity. Because of this recurring theme, his writings inspire controversy.

In pursuing his theme, Michnik at times embraced some who were held by others to be beyond the democratic pale. Among his old friends of the secular left, many felt that an essay he wrote indicating an appreciation for the geopolitical reasoning of Roman Dmowski, an interwar Polish nationalist and anti-Semite, went too far, even though Michnik carefully tried to distinguish Dmowski's protofascist tendencies from his appreciated political insights. Similarly, Michnik's critical approach to Józef Piłsudski included a careful balancing of sensibilities, which stepped on the toes equally of those who remembered only the brilliant fighter for Polish independence and dignity, and of those who recalled only the dictator.

Indeed, Michnik's entire project of bringing together people of opposing positions offended some. False unities can be absurd, even dangerous. They also create new oppositions. Thus, for example, in the paper Michnik read at the democracy seminar in November 1988, when he returned to the problems of the church and the left, he asserted that Polish political culture should include both the venerated religiosity of Cardinal Wyszyński and the rebellious, even sacrilegious secularism of Witold Gombrowicz (the avant-garde playwright, novelist, and essayist). In the context of a Poland experiencing a great religious awakening, for the religious this assertion was difficult to take. For Western leftists and the few radical secular leftists remaining in Poland, it seemed equally strange. But even more challenging was that, by bringing together Wyszyński and Gombrowicz, Michnik was warning that those who would not respect or at least tolerate both were a threat to political and cultural life. Most significantly, Michnik closed his essay with a critique of a cult of Maksymilian Kolbe (the beatified Polish priest who sacrificed his life for another in Auschwitz);

this cult does not address Kolbe's anti-Semitic associations and activities during the 1920s and 1930s. If we consider Michnik's words in the context of his earlier writings, it is clear that he was arguing that the church and the secularists have a common ground for antitotalitarian democratic dialogue only when they clean up their own houses—not just when the secularists forcefully reject their past connections with communist totalitarianism, but also when the religious reject their past connections with xenophobia, racism, and fascism.

Before the fall, these were interesting theoretical judgments, which, along with his bravery, accounted for Michnik's leadership in the democratic opposition as well as for his growing reputation in the West as a political thinker. After the fall, the old theoretical interests and controversies became pressing political problems. At first, Michnik argued for the continued unity of the Solidarity movement. He believed that the common interest of transformation should override the differences within Solidarity, and between Solidarity and various still-marginal political parties. There was a consistency in Michnik's position, and it was broadly respected; but with the collapse of communism, the position was heatedly debated. While in Czechoslovakia and Romania the transformation debate has been conducted in harsh black-and-white terms—the strong anticommunists versus the party of toleration (as they understand themselves) or of collaboration (as the anticommunists understand them)—in Poland the debate has more richly reflected the complexity of the present situation and the well-developed and differentiated political and intellectual traditions of the country: conservative, liberal, and radical.

In the spring of 1990 I spoke to Jan Józef Szczepański, a distinguished Polish writer, president of the Polish Writers Union and participant in the roundtable talks, about the transformations and contradictions of Polish political and cultural life. We were taking a walk around his home town, the city of Kraków. The life in this beautiful but polluted Central European city, Poland's capital of old, is still centered around the town square. Within a few hundred square yards are dozens of churches and a medieval market, the Sukiennice, which is now a tourist attraction where Polish folk art is sold to Western tourists. Poland's oldest university is a few blocks away. Intermingled with the shops of the old order selling their meager, second-rate offerings are enterprises of the new order and venerable cultural institutions.

Strolling through the maze of streets in this ancient capital, I had a sense of grand historic justice. Szczepański took me to a most interesting bookstore, which specialized in books and magazines of the formerly underground press. There, among the translations of Orwell, Brecht, and Hayek and the rows of nationalist, religious, and radical democratic magazines, was one copy of Szczepański's best-seller, *Kadencja*. In this book Szczepański recalls his failed negotiations with General Czesław Kiszczak, at the time the minister of the interior, in the mid-1980s. As president of the Writers Union, Szczepański sought its re-legalization. The negotiations were bound to fail, since the union was a genuinely independent social institution, and the aim of Kiszczak and the other authorities of Jaruzelski's junta was to disarm Polish society. But the book excited wide interest because of Szczepański's brilliant portrayal of the totalitarian mentality.

Szczepański understood that the ultimate decline and fall of communism would mean more than the end of a particularly unpleasant, even brutal regime. He knew that in a certain sense it would represent the end of the modern political era that began with the Enlightenment. He described a decadent totalitarian mentality, having the cynicism of ideological politics without the ideology; an absolute power, in principle ignorant of the reality beyond the ideological script and, in practice, even ignorant of ideology. In the give and take with Kiszczak, Szczepański portrayed the last-ditch attempt of the old regime to sustain itself, and his readers saw the supposed wizard of a bright and beautiful future to be a con man.

When we walked into the store, Szczepański looked for a copy of his book, to give me. Recently published legally, it was hard to find, and he himself no longer had an extra. We looked through the various books and magazines, with Szczepański pointing out particularly interesting items, and finally he asked a salesperson for assistance. I'm not sure whether she recognized him before he spoke. In some ways Szczepański looks like a typical Krakovian gentleman of the old school: tall, conservative, polite, and gentle in his manner. But when he spoke to her, she knew immediately she was confronting the famous author, because his weekly readings from his book had become a hit program on Polish radio. At first she expressed regret. She did not believe they had a copy left, but with perserverance she found one. Szczepański inscribed it, "To Jeff, hoping that this is one of the last glimpses of totalitarian culture. Jan, Kraków 27/III/90."

Our walk and conversation around Kraków was a continuation of talks we had had in New York. Two years earlier, we had spoken about the idea of publishing an international encyclopedia of totalitarianism, as a bookend to the eighteenth-century French *Encyclopedia*. Part of that conversation had been Szczepański's reading and critique of my book *Beyond Glasnost: The Post-Totalitarian Mind*, in manuscript. Since then, the post-totalitarian world we had both hoped for had come into being. We were surveying it on our walk. We both appreciated that totalitarian culture was at the root of absolute domination, and it was appropriate that our first stop was this bookstore of previously banned books.

But all was not so well. His own Writers Union was now ensnarled in the implications of its previous political positions. In the summer of 1989, the writers had advocated that literature be supported solely by the market, without subsidies. Now its leaders were having second thoughts. Publishing houses that had planned to publish two hundred books in 1990 were having difficulty with six or seven. Publishers were now paying authors and returning their manuscripts unpublished. The free-market cost of paper, along with rising taxes, was making publishing impossible. In order to make a profit, forty thousand copies had to be sold, but the houses did not have the money to publish that number. For that reason, only potential best-sellers such as Szczepański's, and Western blockbusters, were accepted. Furthermore, in order to make a profit, bookstores now had to charge prices that few could afford. So no one was buying books. Szczepański observed a bitter paradox: political freedom was yielding cultural unfreedom.

We walked past Teatr Stary, Kraków's oldest and most distinguished theater. Szczepański pointed out that theater too was under very serious economic constraints. Cultural institutions I had studied to exemplify "the persistence of freedom" (the title of my first book on Polish youth theater) were now losing their subsidies. Only 25 percent of their expenses were being covered by ticket revenues.

Institutions that had been able to maintain cultural excellence and advance political critique under communist repression and subsidy were being forced to close. The Ministry of Culture would decide. Cultural traditions were being severely challenged.

The new order right after the fall, not surprisingly, was involving significant disorder and uncertainty. Signs of it were everywhere, from the breakdown in the organization of culture to extremist anti-Semitic graffiti. Szczepański's fear was that the disorder would overwhelm the promise of the new. But along with the fear, I perceived the great satisfaction of this distinguished seventy-year-old cultural leader. We talked about the problems of anti-Semitism and the church. Although he felt that anti-Semitism was politically peripheral, he was critical of the church, especially concerning the controversy over the Carmelite convent at Auschwitz. Parish priests were often anti-Semitic, in the old Catholic way. Sophisticated, urbane Catholic intellectuals didn't help much, because they were satisfied to operate at the elite level, which was more or less beside the point for ordinary Poles. But he was not sure about his opinions, and wanted me to be better informed. So we walked to the editorial offices of *Tygodnik Powszechny*, the major liberal Catholic weekly, so that I could get the more expert judgments of Jerzy Turowicz, the editor. Later, when we spoke about the new entrepreneurial support of avant-garde art, Szczepański took me to a storefront gallery operated by Tadeusz Nyczek (whom I had last met when we were detained togther in Lublin). Szczepański was a man who understood that problems abounded, but in our little walk around the town, he was also able to show me who might be able to meet the challenges of the transition intelligently.

The challenges should be addressed in as careful a way as possible, or the ancient political wisdom might be confirmed once again, that democracy could yield anarchy, which could lead in turn to tyranny. Therefore, Sczcepański supported Poland's odd framework for political change. He took part in the roundtable talks which led to the end of communist tyranny in Poland. At these talks, Jaruzelski and his comrades sat down with their previous enemies, representatives of the church and Solidarity, and agreed to semifree elections and a sort of coalition government. The agreement, in the final analysis, set a framework for the transfer of power from the communists to Solidarity. While before 1989 this result was beyond imagination, except as a distant dream, after the fact many were dissatisfied because it led to a continuing role for communists when this seemed unnecessary. Jaruzelski's presidency was particularly galling. Yet with inherited wisdom in mind, Szczepański was cautious about these imperfections. He knew that the agreements were between individuals and groups who had accumulated authority, and that they were providing the leadership for an orderly dismantling of the communist order—a unique process in the history of totalitarianism. A more perfect transition could reasonably be imagined, but insofar as the agreements were working, only a fool would try to fix them. Such fixing could encourage the emergence of an authoritarian leader, extremist political parties, or wild calls for retribution. Such tendencies existed in Poland. Institutional mechanisms to control them needed to be put into place by utilizing, not revoking, the agreements. Solidarity, therefore, needed to stay together until the task was accomplished.

After the fall, chaos and anarchy were possibilities. Szczepański seemed to be arguing a classically conservative position: that governance, drawing upon accumulated experience, would be most effective, and in this way gain popular support and legitimation. As stated in the Federalist Papers by Alexander Hamilton, the most conservative of the American revolutionaries, this is an important way to assure the people's sovereignty. It is as essential, if not more essential, that government be worthy of popular support as it is that the making of the government respond to the formal demands of reason. The federalists, in their new science of politics, argued that experience and effective results must be considered alongside reason in the formation of a political system. Tyranny was a more likely alternative than a purer democracy.

But a liberal common sense (like Thomas Paine's) provided an opposing viewpoint in Poland. Zygmunt Matynia, a young former law teacher who quit the law faculty before the fall because he found that he was propagating tyranny rather than legality, argued on straightforward legal grounds against the agreement, and by extension against Szczepański's (and Adam Michnik's) position on the transition. Matynia is Szczepański's and my mutual friend. At the end of our walk, we met him and his family for dinner.

For Matynia, the matter of the roundtable agreements was simple: the agreements represented a contract wherein one of the principals, the Communist Party, had died. All agreed that it had disappeared from public life. Therefore, the contract was null and void. Thus the time had arrived to form a new social contract based on the real political pluralism that existed in Poland: political competition among all parties, and agreements built around compromise within the anti-totalitarian camp. Such interaction would create a more democratic order. Even as Matynia made this liberal argument, he recognized the concerns of Michnik and Szczepański. The issue, again, was not whether open political pluralism should be permitted, for it had existed in Poland even before the fall. The issue was when open political pluralism should be institutionalized to replace the antitotalitarian, antipolitical consensus and the framework of the roundtable agreements. Conservatives and liberals agreed that the issue was strategic, but it was also sociological. Conservatives seek to avoid political anarchy as a first order of political business. Liberals seek reasonable change agreed upon by mutual consent.

Sociology gives substantive grounds for and against both sides of the issue. As Polish sociologist Mirka Marody has observed in her writing, since the previous social structure had been destroyed by the communist domination and control of social life, there was need for a unifying force. In the absence of such a force, there would be anarchy. Yet she further observed that enforced unification could also be dangerous: if the important differences in political judgment were not expressed among competing political parties with representatives in Parliament, the government ministries, and other elected bodies and leadership positions, they might be expressed in an extraparliamentary fashion. A period of unity during the course of transition might be necessary, but a transition that lasted too long could yield the very chaos that the advocates of deliberate change were trying to avoid.

The last point has been made quite radically by Czesław Bielecki, a hero of the Polish underground, and also a struggling though successful private entrepreneur, owner of his own architectural firm, Metropolis. According to him and other experienced veterans of the democratic movement, rhetorics of transition are dangerous. Just as the economy requires a quick fix through a clear break with the past and a rapid introduction of market mechanisms, all vanguardisms and political systems of privilege and all false ideologies of unity must be rapidly discarded, and a fully developed political pluralism must be introduced.

In the Warsaw headquarters of his firm, we met to speak politics. His parents were communists, so after the fall, Bielecki was not only impatient with transitions, he feared them. In arguments for political patience he saw the crystallization of a new hierarchy of privilege, the establishment of a new *nomenklatura*. He remembered that his parents and their friends also claimed to be "leading the nation down the road to a better political and economic life." He knew that they were not simply bad or evil people; neither were his old oppositionist colleagues. But in his view these friends were repeating the communist experience. Compromises against democracy had already been made in the name of a better future. The agents of change had only a vague legitimacy. A secret, informal structure, after the fall at first around Wałęsa, but back in his parents' time connected to Moscow, had actually governed. Decisions had been made without clear lines of responsibility. The leadership had counseled patience, while the old rules of the economic and political game had not been changed. For Bielecki, the new order was neither sufficiently democratic nor sufficiently capitalist. He wanted quick and radical change.

Coming from an entrepreneur and a technical expert, Bielecki's radical impatience with the messiness of politics was not surprising. He still faced absurd regulations and, until state monopolies were completely dismantled, unfair competition with state enterprises. The parallels he saw between the new democratic order and the old Bolshevik one were disquieting. But according to many less passionate observers and analysts, quick fixes appeared all but impossible.

Mirka Marody has reported some sobering sociological data. They directly contradict the judgments of Bielecki and others who believe that the more pure the discipline of the market, the more robust the economy and the more democratic the polity. Market ideologists assume that the introduction of economic discipline will yield rational individual and collective economic and political action. In economic matters, people will rapidly learn to link work and enterprise with the pursuit of scarce goods. In politics, they will find leaders and groups (parties) that defend their interests. Neither of these rational configurations has occurred in Poland. A public-opinion poll taken in February 1990 indicated that despite the macroeconomic changes, people only recognized the poor financial situation of enterprises as a perceived change. The Polish respondents were of the opinion that people were not willing to work (42 percent), the organization had not improved (58 percent), and the time and qualifications of employees were not used in any better way (57 percent). They further believed that their living standards were influenced primarily by factors independent of their own efforts (50 percent); 17 percent thought that the most important factor was luck or chance. A full 88 percent felt that obtaining additional income was difficult. And when asked their opinion of the future, people replied that merit would be of less importance than such qualities as cunning, previously possessed wealth, ability to take risks, and personality. The new economic disciplines of the market led people to fall back on their accustomed rationalizations and adaptive strategies: moonlighting and limiting expenses (when 45 percent of the population was already no higher than the level of biological survival). According to Marody, these adaptations reinforced old ways. They were old habits blocking new possibilities.

It can be argued, as Marody has conceded, that in the economic sphere, the changes were too young and as yet insufficiently radical for new attitudes and actions to have taken hold. But in contrast to places like Czechoslovakia, in Poland political change was long developing, and even there, old habits seemed to be blocking what many assume to be "natural," a multiparty system. People have continued to think in old ways, either supporting or disobeying the authorities. As the uncertainties and hardships of the transformation were personally felt, potential electoral support of Solidarity dropped by 15 percent (between November 1989 and February 1990); but at the same time, the very meager support of the other political groups and parties did not increase. People were not seeking other political alternatives, even when these had access to the mass media and operated freely.

Marody reported her data in a paper entitled "New Possibilities and Old Habits." Her empirical conclusions can be summarized in two points: first, Western models and expectations are not easily applied to Polish circumstances; and, second, people change slowly. Traditional conservatives are not alarmed by this situation, although both liberals and radicals are. Conservatives know the limits of change. They even elevate the limits to a normative principle. Liberals and radicals advocate change, find it both natural and desirable, and must explain why it does not occur. In the Polish circumstances, the liberals and radicals feared that absence of change would lead to chaos. Conservatives, to the contrary, believed that chaos would result if change did not occur within customary and evolving limits. This is an important and significant, even universal, debate. The question is: Where should it occur, and how should it be politically articulated? All three parties of Poland's roundtable talks contained conservatives, liberals, and radicals. In the old official parties, in the church, and in Solidarity, there were true believers in market magic, and there were nationalists, moralists, and those who were primarily concerned with the effects of various changes and stagnations on the weak and disadvantaged. Since the church, as a matter of principle, did not directly engage in politics (especially because of the pope's edicts against such involvement), and since the old parties' effectiveness receded rapidly, political pluralism emerged in two locations: among former oppositionists inside and outside Solidarity. The problem was that fully developed pluralism was frustrated in both instances. Inside, Solidarity's ethos of unity made differences seem like petty factionalism. Outside, the emerging parties had more to do with national nostalgias and ideological fascinations than with pressing political problems, and they seemed to have only very narrow appeal. The political paradox was that the society was still mobilized primarily on the old antipolitical, antitotalitarian consensus (in Solidarity's citizen committees), while political contestation in political parties was slower in developing.

This situation accounts for the peculiar character of Poland's 1990 presidential election, though it was Poland's first fully free national election. The political culture and institutional context of this election set very severe limitations. A politics of the left and the right was emerging, but ultimately an antipolitics overwhelmed it. There was the antipolitical concern of those who wanted to forestall the election (Michnik and Szczepański among them). There was the antidemocratic demagoguery of Wałęsa. And the most bizarre was the last to come—the Tymiński phenomenon. All of these phenomena revolved around the extraordinary personality of Lech Wałęsa. There were reasonable grounds to be conservative, liberal, or radical after the fall, but the less than reasonable politics of personality, along with traditional affiliations of nation and church, threatened to overwhelm reason.

CHAPTER 7

Wałęsa: Washington or Piłsudski?

Lech Wałęsa, like Václav Havel, is a generally recognized national leader, symbol of national traditions of resistance and of civil society's victory over the communist party-state. His actions, like Havel's in Czechoslovakia, were crucial in deciding the fate of Polish democracy. A key to his power, as with Havel, is facility with language; but in this regard his strengths are very different from Havel's. He is less the poet, more the democrat. Wałęsa is a master of the vernacular. He speaks the idiom of the countryside, combined with urban street-smarts. He uses a self-mocking bravado, powerfully laced with subtle understatement. He is a populist empowered by his speech.

Wałęsa apparently knows when to give and when to take. At the outset of the famous negotiations at the Lenin shipyards, he was a union leader. But by their conclusion, in August 1980, he was something more. At one point during the negotiations, all of the union's

demands had been met but one—freeing the major intellectual oppositionists of the Committee for Worker Defense (KOR), who had
been imprisoned when the strikes began. Wałęsa and his colleagues
held firm, not ending the strike until the oppositionists were released.

After the pact was signed, Wałęsa addressed the workers. His audience was tense, prepared to be euphoric. Wałęsa announced the successful conclusion of the negotiations, and a worker called out, "What
about our colleagues from KOR?" Wałęsa answered with a question:
"Who do you think I am?" Then he paused and answered his own
question, in language that was simple and direct: "We don't sell out
our friends."

The cadence of Wałęsa's language expressed the confidence and
cunning of a new social and political force. That exchange was filmed,
along with excerpts from the negotiations, and shown around Poland
in the documentary *Workers '80*. Through that film, and through the
growing self-awareness of its actors, the political position of Solidarity
took shape, and Wałęsa emerged as its leader.

During the tense 1980–1981 period, when legalized Solidarity
fought against a hostile party-state, the electrician from Gdańsk
repeatedly displayed his leadership. He knew how to be both tough
and conciliatory. He spoke for the union and its leadership, availing
himself of the advice of Poland's foremost intellectuals, scholars,
scientists, and technical experts. He bravely attempted to reconcile
the unreconcilable—"the independent self-governing trade union
Solidarity" (as it was officially and ironically known) and the Polish
United Workers Party, with its self-defined Leninist leading role.

At times Wałęsa was tough with his communist adversaries, particularly Mieczysław Rakowski (who ten years later became the last leader
of the deteriorating Communist Party). Wałęsa knew when the Party
was seeking fatal compromises, and at those times he avoided them.
At other times he was much more flexible than some in the union
leadership and among the active unionists. To them he even seemed
autocratic, too often circumventing union democracy. Yet his actions
were popular with the rank and file and the general public, which
strengthened his position.

Wałęsa later faced serious challenges, but during the state of war, the
circumstances and his actions elevated his leadership. His resolve, his

Nobel Prize, and, in the late eighties, the support he received from a new generation of disgruntled young striking workers, made him the primary negotiating partner with the collapsing party-state. During the martial-law period, when the rest of Solidarity's leadership was either in jail or underground, Wałęsa continued his political activities. Because of his international fame, he remained free. The Polish regime had hoped that its repression of other oppositionists would make him simply ineffective, but with underground resolve, this proved not to be the case. Even after the end of martial law, when Solidarity functioned with difficulty as an underground structure and the regime's strategy of repressive tolerance seemed to work, Wałęsa, thanks to his national and international celebrity, was a key player on the Polish political stage. Although Poland's chief government spokesman, Jerzy Urban, repeatedly called him "the former leader of a former union organization," Wałęsa prevailed. The danger of intervention by the neighbor from the east receded. Jaruzelski's various political and economic reforms failed. And by the beginning of 1989, it was clear that the regime's need for Lech Wałęsa outweighed the threat he posed.

The Polish roundtable talks began. The jailed sat down with their jailors; the informal authorities in the worlds of literature, theater, sociology, and economics, along with leading Solidarity activists, met face to face with respected church authorities and totally disrespected party-state officials. The outcome is well known: a half-free election, guaranteeing a communist majority in Parliament, Jaruzelski as president, and Communist Party control of the defense and internal (police) ministries. And even so the Party lost control. All of the negotiated guarantees for continued communist power collapsed. Solidarity won ninety-nine of the hundred seats in the newly formed Senate. It won all thirty-five of the seats it could contest in the lower chamber of Parliament, the Sejm. The Peasant Party and the Democratic Front, both traditionally subservient to the communists, rebuffed their former masters, and with the support of these parties, Solidarity formed the new government. All of the Solidarity candidates were endorsed by Wałęsa. He picked the new prime minister, and then Tadeusz Mazowiecki named the new government. And at this point a more normal politics began.

Previously, politics had had two faces in Poland: anticommunism and antipolitics. The unity of Solidarity had been a unity against the dominating authorities, a united civil society against a totalitarian power. The unity of society was the result of an antipolitical practice, which took as its major task the disengagement of the civil social order from political control. Thus, during the period of legitimate Solidarity, Wałęsa and other union representatives repeatedly insisted that Solidarity was merely a trade union, perhaps a social movement, but certainly not a political organization. They doggedly insisted that they respected the "leading role" of the Polish United Workers Party. They took as their major task the substitution of social control for political control.

During the martial-law period, this mission was continued. They did not establish an underground political force, political parties, an underground government, or a government in exile (as the Poles did during the Nazi occupation). Rather, they concentrated on the development of oppositional cultural activities and social networks, from publishing houses, to various educational enterprises, to ad hoc welfare institutions (especially for families of the politically repressed). This social practice provided Solidarity with a significant social infrastructure for governance. It also provided a sound social basis for democratically controlled political contestation. But with normal politics began democratic difficulties, and overriding them all was the Wałęsa problem. In November 1988, before the fall, an oppositionist friend once joked in frustration, "The moment we win, I'll get on the first flight abroad." He seemed to have anticipated the dangerous aspects of the difficult transition from antipolitics to politics.

Havel's overwhelming authority exists in a virtual social and political vacuum. Wałęsa's does not. For Czechs, though to a lesser extent for Slovaks, Havel provides not only political leadership but also moral leadership. His is the moral leadership achieved by a persistent opposition to totalitarian power. He "lived in truth" and suffered the consequences, while the vast majority of his compatriots lived the lie. The contrast between Wałęsa and his fellow citizens is not nearly so great. Wałęsa was part of a great social movement. He was an archetype of the resistant Polish workers. But when Poles look for high moral leadership, they turn to Karol Wojtyła, Pope Jan Paweł II. Although this too may involve significant problems, it does avoid an overconcentration of moral authority in Wałęsa as a political leader.

There was even a Polish joke displaying an ironic sensitivity to these matters. It involved the miracle of the Black Madonna of Częstochowa, whose image Wałęsa always wears on his jacket lapel. According to the joke, when the Madonna returned to Częstochowa, she wore an image of Wałęsa on her dress. He associates himself with a national religious icon, "the Madonna Queen of Poland," but a too-close association of the two is ridiculous.

In a certain sense, Wałęsa has been strengthened by the fact that he is clearly a practicing Catholic, but not a Catholic politician. He is an autonomous political authority in the sense that he has been quite willing to resist (and has been successful at resisting) the political directives of church authorities, from the venerated Cardinal Wyszyński to the ridiculed Cardinal Glemp. But as a political author-ity, Wałęsa, unlike Havel, operates in a well-developed political field, something he has sometimes failed to understand.

Mazowiecki was actually named prime minister by Wałęsa. According to the rules of the roundtable game, President Jaruzelski formally had this power, subject to the confirmation of Parliament. But when Solidarity and the Communist Party's coalition partners together refused to confirm Jaruzelski's nominees, the president, the Party, the church, and Solidarity, after predictable jockeying, agreed on a Solidarity candidate. When Wałęsa made it clear that he would not take the position, the most likely person seemed to be Bronisław Geremek, a world-renowned medieval historian, expelled member of the Academy of Science, and close adviser to Wałęsa. But Wałęsa did not give him the nod, perhaps because of Geremek's communist past, or his Jewish background, or his independent cast of mind and pol-itical base, which might make him Wałęsa's competitor. Instead, Wałęsa chose a well-respected but less independently powerful lay Catholic journalist, editor of Solidarity's weekly newspaper, *Tygodnik Solidarność*. This selection set in motion interesting political dynamics.

Mazowiecki's appointees to high government posts included oppo-sitional activists, university professors, journalists, researchers and technicians in state enterprises, and union activists, among others. Unlike Czechoslovakia, Poland had a broad range of people within and outside official institutions with an open record of ethical and effective action, though they had different political orientations, past experiences, and present priorities. Mazowiecki chose among them. Some of his choices proved to be more popular than others; for example, Jacek Kuroń, the minister of labor. Some were more controversial, such as Leszek Balcerowicz, the architect of the economic reforms. But all were chosen after consideration of their past track records, which were visible for public inspection.

From the beginning of the Solidarity government, there was tension between Mazowiecki and Wałęsa. Wałęsa seemed to be torn between a noble withdrawal from political life and a desire to continue to lead society in an unofficial capacity. At first he indicated his support for Mazowiecki, but when it became clear that he would not be the real power behind Mazowiecki's throne, grumblings were heard from Gdańsk around two distinct and contradictory themes. On the one hand, the government was seen as acting too slowly, without enough resolve. On the other, its actions were judged as being insensitive to their impact on ordinary people. In April 1990, at the second Solidarity Congress (the first was in 1981), Wałęsa (a rich man) even maintained that his wife Danuta was having a hard time making ends meet. During the congress (where Wałęsa's position as union leader was reconfirmed), as well as in interviews, Wałęsa spoke about the need for firm executive actions in order to protect the disadvantaged and expedite economic transformation. And clearly the presidency was on his own agenda, from the roundtable talks onward. This was the Wałęsa problem: when personal ambition was the issue, did he know when to come forward and when to withdraw? Did he know how to act democratically?

Wałęsa's decision not to become Solidarity's first prime minister indicated real political wisdom. Like Washington, who was also a man of considerable ambition, he seemed to understand that his own personal authority could overwhelm democratic constitution. Washington could have become the first military dictator of the new nation after the success of the American army. Instead he bade farewell to his troops. When he returned to public life at the Constitutional Convention, and later when he took office as the first president, he could have become the first American monarch. But instead he limited his presidency to two four-year terms. Washington's power of resignation was as important in the making of the American republic as were his positive military and political actions. By not becoming Poland's prime minister, Wałęsa too exhibited such power. When he acted in this wise fashion, it became clear that he might return as Poland's first democratically elected president.

The half-democratic nature of the roundtable agreements made many Poles uncomfortable. Some strongly opposed them, while others, probably most people, felt that they were a significant step toward democratic rule and national independence. The prospect that after a period of transition Wałęsa might become president satisfied many on both sides of the question. In place of President Jaruzelski, there would be President Wałęsa. This would indicate the completion of the political transformation, the successful conclusion of the self-limiting revolution, as Poles had described their antipolitics since the mid-seventies.

But as normal politics began to function in place of antipolitics, judgments changed. For some, Wałęsa began to look like a simple solution to a set of very complex dilemmas. For others, he began to represent a major problem. The politics around the Wałęsa problem were initially conducted in whispers, or indirectly. Relations between the union leader and his former advisers grew tense. When Mazowiecki became prime minister, Wałęsa, without consulting his staff, appointed the new editor and editorial board of the Solidarity weekly. Many of the journalists there protested; some resigned. *Tygodnik Solidarność* became the pro-Wałęsa journal, while the Solidarity daily, *Gazeta Wyborcza* (edited by Adam Michnik), stayed closer to the Mazowiecki government.

Important polemics developed in the Polish press around numerous issues concerning old communist monopolies and properties, the continuing validity of different aspects of the roundtable agreements, the funding of radio and television, and the Polish presidency. But, significantly, it was in *Tygodnik Solidarność* that vigorous polemics for a strong presidential government were published. It began to appear that Wałęsa's model was not Washington but a more likely and closer source: Józef Piłsudski, the Polish military leader who fought heroically for independence, withdrew from public life when independence was achieved, then returned as a popular dictator in the 1920s.

At first people seemed to agree that Wałęsa would be the next president. What they questioned were the powers the president should have, some in a general way, some with Wałęsa specifically in mind. There were two interconnected concerns about Wałęsa personality: that his talents were antipolitical ones, and that when he entered the more explicitly political realm, he would reveal authoritarian tendencies. The more general, principled arguments against a strong presidency were those favoring decentralized authority in the name of pluralism, local autonomy, and the (antipolitical) ethic of Solidarity.

Wałęsa's critics observed that he was a smart negotiator and a foxy opponent against the communist authorities, as well as a master of the politics of resistance, but it was far from clear that those were the talents needed for a successful presidency. In the course of normal politics, a willingness to use unconventional methods, including a willingness to suspend democratic procedures—a necessity during resistance—could be disastrous. Wałęsa's talk about the need for strong executive rule troubled them.

Even so, there was no doubt that Wałęsa had been Poland's most respected and effective leader. And during a difficult period of political transition and economic transformation in the life of any nation, a leader with the ability to keep the nation unified and working together on the most daunting tasks is an invaluable resource.

These arguments for and against Wałęsa were serious. They became public in the presidential campaign of 1990. Insofar as none was enforced in an absolutist fashion, they were part of the developing democratic game. When Wałęsa came to be viewed as indispensable by some (including himself) as a national savior, there appeared to be the danger that his presidency might follow Piłsudski's path from popular patriotic hero to political dictator. There was a real danger that the political resources Poles already owned could be dissipated. From the other point of view, if Wałęsa's critics projected this development too strongly in their own minds and assessed Wałęsa too quickly as a major threat to democracy even when he was not acting in an antidemocratic fashion, then democracy could also be compromised.

The fundamental threat of Wałęsa was that of the authoritarian leader with a cult of personality. Other preceived threats to democracy, both from Wałęsa's opponents and from his supporters, depended on their specific political positions. Some were narrowly partisan, others were based on imagined overarching unities. They were based on specific ideals of politics, religion, economics, and nationality.

The purely political question—in other words, the formal political question—concerned the relation between political leadership and other political forces and the balance between consensus and articulated conflict. When the answer to all political questions revolves around the leadership of one person, or of a mythically presented party unity for that matter, political life is reduced to intrigue. Who has and who has not the ear of the supreme leader or supreme party organ? How does one gain access or get something done without it? This was not the situation after the fall. Instead, real, even if unusual, political questions came to the fore. While there was a great deal of concern in Poland about Wałęsa, his edicts did not decide political issues, and it was broadly understood by both his supporters and his detractors that with or without Wałęsa, there were pressing political problems to be addressed. A vital problem was one that had plagued the American founders—the question of faction.

The American federalists and antifederalists feared factions. They knew they were an inevitable part of republican life, and at the same time a fundamental threat to the viability of republics. Factions must be controlled. According to the antifederalists, the Constitution would create a republic so large, and with such a diverse population of warring factions, that disorder would be inevitable. They preferred a confederation of decentralized, smaller, economically and ethnically homogeneous polities, more resistant to the factionalism of crystallized opposing interests on the one hand, and a tyrannically enforced order necessary to suppress interest-group formation on the other. The federalists took the contrary position: factionalism could only be transcended in a larger union. Madison eloquently argued in Federalist Paper number 10, his most original contribution to political theory, that in a large republic petty factions would be numerous enough to balance one another, permitting the common good to emerge. After the fall, this debate was repeated with interesting variations on the old American themes.

There is a tremendous irony here. While America's economic weakness is evident, American theoretical experience may be gaining importance. Perhaps this century of American military, political, and economic hegemony will close with the ascendance of half-forgotten

American political wisdoms. I, for one, hope that the charismatic personalities of Central Europe pay some attention to George Washington, and that the discussions about the need for and the roles of political parties consider classic American arguments.

Confusion has been widespread in the new democracies. People look for simple models, or a set of easy-to-follow democratic rules. But there are none. In the democratizing European nation-states, citizens are struggling over these classic political questions. No simple answers have been generated. Few general rules seem applicable. Indeed, the commonalities shared by these societies are less pronounced than during the communist era. The differences are ever more apparent. They shared Stalinist histories, but de-Stalinization and democratization have taken very different courses: some fast, such as Romania; some slow, such as Poland; some apparently complete, such as Poland, Czechoslovakia, and Hungary; some strikingly incomplete, such as Bulgaria and (centrally) the Soviet Union. If we look closely, we see that complex political problems rather than easy formulas (such as "the end of history") contributed to these varied outcomes. Nevertheless, there are general lessons to be drawn. Standard social and political interpretations must be revised, but the events of the fall are not beyond interpretation, or even beyond the categorization of politics.

As the old Marxist cliché goes, it is not an accident that at crucial points in this account of democratic problems, I have turned to American political precedents. For, I believe, the events of the fall discredit one modern revolutionary tradition—the one that connects the Chinese, Russian, and French experiences—and highlight the continued importance of the other modern revolutionary tradition, archetypically represented in the American experience. Marxist common sense, accepted by many non-Marxists, dismisses the political importance of the American Revolution, viewing it as merely political, nothing more than a war for political independence, conservative in its social implications. It has been contrasted with the social transformations realized in the French, and especially the Russian, revolutions. The fall of communism demonstrates that this interpretive script has to change. The American Revolution constructed a republican political foundation that made a struggle for democracy possible.

The revolution did promise more than it delivered: contradictions between the reality of gross inequalities and social injustices, and theories of political equality and democracy, have persisted. But the grounds for addressing these problems also persist, whereas the Russian Revolution has self-destructed. The Americans did not think they had easy solutions to complex problems. They had, rather, a set of political principles, enshrined in the Declaration of Independence and the Constitution, which they struggled to enact through mutual consent, along a rocky road. The citizens of the "other Europe" have been trying to do the same thing. Therefore it is not surprising that they have been facing similar problems in democratic constitution.

Such a politics seems to present a common set of problems independent of the social circumstances in which they occur. The democratic legitimacy of the political system and its leaders, and the balance between consensus and conflict, are the basis of a new politics. Some emphasize more the legitimacy of the leader, some emphasize more the system, some are more concerned with the problems of conflict and seek to nurture consensus, and some are primarily concerned with the problems of consensus and nurture conflict. On these political grounds, a new basis for a left-right distinction emerges. We observed the basis of conservative, liberal, and radical sensibilities in the judgments of Jan Józef Szczepański, Zygmunt Matynia, and Czesław Bielecki on the political transition. These sensibilities may provide a new basis of politics, addressing the issues of leadership and representation, the balance between conflict and consensus when dealing with problems of nationalism, the relationship of religion and politics, the institutions of the economy, and the organization of cultural life.

III

NATION

The Problem of Nationalism: On the Road to Harmony with the Minister of the Interior

The day after my discussion with Jan Langoš, the Czechoslovak minister of the interior, we drove together to Harmonia, a retreat thirty kilometers outside Bratislava. During this trip, and in Harmonia, I started a fundamental reconsideration of the question of nationalism in the post-totalitarian world. My position had been one of tolerance. But I began to appreciate the pressing need for distinguishing between nationalism as a political pathology and nationalism as a normal political phenomenon. As a pathology, nationalism overwhelms the democratic politics of the left, right, and center; as a part of normal politics, it respectfully articulates the differences between various groups.

On the road to Harmony, Langoš and I no longer had the benefit of a translator. The Polish-Slovak conversation provided for a simple exchange of opinion, and quiet for reflection. Langoš had picked me up at my apartment in his black Czech limo, Tatra 613, together with his assistant, also from Bratislava, his bodyguard, and his chauffeur. While we traveled cross-country at about ninety miles an hour, we talked about his becoming an official, about the issues of religion and nationalism, and about the politics of fear and the politics of dialogue. He seemed much more tired than the night before.

Halfway through our journey, two Czech traffic officers waved us down for speeding. But when we slowed down and approached them, our bodyguard flashed the minister's identification. The Czech cops saluted smartly and waved us on. As we drove off without stopping, a momentary sense of fear came over me. I realized that the highway militiamen were surely holdovers from the old regime. It was not necessary or desirable or even possible to change such personnel. What about our driver and guard? Could it be that they too were holdovers? I had heard that Havel and his people felt surrounded by the old officialdom. Some people complained that he was too much influenced by them, others that he did not distinguish between them and anyone else outside his small circle of dissident and artist colleagues. In the lap of luxury, there in the official limousine, I realized that the luxury could be a seat of danger. Langoš was charged with the task of dismantling the Czech secret police. But was he at its mercy?

I had an urge to turn around and see whether we were being followed. Three quick images came to me. I recalled approaching the courthouse in the city of Gdańsk in Poland, in May 1985, attempting to observe the trial of Adam Michnik, Władysław Frasyniuk, and Bodgan Lis. I had been advised to act as normally as possible, but also to be aware that most of the undercover police were probably women—some elderly, and some strolling with their children. And there had seemed to be an unusual number of strolling mothers that day. Then I recalled riding in the car of Michnik's fiancée that same day, and turning around and seeing two "undercover" police ostentatiously and recklessly following us. And last, I remembered a walk with Michnik months later through the Old Town of Warsaw, after he had been released as part of Jaruzelski's "normalization process." In the narrow streets, a car had passed rather quickly and closely, and Michnik had jumped like a man who knew he had enemies in the secret police.

Now I was with the head of such a police force, and I wondered how much safer I was with him than I had been with Michnik in darker days. But then I consoled myself by thinking that Langoš certainly knew more than I did about the hard facts of the way things were, and therefore our bodyguard and driver were probably trusted old friends.

My mind, momentarily at ease, shifted to thoughts about the unsettling problems of nationalism. Langoš had told me about the xenophobic basis of Slovak nationalist tendencies. For the nationalists, he had explained, the Hungarian minority was a symbol of nine-teenth-century exploitation, the Czechs were a symbol of 1930s exploitation, and the Jews were the universal Other. "We have anti-Semitism like Poland's, without Jews," he had declared. "Therefore the only aggressive act is the desecration of cemeteries." He viewed the rise of nationalism negatively and believed it was caused by fear of the future, "the fear of entering a confusing world unprotected." He maintained that there was little connection in Slovakia between nationalism and religion (that is, the Catholic church), though the Slovaks in their Catholicism did distinguish themselves from their more secular and Protestant Czech compatriots. But it was not the nationalism or Catholicism of the Slovak Christian Democrats that primarily concerned Langoš; rather, it was the fanatical Slovak National Party. He himself was allied with The Public Against Violence, the least nationalist political grouping in the Slovak political arena.

Langoš told me about the plans for the meeting in Harmonia. It was to be a closed session to formulate the position of The Public Against Violence on the national question. Leading representatives of the Slovak and Czech governments and federal authorities would attend. It was hoped that the connection between The Public Against Violence and Civic Forum would provide a basis for compromise. Christian Democracy could not do this, according to Langoš, because in Slovakia the Christian Democrats were too nationalist, and in Bohemia they were too weak. But the difficulty of working out an adequate compromise through The Public Against Violence and Civic Forum was also immense, arising from nationalism's historical roots and its ambiguous relationship with democracy.

Historically, nationalism and democracy developed together. The notion that the people should have a say in political affairs coincides with the idea of the nation as a large-scale primordial human collectivity cutting across class and status boundaries. The nation is made up of the people of a discrete geographical area with a particular set of customs, and usually with a common language. Its political legitimacy is built upon the sovereignty of its people (however this may be represented). The organization of political life around the idea of the nation has become a reality that is taken for granted; both its universal and its problematic nature are probably best represented in the world body, the United Nations.

The universality of nation and nationalism, of course, is a relatively modern phenomenon, and the universal is paradoxically based on a series of distinct particulars. While the nation state has become a worldwide mode of political organization, each nationalism purports to be distinct. Nationalism involves a unique blend of commonality and difference: "We—, like other nations, have our rights and responsibilities. We must realize our unique inheritance." When Edmund Burke inserted "English" into this proposition, he was attempting to indicate that liberty was constituted through communal tradition, and not through reason.

In the twentieth century, for those who have thought seriously about totalitarianism, Burke's arguments have considerable cogency. Hannah Arendt has shown that those who were excluded from nation-states were without rights. They became stateless victims of National Socialism. Because it both included and excluded membership, the idea of nation protected some and banished others. But that the name of the "socialism" was "national" indicates something more. Not all nations were England, the society in which the idea of nation first mobilized the population. Tyranny, as well as liberty, could constitute the nation's unique inheritance.

When Russia was mobilized as a nation, for example, national distinctiveness was based more on resentment of the Other—the Western—than on a positive national inheritance. The insecurity of the ruling elite, and their resentment, were two integral elements of the idea of the nation as a people subjected to a despot, benevolent or not. To be included in Stalin's polity did not protect citizens. It endangered subjects, very much in the czarist tradition of Ivan the Terrible and Peter the Great (who, for his subjects, may have been even more terrible than he was great). This tradition hangs over Eastern Europe.

Embedded as I am in American political discourse and life, the balancing of pluralistic and national (or patriotic) commitments seems normal. But even for Americans, serious difficulties are involved in such balancing. In the new democracies, the task is even more difficult. In Harmonia, I realized the dimensions of the problem. All at the gathering were committed democrats, and therefore understood that their major opponents were Slovak ultranationalists. At one point, when the very serious problems they faced were still far from resolved, the hundred delegates at the meeting watched a film of a Slovak National Party rally. The speaker in the film denounced the assembled Slovak delegates as traitors because of their part in modifying a law making Slovak the official language of Slovakia. What they had done was provide the ethnic Hungarian minority certain minimal rights. For example, if in a locality there were more than 20 percent Hungarians, the minority language was permitted though not required in official transactions. For those assembled, this was a tolerable compromise; most, in fact, would have preferred a much more liberal law with more substantial guarantees of minority rights. But among the extreme nationalists, the law was criticized for its liberalism. They saw it as proof of national treason.

Havel's new regime was denounced as a new totalitarianism, executed in Slovakia by The Public Against Violence. The slogans were wild and demagogic: "Enough of Prague!" "The Slovak Gold and Treasure for the Slovak People!" "Long Live the Slovak National Party!" "Mečiar (the Slovak prime minister), Do You Think You Are Wiser Than the Slovak Nation?" "Slovakia to Victory!" "Slovak Independence!" The speakers portrayed a fascistic vision: "Brothers, Christmas is coming and our wives, mothers, and grandmothers need something to feed us." "They (The Public Against Violence) call us the mob and declare they don't have to obey the mob. We the Slovak people put them in their posts and now we are not good enough for them." "Our tenderness and love have been replaced by a new totalitarianism." Slovak fanatics on hunger strikes over the concessions to the Hungarian minority were glorified as heroes: "I bring flowers for the hunger strikers. I am concerned about their fate. Those boys will be parents too! They want something different for their children, and that is why they are on their hunger strike." "The language law that passed yesterday is the lowest chapter in the history of the nation." "Strengthen your national consciousness! Be better Slovaks than those in Parliament who betrayed the nation for the sake of membership in Europe and tolerance!"

The rally continued with demands for a national army to protect Slovak security, with paranoid visions about television, about those in Prague, about those who didn't have a true Slovak consciousness. While it was shocking for me to see thousands of people listening to these diatribes, it was not clear whether those assembled were mostly curious passersby or committed nationalists. Nevertheless, hearing tolerance and Europe used as slogans of derision in Central Europe seemed outrageous, and not only to me. I was watching the film with Soňa Szomolanyová, a sociologist at Comenius University in Bratislava and, since the Velvet Revolution, a very active member of The Public Against Violence. She was translating, and added her editorial comment, which was expressed with horror: "We didn't expect this last December."

For democrats and reformers in Slovakia and Bohemia, and in Poland, Hungary, Romania, and Bulgaria as well—and, indeed, in the Soviet Union—unexpected horrors were now happening. Democratic wishes were being fulfilled within very difficult realities, and nationalism was one of the most difficult. They wanted to balance positive nationalist commitments with pluralism and a modern European identity, but others were mocking this position as treachery. Fedor Gal, leader of The Public Against Violence, told me he personally faced the problem directly three or four times a day, when people came up to him on the streets and verbally abused him. Gal is a democrat and also a Slovak patriot. When we first met in New York in the summer of 1990, he presented me with a beautiful book of photographs taken in Bratislava in 1968 and 1969. It was a very nice gift, but also a reminder that the Prague spring and the Soviet crackdown had not been just a Czech affair. When we met in Harmonia in November, 1990, Gal was a harassed man subjected to daily nationalistic attacks in the press and on the streets.

There was also the problem of his parentage. Gal was born in a concentration camp. His father had been exterminated by the Nazis, and at the time we met in Slovakia, he was being attacked as a Jew and the leader of a Jewish political movement. He seemed bewildered and angry, determined to be politically effective but uncertain about the means. He told me he would be offering his resignation to his colleagues the next day, but was not sure about the outcome of this act. He believed that if he did not hold the leadership, it would be taken by the Slovak prime minister, Vladimír Mečiar. Aside from his and others' evaluation of Mečiar as an ambitious political personality, willing to play with nationalist xenophobia, Gal viewed political leadership by the premier as undesirable. Gal was committed to a separation of powers, and distrusted an overconcentration of power in any single leader.

The major issue upsetting Gal and The Public Against Violence was demagogic nationalism. Gal believed that his Jewish heritage was complicating the political equation, but that the real problem was the distant relationship between the sophisticated intellectuals who made up his movement's leadership and the average Slovak. This problem, in fact, existed throughout the developing Europe. The nationalists claimed that the political leadership had lost contact with the situation of ordinary Slovaks; they were too busy worrying about smooth relations with Prague, and about being "part of Europe." They did not understand or care about the good of the Slovak nation.

Gal conceded that there was some substance in this complaint. He knew that during the revolutionary changes, his movement had been the only significant antitotalitarian social force. The movement had helped with a prison strike in December 1989 and had overseen major changes in personnel in all sorts of institutes and enterprises. Movement activists had been broadly popular; but since then, their popularity had been declining. Now Gal himself was the third most unpopular figure in Slovakia (after the heads of the Communist Party and the Christian Democratic Party). There was a distrust of all politicians, and an openness to demagoguery. He was the only Jew in the leadership of The Public Against Violence, and he knew of only two others who were activists. Yet the organization was commonly denounced as being Jewish. Nationalism as an integrative force was degenerating into xenophobic paranoia.

As a child of the Holocaust, Gal felt a responsibility to his father and other relatives who had died in the camps. He saw his political activism as payment of a debt to his ancestors. For him, tolerance and minority rights were not abstractions but absolute and personally felt imperatives. He saw the Velvet Revolution as having provided a unique opportunity for political and personal development. In Bratislava, the central leaders had been a group of social scientists, not the artists and professional dissidents of Prague. Gal and his sociologist colleagues had immediately become active, but he was not at first the leader of the movement. He took charge when it was revealed that the first leader, Jan Budaj, had signed an agreement to cooperate with the communist authorities as a way of receiving a passport.

Budaj withdrew very reluctantly, under pressure. His reluctance to withdraw was something of which Gal was quite critical, not because of a sense of political purity, but because of political realism. Gal believes in the democratic role of The Public Against Violence, and therefore is himself willing to withdraw from its leadership if that will strengthen the movement. (The fact that his Jewish ancestry is a political liability doesn't speak well for the politics of Slovakia, a nation that enjoyed its only form of independence as a Nazi puppet regime, the problems of which are being glossed over by the nationalists.)

In Harmonia, Gal did not seem to think that a test of his compatriots' liberalism was of the utmost importance. Rather, his primary concern was working out an effective way to overcome the gap between the populace and the leadership of the political movement. The task, as he saw it, was not to compromise with ultranationalism, to try to "out-nationalist" the extremists. He astutely foresaw that the nationalists' popularity was waning—two weeks after our conversation, the Slovak National Party was badly beaten in local elections. The task was to develop a popular politics that would speak to the concerns of the populace in an understandable way.

We talked during the evening hours of an all-day session. The deliberations at Harmonia took place in two locations. In the main hall, the delegates attempted to work out a formal agreement concerning the problems of federalism, nationalism, and the political positions of The Public Against Violence; in a smaller adjacent café, informal discussions took place. Smoking was prohibited in the hall, so the delegates had a built-in excuse to absent themselves periodically from the formal gathering. Gal and I conversed during one of his smoking breaks. I learned later to my surprise that he had been more candid with me about his plans and concerns than he had been with his colleagues. They had never openly dealt with the issue of anti-Semitism, and both he and they didn't know how to begin to do so.

I listened discreetly to the formal discussions (officially they were closed deliberations). There was significant political division between those who were most concerned with being true to their fundamental political principles and those who were primarily concerned with the movement's declining popularity, what the German Greens call the fundamentalists and the pragmatists, or what Max Weber called those with an "ethics of ultimate ends" and those with an "ethics of responsibility." The delegates as a whole did not seem very nationalist in their political orientation, but some argued for a more clearly nationalist rhetoric as a way of reaching the populace. One delegate, a professional actor, argued for nationalism with open cynicism. He maintained that in politics, as in drama, one must reach an audience, and to reach the audience one requires a good script. He considered the leadership's doubts about inflaming the prejudices and passions of the masses to be naïve and elitist. If the movement succumbed to such elitism, he argued, only those who were more nationalistic would prevail.

Many delegates had a sense of impending doom. One biologist, a representative to the Council of Europe, was in despair. To his mind, such demagoguery in The Public Against Violence, along with proposals to create the position of president of Slovakia and other constitutional assertions of Slovak autonomy, was leading to de facto Slovak sovereignty without proper guarantees of human rights. To his federalist mind, the result would be Slovakia's exclusion from Europe, "drawing the frontier of Europe at the Czech-Slovak border." Slovak separatism meant authoritarianism and, for him personally, emigration.

I learned from this man and his close colleagues that the most adamant Czechoslovak federalists were Slovak antinationalists, who make up a cosmopolitan Slovak intellectual circle. But for a less sophisticated delegate from the countryside, much of what they said was hard to follow. To such a person, dignity meant independence, and the independence of the Slovak people meant Slovak pride and autonomy, not deference to the talk of a new elite that he and his people did not understand. They had had enough of submission with the Bolsheviks. Such was the political dilemma that Gal, as an astute politician, had to address. An honest—as well as a dishonest—Slovak patriotism was now a significant political factor, along with a distrust of such patriotism as a rhetoric of intolerance and ignorance. He wanted to give the manipulators of nationalism less grist for the mill of xenophobia.

Gal's supporters were dismayed by his possible resignation. One woman actually approached me asking *why* I thought he might resign. Knowing I was Jewish, she asked me if I thought it had to do with the fact that Gal was Jewish. When I indicated that I did think so, she inquired whether I believed the issue should be brought out into the open. It was an odd situation. I was on my first visit to Slovakia. I didn't speak or read the language and didn't know whether, or how sensitively, the issue of anti-Semitism had been discussed in the press. The situation was similar to Poland, where anti-Semitism was still a significant social force without Jews, but not like Hungary or Russia, where the ascendant anti-Semitism is flourishing with a Jewish presence. In the Central European tradition, anti-Semitism was connected to fear of the modern, the democratic, the Western, and the unfamiliar, but my own unfamiliarity with the present political culture in Slovakia made it hard for me to answer her question directly. I could only report recent events in Poland, where I had just been.

In Poland, I told her, Adam Michnik, a friend and colleague of Gal, who also has Jewish ancestry, was openly attacking the issue of anti-Semitism and its link with authoritarian nationalism, both in his writing and in his capacity as the editor of Poland's major newspaper. The topic had been discussed for the past decade in the Polish legal and underground press, though for the most part Michnik had taken no part until recently. But now that authoritarian nationalism was threatening to function as a real and reprehensible alternative to democracy in the post-totalitarian period, it might be necessary to address old demons frontally. Further, I admitted that after the Holocaust, especially on the ground of the Holocaust, I was not predisposed to be particularly diplomatic about this issue.

I was being blunt, but also, I realized, not particularly helpful. I found out later that there had been hardly any discussion of anti-Semitism either in the popular press or in The Public Against Violence. Starting such discussion would be difficult, and people were not at all sure that Gal would approve. As it turned out, in an all-night session, they attempted to work out a way of skirting the issue. Gal wouldn't resign but would ask for a vote of confidence, and someone else would be appointed to begin speaking for the movement in the media.

But in the end, even this arrangement was unnecessary, because Gal's chief rival, Prime Minister Mečiar, initiated a discussion of the movement's leadership by voicing support for Gal. So a momentary crisis was averted. But central underlying issues were being left unaddressed. The distance between the political elite and the general populace was being overcome by pandering to nationalism, and the paranoid politics of interethnic hate were being left largely unexamined.

I decided to depart from Harmonia on my own, and asked the reception clerk to order me a taxi. Since it had to come from Bratislava, I had to wait about an hour. I spent the time questioning the clerk, who turned out to be an underemployed physicist, about what he thought of the people gathered at the retreat. His answer expressed the disillusionment that I knew to be spreading throughout the region, one year after the fall of 1989. While these people were probably better than the communists, he maintained, they were politicians, more interested in themselves than in others. He knew big changes were coming, but they didn't make sense to him. "What really bothers me is that the communists were no good, and we didn't like them, but when they were in power there was money. Now, with these guys, the money is gone. What I want to know is, where has the money gone?"

This university-educated young man clearly had no idea of the nature of the economic crisis, and he was frightened. So, as it turned out, was my taxi driver, a Hungarian living in Bratislava with his Slovak wife. His teenage daughters were suddenly the objects of ethnic hatred at school, and he had no sense that his government—and, more importantly, informed social consensus—would protect them or him. It was brought home to me again in the taxi that one important legacy of communism was social confusion. And at Harmonia I had seen a dramatic illustration of the truth that such confusion, along with ascendant national pride, leads to nationalism of the worst kind.

CHAPTER 9

The Dialectics of
False Solutions

Pluralism is not an easy political ethic, even when men and women of goodwill seek it. It seems that different races, nationalities, and religions, with histories of mutual suspicion and conflicts, are inevitably bound to work against one another and not with one another.

The socialist project presented one way to overcome the problem. Whether it stemmed from the Marxist-Leninist, the social-democratic, or the trade-union tradition, the project built upon the dream that shared class interest would make national, racial, and religious antagonisms obsolete. In the course of a common struggle for the primary cause of social justice as it was defined by economic structures, such "minor" conflicts would recede. But in the more democratic socialist experience, political and union leaders and members soon learned that the human world was more complicated than their models. Worker fought worker in World War I, with trade union and socialist party

support. Class interest did not supersede patriotism as a political moti-
vation. As a last stand for proletarian internationalism, Lenin's party,
then his country, and then its empire staged a massive revolt against
this lesson. Now the ideological chickens are coming home to roost.

The specter of nationalism was repressed in the communist world.
The prevailing policy was to silence nationalist rhetorics and aspirations. At first, this political move was probably made with principled
purpose. The Bolsheviks probably did expect the workers of the world
to unite and worldwide socialism to put an end to petty nationalisms,
just as Marx thought revolution would finally answer the Jewish question. But with the Bolsheviks, as with Marx, intolerance was deeply
embedded in political principle. Marx identified the Jewish problem
with capitalism, accepting a major anti-Semitic theme. The Russian
revolutionaries, in a twentieth-century echo of czarist practices, identified "internationalism" with their version of Russian national interests,
and "progressive national liberation movements" with the nationalist
movements that supported Russian interests; and they confined their
condemnation of nationalism as a negative phenomenon to those
which opposed Russian interests. Deportations by the millions, mass
imprisonments and murders, were the instruments of the internationalist project. The repressive police and military apparatus assured its
perverse successes. Nationalism as a significant mobilizing and
destructive force appeared to be a thing of the past in the Soviet bloc.
A totalitarian progress was apparently realized.

In the postwar period, the captive nations of the Baltics, along with
the socialist People's Democracies of Eastern Europe, were forced to
bury their national patriotisms. The Red Army, along with allied
People's Armies, had liberated these nations from Nazi occupation or
indigenous fascist oppressions. The new order would put an end to the
old national and ethnic conflicts and identities. Under the umbrella of
a Soviet-imposed socialism, the destructive forces of nationalist conflicts would cease to exist. Although the new regimes were not very
popular, their theoretical and historical schemata did have persuasive
power. The people of Eastern and Central Europe had experienced
unimaginable horrors. A strongly enforced new order, which promised
to put an end to the national antagonisms and ethnic and religious
strife, did seem to have an historical inevitability on its side. Not only

explicit leftists and communists, but also former rightists and nationalists, recognized it. The simple if brutal theory and practice of the victorious Soviets was quickly and conveniently putting modern horrors into the past. A brave new future was being constituted.

This schema had broad attractions, and it created a new synthetic "Captive Mind," as the Polish Nobel laureate, poet, and essayist Czesław Miłosz put it in 1951. Lithuanians, Latvians, and Estonians no longer had to worry about fascist overlords. Poles might experience problems with West German nationalists, but their relations with the progressive forces of the German Democratic Republic were secure. The antagonisms between Hungarians and Romanians concerning the political identity of Transilvania were things of the past, as were the antagonisms among the nations of Yugoslavia and the Soviet Union. A unified commitment to the building of socialism, supported by relations among all of the national Communist Parties under the leadership of the Soviet party, would help create a just international peace.

All of this, after the fall, seems extraordinarily absurd. But we should realize that it was a variation on a widespread progressive theme. A more liberal variation hoped to resolve national differences in deliberative bodies such as the League of Nations and the United Nations. There was a generally recognized nationalist problem, and for some, socialism did appear to offer an effective and humane solution. But unlike the at least half-successful projects of the League of Nations, the United Nations, and the World Court, the Soviet socialist solution never really attempted to address the problem of nationalism; rather, it repressed or cynically used it. In the Soviet Union during World War II, nationalist motivations were employed to mobilize the population. And in the postwar era in Eastern Europe, the struggle against "rootless cosmopolitans" and Trotskyists reintroduced anti-Semitic nationalist themes. The nonsensical theoretical distinction between retrograde "cosmopolitanism" and progressive "internationalism" allowed Eastern European communists to utilize national prejudices for their own political purposes. The 1956 revolt in Poland, unlike the one in Hungary, was contained by Władysław Gomułka's popular nationalist program of a distinctively Polish Road to Socialism. At times, particularly during the post-Stalinist era, nationalism was introduced as part of a liberalizing reform. But whether used in liberal or illiberal ways, official nationalist policy was a cynical instrument of Party rule.

It is not surprising, therefore, that a genuine nationalism provided a primary basis for anti-totalitarian politics and, in the post-totalitarian world, provides a basis for political mobilization and renewed antagonisms. While nationalism was kept alive in a cynical form in the official ideology, an unofficial nationalist memory served as the basis for a broadly understood criticism of official practices. Playing with nationalist matches, the communists of Eastern and Central Europe and the Soviet Union incited later nationalist fires. The unexamined and unselfconscious nature of Eastern and Central European nationalism, after the fall of communism, makes it particularly dangerous.

To the democratically minded in the context of a totalitarian cultural world, in contrast to their Western colleagues, national independence and patriotism may have appeared to be an unambiguous good. As with freedom of religion, the cause of national freedom was able to provide a broad societal basis for resistance and commonality. In today's situation, to use Hungary as an example, much divides Hungarians, like all national groupings, and communism signally failed to eliminate structures of competing interests and values. Old privileges have been inherited from the precommunist era, if not in the form of extensive private property, certainly in the form of what sociologists call cultural capital: knowledge of how to project power through the manipulation of cultural symbols; a favorable position in social networks of influence; and a high level of education and expertise. New advantages have also fostered significant inequalities, from the power and privilege of the *nomenklatura* to small-scale but sometimes highly successful capitalist enterprises promoted by a variety of economic reforms. The interests of town and country, the workers and the peasants, are often in conflict. And national minorities, particularly Jews and gypsies, inflame passions. Despite all this and more, a commitment to Hungarian independence and sovereignty unites just about all Hungarians. There are differences in emphasis. But both of the main parties, the Democratic Forum and the Free Democrats, strongly emphasize patriotic themes. In Hungary, this patriotism has meant a deep commitment to the fate of Hungarian national minorities living outside the country, particularly in Romania. The less nationalistic Janos Kis, the distinguished philosopher, theorist of human rights, and moral leader of the Free Democrats, equally with Jószef Antall, the leader of the more nationalistic Democratic Forum, has emphasized the importance of defending what they both underscore is Europe's largest minority population in the contested lands of Transilvania.

Like Havel and Gal of Czechoslovakia and Michnik of Poland, Kis comes out of a leftist tradition that has radically examined and rejected totalitarian politics and culture. Central to this process has been a renewed appreciation of national identity and attachments. An independent national community with political sovereignty (from its Soviet overlord) was understood as a precondition for democratic politics. An independent nation presents the possibility of an independent public life. And without these autonomies, democracy as self-governance is impossible; in other words, there must be a self-identified body of subjects to act politically. The democrats of Eastern and Central Europe perceived that national autonomy and democratic rights were two sides of the same political coin. While in the past the church—most strikingly in Poland—may have been a place to constitute a beleaguered autonomous common world, a refuge, an autonomous nation permits the systematic constitution of democracy.

But sovereignty and nationalism present both internal and external problems. Who should be a full-fledged member of the nation is a renewed issue, as is the relationship of the nation and its neighbors. The Pax Sovietica eliminated Hungarian-Romanian territorial conflict. There were certainly persistent social resentments, but they were not politically articulated. Officially, the Romanian and Hungarian working classes had united, and under the leadership of the Communist (especially Soviet Communist) Party, they had no conflicts. Only with the weakening of the Hungarian socialist regime did open international tensions reemerge. These tensions present serious problems for democrats. National misunderstanding and conflicts are inevitable.

Consider the beginning of the Romanian revolution, across the border. It started in Timişoara, a city in Transilvania. Lászlo Tökés, a pastor of the Hungarian Reform Church, was about to be deported for preaching against the government's policy of destroying rural villages and replacing them with new agricultural-industrial towns. When the police came for him, his (ethnic Hungarian) parishioners tried to protect their minister. They were joined by students and others of Romanian ethnicity. The Securitate fired upon their protest rally. Dozens were killed. Nonetheless, Ceaucescu went on a previously arranged state visit to Iran. Upon his return, he called for a mass demonstration in Bucharest to denounce the "counterrevolution." In a dramatic break from the official script, the dictator was booed. Before television transmission could be cut off, images of a horrified dictator reacting to the momentary failure of totalitarian control were broadcast nationally. The population revolted nationwide. The regime crumbled. A brutal, even if relatively short-lived, civil war broke out between forces of the army who supported the changes, and members of the security police who supported the old order. This was the only violent uprising in the fall of 1989.

In view of Ceaucescu's brutality and the thoroughness of his repressive policies, the violent nature of the Romanian transformation is not surprising; nor is the ambiguous political nature of the new leading party, the National Salvation Front, and the uncertainty about its democratic commitments. What is particularly noteworthy, however, is the fact that in Ceaucescu's atomized order, a temporary link between Romanians and Hungarians was at the root of the revolutionary changes. If the Securitate had fired on an exclusively Hungarian crowd, the pressure for systemic change might not have spread so rapidly. Ethnic prejudice might have been utilized to contain the disruption. The solidarity across nationalities significantly contributed to a general resistance. Suddenly the citizenry of Romania decided en masse to live in truth.

Yet in Timișoara, and in Romania more generally, conflicting truths soon emerged. Ethnic Hungarians and Romanians were able to agree that just about everyone was oppressed by Ceaucescu. Most people of goodwill were also able to agree that Hungarians had experienced particular injustices, specifically, severe limitations on their cultural life such as the closing of schools and various sorts of community centers. They had been treated as aliens in lands long connected with Hungarian history. The official history itself had minimized their presence; moreover, to their minds, it had exaggerated Romanian claims to Transilvania. There were—as there continue to be—clear grounds for nationalist conflicts. With the dictator gone, these competing nationalistic claims were more clearly articulated. Even with goodwill (which was not always present), serious confrontations appeared. Hungarians demanded immediate renewal of their cultural and social institutions, from schools to hospitals. Romanians, while they may have been sympathetic and even supportive of the Hungarian cause, defended their own interests. They too had suffered under the dictatorship. As Hungarian grievances were addressed, Romanians increasingly felt that their access to education, hospitals, and the like had to be assured. Inevitably, with cause, ethnic Hungarians were predisposed to sense a reluctance to change on the part of the Romanians, and the Romanians were predisposed to resent the fact that they were being forced to undergo further suffering, even after the revolution. Hypothetically, compromises could have been worked out to satisfy and balance their competing claims. But in a situation lacking a generally recognized political authority, nationalistic antagonisms were easily inflamed.

On March 23, 1990, ethnic Romanians attacked Hungarians in Tirgu Mures, leaving four dead. People on both sides perceived themselves to be defending national integrity and interests. The Romanians, including those bused in from the countryside, engaged in an organized attack, a pogrom of sorts, to put the Hungarians back in their place. Someone without interest in a democratic resolution to the Romanian problems, who understood the delicacy of the political situation, had provoked the attack. It could have been an agent of the old order from the Securitate, or a Romanian nationalist extremist. It could even have been a Hungarian nationalist, trying to increase tensions between Hungary and Romania and influence the Hungarian elections, held four days later, in favor of the more nationalistic Democratic Forum. Although the last speculation seems to be the least likely, in the uncertain political situation, without any commonly recognized political authority, almost anything is possible. Even an idea that I heard in Budapest, where I happened to be at the time— that an alliance between the prewar fascist Iron Guard and the Securitate was behind the events—cannot be discounted.

But such speculation does not and indeed cannot deal adequately with the dilemma. Even if the "truth" of the events should be revealed, if the agents behind the pogrom should be exposed, it would not solve the underlying problem of nationalism. We are reminded again that patriotism and democracy are both mutually supportive and problematically related. If people are to engage in self-rule, they must have a sense of being part of and committed to a community. But competing political allegiances can tear a polity apart, if patriotism leads to conflicting absolutist and exclusivist claims. Hungarian and Romanian patriotism were compatible when they shared the same anti-totalitarian focus. They could still be made compatible, with mutual respect and a commitment to pluralism as a first principle. Without such respect and commitment, or even with them but without firm institutional supports, a politics of manipulation and domination will overwhelm democratic prospects, as was demonstrated in Tirgu Mures.

Back in Hungary, in the parliamentary elections, the events in Romania did assure the victory of the more nationalistic party. While all of the political parties expressed their outrage about the events in Tirgu Mures, the Hungarian electorate knew that some nationalistic credentials were more authentic than others. The runoff elections in Hungary took a particularly mean turn. Charges of anti-Semitism and Bolshevism were exchanged. Spokesmen for the Democratic Forum's right wing not very subtly hinted that the Free Democrats were not truly Hungarian (in other words, they were Jews), while the Free Democrats attacked this anti-Semitism and questioned the Forum's more accommodating approach to the Communist Party in the past.

There were real issues in the campaign. The Free Democrats, the party of the most radical democratic oppositionists, proposed a more radical economic program and a clearer political break with the old order. The leading members of the Democratic Forum were more cautious. Before the fall, they had been more willing to compromise with the communist authorities; after the fall, they proposed a more gradual transition. But in the end the election rhetoric did not revolve around such reasonable differences of opinion. Rather, it centered on the seamy side of nationalism and political identity. Put perhaps a bit too bluntly, as the opponents stereotypically viewed each other, the choice was between Jewish cosmopolitan Bolsheviks, and ultranationalist village collaborators. Although both sides agreed that the Romanian authorities should be held responsible for the events in Tirgu Mures, they violently disagreed on just about all other nationalistic issues, particularly who was or was not a real Hungarian and who would or would not defend real Hungarian interests.

Remarkably, the heat of the campaign quickly cooled. The Forum won a decisive victory, but developed a means to work with the Free Democrats as the loyal opposition. On issues that require a two-thirds majority in Parliament (ones that have to do with constitutional questions), the two opposing parties agreed on a common political strategy, and a Free Democrat has been appointed president, with the support of the Democratic Forum. The common commitment to democracy has controlled potentially destructive nationalistic tendencies in the area of internal divisions.

Foreign relations are another matter, as are the internal problems of nationalism in more complicated circumstances, such as those in Czechoslovakia, Yugoslavia, and most crucially the Soviet Union. In those situations the problematic relationship of democracy and nationalism reveals itself in all its complexity. To varying degrees, the very existence of the Soviet Union, Yugoslavia, and even Czechoslovakia is open to question after the fall, and the peace of Eastern and Central Europe, which was one of the few truly positive aspects of Soviet domination, may be a thing of the past. The rebirth of independent nations may just as likely lead to the pain and suffering of international and civil conflict as to attempts at constituting democracy. Pessimism is easy. The obstacles to democracy are great. Ironically, the idea of Central Europe, an echo of an earlier imperialistic domination, may be used as a means to overcome political tragedy.

CHAPTER 10

Europe

Central Europe is an artificial creation. It is a state of mind. As a political notion, it is not primarily about geography. It is a term associated with horrors, especially in the German part of "Mitteleuropa," though in the recent past it has been politically invested with democratic hopes. The renewed interest in "Central Europe" in the early 1980s involved an act of symbolic secession from the Empire of the East. The investment represented a conscious, if somewhat utopian, decision to desovietize a political culture. Milan Kundera, Czesław Miłosz, and George Konrád, among others, juxtaposed center against east, pluralism against monism, antipolitics against (Communist Party) politics. They remembered, glorified, and celebrated the diversities of the presovietized past, hoping to help constitute a more liberal, pluralistic, and democratic European future, a new spring of independent national cultures.

119

But such dreams confront hard and complex realities. In the cosmopolitan Central European culture of old, German was the *lingua franca,* and a Jewish creative intelligentsia was a, if not the, primary social carrier. Yet in recent Central European dreams, the Germans have been left out, and there can only be—at best—nostalgia, tolerance, and appreciation regarding the positive international Jewish legacy (not a bad thing, considering past experiences and present alternatives). Now, new German problems must be confronted. Distancing from the West along with the East is at issue, as is German hegemony.

In Germany, the debates about Central Europe are markedly different from and have little to do directly with the discourse elsewhere in the region. They concern a confrontation with German history and the pursuit of German interests. The original German formulation of the idea of Mitteleuropa was made by Friedrich Naumann in 1915. Because it was discredited by the Nazi experience, the notion was picked up after the war with significant reservations. It was cautiously reintroduced into political life in the mid-1960s, with the Social Democrats' attempt at devising an approach to minimizing the divisions of Europe. By the seventies and eighties, the notion was politically linked with West German *Östpolitik* and the movement to reduce or eliminate nuclear arms and foreign troops on German soil. It also rationalized the intensification of West German commercial ties with the German Democratic Republic and Eastern Europe.

Such practical activity has led to a robust intellectual debate that cuts across the political spectrum, from those who call for a rediscovery of lost cultural and social ties with the East, promoting an anti-politics, to left- and right-wing nationalists, and to mainstream Social Democrats. Mitteleuropa, with or without a reascendance of German nationalism, has become the political ground of German foreign and domestic politics. The issues are: How far east is this "Central" Europe? How far west? How important are the Western values of political freedom and democracy in the German and non-German versions of Central Europe? Do intra-German issues take precedence over Western European and Eastern European ones? What is the relation between German unification and European integration? These German problems are located, like Germany geographically, at the center of Europe. They also form one of the central geopolitical and theoretical concerns of our age.

A little farther east, the idea of Central Europe was idealistically revived when the collapse of the Soviet empire was not even a reasonable dream. Now that the rewriting of the map of Europe is eminently practical, the idea of Central Europe is a necessity for the domestication of nationalism and imperialism. The democrats and nationalists of the democratizing nations do not seek to "join Europe" in order to be politically or economically dominated by a unified Germany. Rather, the Central Europe they envision is based on two negative propositions—neither German-imposed nor Soviet-imposed unity—plus the positive one of national pluralism.

Jacques Rupnik, a noted observer of European affairs, reminds us that two ideas concerning nationalism and cultural identity have competed in Central Europe since the nineteenth century. One celebrates plurality and democracy and politically views the nation as "a community of citizens." The other, more German, is a more romantic "blood and soil" concept and identifies with "the Volksgeist unique to each nation." The struggle continues, with some significantly hopeful news coming from Central Europe, and much more disturbing news coming from the East, particularly on the southern periphery of the Soviet Union.

A key issue is whether the resurgent moves for national independence will serve democratic or authoritarian political practice. "Central Europe" as an idea currently points in a democratic direction. It is concerned with national identities as they come together and enrich politics and culture. It is, as Rupnik puts it, "an attempt to reclaim a world that is lost, a culture that was and is fundamentally pluralist, the result of centuries of interaction between different cultural traditions." For this reason, Rupnik argues that the concern with Central Europe involves a rejection of the ethnic nationalism and anti-Semitism that bedeviled it in pre-Soviet times. Along with the constitution of civil society in opposition, most spectacularly by Polish Solidarity but also by the Czechoslovak and Hungarian oppositions, this view suggests that on the outer peripheries of the decaying empire, nationalisms in plurality may be democratic supports.

Yet there are competing notions of Central Europe. The principals involved, and their purposes, determine the degree to which the transnational ideal will promote pluralism or international conflicts. Some people take the concept quite literally, both in the geographic and in the historical sense. For them, Central Europe includes a reincarnation of the old geographic ideals, albeit without German imperialism. In this way, Central Europe can become an ideology of ill-will and bad faith, with or without malice aforethought.

A respected senior scholar in Prague explained to me that his mind is now centered on four cities: Budapest, Vienna, Berlin, and Prague. This urbane expert proposed that with the decay of the Soviet empire, historic links among these cities are being, and should be, reinforced. The common philosophic, artistic, architectural, and economic histories of Mitteleuropa should now flourish. He knew of my past connections with the Polish democratic opposition and with the Solidarity government. He expressed regret that "Warsaw now seems [to him] quite distant." He professed an admiration for Polish national resistance, and confessed that in darker Stalinist times, he and his colleagues looked to Poland for the free access to European culture that the Poles had won. But now he has a clear sense that it was all a result of the distortions of Soviet domination. Take away the domination and Warsaw seems backward, Eastern, not really part of Europe's center.

When this scholar thinks about Central Europe, he thinks about an idealized interwar period free of German domination, or even an idealized Habsburg period. He remembers the simple geographic fact that Prague is west of Vienna, and the fact of economic history that Czechoslovakia in the interwar period was much wealthier than "backward Austria." This was the world of his adolescence. He wants to rebuild it, free of the twentieth-century horror that has done so much to define his life. It is a noble cosmopolitan desire, but it has a mean parochial side. It includes the affectations of a European superiority and hierarchy and, in American radical jargon, a Eurocentrism.

This Czech gentleman focuses on European glories, hoping to ignore European follies without sufficiently considering European responsibilities. He draws the Central European line around Hungary, Austria, Czechoslovakia, and Germany. This is the multinational set of democratizing nations to which he believes he naturally belongs.

When one draws the line in this way, one overlooks the forty-five-year period of communist domination of Eastern Europe. Such an approach is quite convenient for a newly appointed department chair in a Czech academic institution.

The way nationalism and regional relations are formulated is not only connected to geopolitical reasoning and economic interdependence. It is embedded within the mundane activities of daily life. Most of the citizens of the "other Europe" did not themselves oppose communist and Soviet domination; they lived the lie. Our senior scholar was implicated. He found himself abroad in the West in 1968, but after some hesitation, he chose to return to his embattled nation. He paid for this decision. He lost his position as an academic, but by carefully accommodating the powers that were, he became a technical expert. He was able to maintain professional integrity without gross political compromises. Neither a member of the Party nor an open oppositionist, he could maintain some self-respect while he lived a comfortable upper-middle-class existence. But petty compromises had to be made. When he was visiting the United States, in 1988, he publicly criticized Dubček's politics perhaps a little more than he would have done if he had been a free man. He cautiously avoided political statements critical of the communist regime and questioned the political realism of his more overt oppositionist acqaintances from Hungary and Poland. He did not lie, but he also did not tell the truth as he really saw it. After the fall, he was not proud of his past actions. He could openly reflect on his own limitations. He took solace in the fact that not everyone could be a hero, and a new political order based on the rule of heroes would be undesirable.

It is difficult to reject his reasoning too harshly. Nonetheless, we must look at the facts as they shape post-totalitarian politics. During the period of communist domination of Czechoslovakia, he did not frontally oppose the totalitarian order in the name of the European values of freedom and pluralism, the very values that he and his compatriots understand as being the key to membership in "Europe." Instead of making such principles the core of his conception of today's Central Europe, he falls back on nostalgic and distorted memories of a Central Europe that constituted, in fact, the seedbed of twentieth-century barbarism.

Unfortunately, vague notions of national character orient not only this particular scholar, but a great deal of (inter)nationalist logic after the fall. When a German-American businessman looks East, he remembers from his youth the negative stereotypical meaning of "Polish work" (namely, poor work), and then, for him, Poland's poor economic circumstances are explainable without examination. When sophisticated Hungarian intellectuals, long associated with the circles of the democratic opposition, look at the politics of the Soviet Union, they discount the possibility of a democratic alternative to Gorbachev, for "the Russian nation is really oriental," not capable of European democratic refinement. A Polish intellectual judges the situation in Bulgaria and comes up with the same appraisal. These are but a few examples of a kind of nationalistic reasoning that threatens the democratic potential of the European ideal.

When Eastern Europeans were still locked into the Soviet system, Central Europe represented the ideals of freedom and plurality. Now, after the fall, it may become a rationalization for various nationalistic prejudices. For the Germans, ideas about Central Europe have always oscillated between intra-German questions and *Östpolitik*. Might it be otherwise? The idea of Central Europe used to suggest to Germans that their destiny was somehow different from that of their Western neighbors. Such argument has momentarily quieted after the fall. Now Germans of almost all political persuasions link German reunification with European integration. But the West Germans' greater acceptance of the tyranny of the East, which was an essential part of its *Östpolitik*—for instance, their too-quick appreciation of Jaruzelski's normalization of Poland, and their nationalistic reluctance to settle clearly, formally, and definitively all questions concerning their eastern borders—suggests that the centrality of Germany may again involve significant nationalistic problems. If Germany was officially willing to overlook the tyrannical qualities of its eastern neighbors once, if it was willing to overlook the central questions of freedom and pluralism in order to pursue a realistic foreign policy with the Soviet bloc when it was still perceived to be strong, will a united Germany as the dominant European power overlook such principles in the pursuit of its own national interests? Many people in Europe and the United States worry about such issues when reflecting on the experience of the two world wars, and especially of the Holocaust. And things get more complicated when we turn our minds east toward Russia.

An ideology of Europe, Milan Kundera's for example, may exclude Russia and the Soviet Union. From this point of view, the Soviet Union is in western Asia, not Eastern Europe. Before the fall, such ideas represented playful rejections of the sovietization of Eastern European life. Now they amount to a narrow and negative Eurocentrism, pure and simple. An eloquent rebuttal of such narrowness would begin with the names Tolstoy and Dostoevsky to underscore the absurdity of this position. But the problem is serious. If Europe is to be viewed as more than a small corner of the world from which a great deal of suffering has emanated, it must be seen as the original seat of a set of political values with universal applicability. Democracy, human rights, and freedom have important European histories. Although Europe has included much more and much worse (modern warfare, totalitarianism, imperialism, and the Holocaust), and the positive values have taken root elsewhere, it must be appreciated that the modern political ideals of democracy and freedom, along with socialism, liberalism, and conservatism, are the fruits of European political culture. If the culture is to have any meaning apart from domination and imperialism, it must apply beyond the western sector of continental Europe.

The tragedy of Russia and its empire is the tension that binds the Russian experience to the European West. Ambivalence about its relationship with Europe is at the very core of Russian political culture. The key national issue is: to be or not to be part of Europe. The question has been posed in extreme forms over the past two centuries, and has been answered with great poetry and human suffering, acute insights and grand delusions. The issue has more than particularly Russian significance. Today, world peace depends on how the Russians address the question of nationalism. This is the only disintegrating empire in history with an immense stockpile of nuclear weapons. Furthermore, the way the national question is posed in Russia reveals in extreme form the dimensions of the problem as it appears elsewhere.

The battle is between the westernizers and the nationalistic Slavophiles. The battle lines constantly shift. In the nineteenth century, those such as A. I. Herzen who advocated westernization often did so in the name of Russian interests; when faced with disappointments, they themselves often became Slavophiles. In our century, what was once clearly and self-consciously a move toward the West—the study of the Western "scientific theory" of Marxism and its application to Russian circumstances—became a means to construct a very Russian despotic regime, which at crucial points legitimated itself through the use of nationalistic rhetoric. The main opposition to the regime was, at first, developed on Western grounds. The dissident movement was focused on a defense of human rights as a universal principle. Yet it has produced Russophiles of extraordinary literary talents such as Aleksandr Solzhenitsyn, and of clear nationalist-fascist convictions such as Igor Shafarevich. Gorbachev's *perestroika* and *glasnost* have also flip-flopped. They had as their primary goals a concerted incorporation of Western culture and technology into the Soviet system, but they have also given official license to nationalistic sentiments. Indeed, *glasnost* has provided real political opportunities to advocates of Great Russian ultranationalism—the Black Hundred of the past, Pamyat today—and to the anti-Semites whose ancestors produced the *Protocols of the Elders of Zion*. The resurgent popularity of such protofascist messages is as significant a consequence of the new Soviet political and cultural openness as is the publication of previously banned novels, poems, and historical monographs.

The Slavophiles inside and outside the Party are making alliances. Some apparently want to distinguish good and bad communists, the Good Lenin and even Stalin versus the Bad Trotsky and Kaganovich, in other words, those with Jewish ancestry. Others only see bad communists. But the alliance between Party and anti-Party nationalists is based on their common hatred of liberalism, which, they contend, saps the nation of its natural talents. There is a broad public for such "new right" ideas, particularly in cities in decline such as Leningrad, in Party-administered cities with outmoded industries and acute ecological crises, and in regions where there is ethnic pressure against Russians. The strength of this public may make impossible the resolution of the Soviet problem. The Soviet empire is disintegrating. Like the nations of Central Europe, some non-Russian nationalities, particularly in the Baltic republics, are attempting to link their struggle for independence with liberal and democratic principles. While the Ukraine may eventually present a similar but more profound challenge, the international conflicts within and between Soviet Georgians, Armenians, and Azerbaijanis pose nationalistic problems of a different order: civil wars. Some, therefore, would interpret all of the nationalistic agitations negatively.

This interpretation does not make important distinctions and denies the potentially valuable democratic contribution of national identity. Previous Soviet policy was ambivalent about nationalism. It openly used Russian nationalism from time to time, and covertly promoted Russian dominance of the Soviet Union and the international communist movements, both inside and outside the Soviet empire. While the Revolution was fought under the slogan of internationalism, it is ironic that it led to the organization of a federated political structure on ethnic grounds, which promoted the crystallization of national identities that were not previously well formed. These identities, along with the Russian, are real. They have histories with people committed to them. The question is not whether they should exist, but whether they should serve democratic or authoritarian purposes.

Authoritarian mythology, not nationalism itself, is the real danger. Shafarevich has declared,

> The spiritual image of the people is formed during many centuries, during which the traditions of social existence, organically connected, are forged—and only if it is based on [those traditions] can the historical evolution create stable forms of life, natural for this people. . . . If following the advice [of the Russophobes] we abolish the role of the state . . . the result could only be the speedy and complete disintegration. . . . [T]he state evidently should for a long time play a great role in the life of our country.

This is part of a polemic against "little people" (in other words, Jews) who would cut off the Russian people from their organic spiritual roots and deprive them of their (authoritarian) state instrument of defense. Abstract ideas about pluralism, democracy, and tolerance are part of the problem. Primordial attachments of a fascist kind are the solution. All who oppose the solution are not real Russians; therefore, they are Russophobes.

This position presents a set of simple solutions to highly complicated problems. According to this thinking, the imposition of Western russophobic ideas created the negative legacies of the Revolution. The attempt to liberalize political and economic life represents an extension of the diabolical russophobic project. Only the stern hand of the Russian state, in Russia and its empire, can halt the spiritual decline of the Great Russian nation and its people; then a proper Soviet order can be reestablished.

Some holding this position seek a revitalized Russian empire, others an independent Russian nation. Neither the imperialists nor the nationalists concern themselves with a democratic federation or confederation of nations, that is, a more democratic and liberal position.

Federalism came (relatively) easy in North America, has developed with greater difficulty in Western Europe, and will possibly develop in Eastern and Central Europe. The coming together of people from distinctly different groups so that they may meet, express themselves and their judgments and interests, and then act on an agreed common good, involves great political sophistication. Mutual respect must be solid. A constituted political means of expressing strong differences of opinion and interests and, at least temporarily, of resolving the differences, must be worked out. These liberal requirements are only now being attempted in the Soviet Union, under the most adverse circumstances. How they will be worked out, and who will or will not be included, cannot be known in advance. All that can be predicted safely, if somewhat facilely, is that the future structure will be something between a complete breakdown and an unchanged unity. National, economic, political, and cultural interdependence will support some unity; the assertion of national identities will lead to at least some national independence. The hope of confederation and democracy is that citizens will turn away from primordial authoritarian mythologies and toward pluralism and tolerance. Events in the Baltics, where the ascendant political forces have cooperated, and even attempted to mediate between Armenians and Azerbaijanis, suggest reasons for hope. The conflict in the Caucausus is more ominous. In the end, as Russia goes—either toward authoritarianism or toward democracy— so will likely go the other nations. At least, if Russia goes the democratic route, real democratic possibilities will be open to others.

The odds against democratic constitution in Russia are great. Nationalism, as I have already suggested, is a direct obstacle. But it is also a resource. Within an imperial context, the nation is a self-limitation. Shafarevich and others claim that Russia has been the nation to suffer most under the Soviet regime. They maintain that its standard of living has been lower than many others under Soviet domination, and that only Russia lacks its own republican institutions (including its own Communist Party). Critics of the ultranationalists point out that these claims are disingenuous, particularly since all unionwide institutions are in fact dominated by Russians. Nonetheless, a commitment to constitute such national structures and diminish and dissolve union structures, linking national institutions with the official and unofficial local ones, can move Russian politics in a democratic and "European" direction. A politics of national identity is being directed against the (Soviet) political union of ideological construction. A wide variety of local political institutions, united in the Russian Democratic Union, push the nationalist ferment toward democracy. The repeated election victories of this union's representatives over xenophobic nationalists (with the old apparatchiks left in the dust) suggest that democracy is not impossible. We should keep in mind, however, that the confrontation between democratic and "new right" nationalist forces may not be decided at the ballot box. The power of the new right is that its ultranationalism appeals to key political actors in the military, the police, and the Party, with its broader constituency in particularly oppressed localities. If the new right is to emerge as the ascendant force, it will probably be through the direct repressive power at its disposal.

The development of new nationalist and democratic politics to replace the present Soviet structure is a possibility. But the political and cultural problems already considered here with reference to the more advanced democratizing nations are even more pressing within the Soviet Union. Nevertheless, we should not confuse tension and disorder with chaos and breakdown. The transition to democracy, if it is to occur, will be difficult. The articulation of long-suppressed conflicts is desirable; only then can they be resolved through public deliberation. Although the tasks are immense, they are not hopeless.

An ultranationalism is the new ideological threat. National identity can mobilize a population, especially if the identity was suppressed or distorted in the population's sovietized past. Real political and economic problems can then be explained away as the result of anti-national elements. If the problems persist, a political circus can spring up, centered on conflict with internal or external enemies. If such a script were to move the people of the Soviet Union and its old bloc, a popular mobilization could avoid dealing with real challenges for years—perhaps decades.

The physical and moral damage of the old ideological politics may be extended, it is true. But nationalism can also be part of a civilized politics of independence and national interdependence, of confederation or federation, of democratic left and right. People seem to be growing weary of ideological enthusiasms. Just when Slovak nationalism was ascendant in Czechoslovakia, the people moved away from it. As soon as the parties using covert xenophobic appeals won the Hungarian and Polish elections, they overtly repudiated xenophobia.

But the politics of nation, confederation, and federation should not be repressed as they were during the time of "previously existing socialism." The democratic left will resort to the reasonable appeals of abstract human rights. The democratic right will emphasize the more concrete experience of particular historical communities and their relations. People on the left will probably be more anxious for change; on the right, they will more likely be anxious about change. There will be no clear formula to settle the problems nationalism solves and poses. Neither a Wilsonian belief in the right of historic nations to state sovereignty, nor a regionalist confederalism, federalism, or internationalism, will be "right" or the only thing "left." While national sovereignty could be the only democratic route for the Baltic states, in Slovakia, as the federalists believe, national sovereignty could put an end to democracy.

Only political deliberation using the "rightist" resources of tradition and experience and the "leftist" resources of reason and reform will resolve these dilemmas on a case-by-case basis. It will take enlightened judgment by political leaders such as Havel, Gal, Michnik, and Kis, and by the general citizenry. Jan Urban, a Czech journalist, is a widely respected social activist who has focused his professional and political energies on this issue. For me he reveals, both as a writer and as an activist, a strategy for the democratic resolution of the problem of nationalism.

I first met Jan Urban a year before the fall of communism. Alena Hromádková introduced me to him when we were making rounds together of the Czech opposition. Jan is an extremely attractive political personality. As a young dissident in his thirties, he was engaged mostly in sustaining and expanding the underground newspaper *Lidove Noviny*. As a major political celebrity after the fall, he has refused all offers of high official positions, key ministries, ambassadorships, and so forth, and has started a career as a professional journalist, writing important editorials for *Lidove Noviny*, now the most important Prague daily.

Urban struck me immediately as a potential leader. Bright, young, with an acute sense of humor and intelligence, and an austere sense of duty and priority, he is capable of acting realistically without losing sight of his idealism. We have developed a close friendship, cemented on my first visit to Czechoslovakia, when he explained to my New School colleague and friend Ira Katznelson that he was "an enemy of all isms." Prompted by Katznelson, we had been talking about Marxism, actually existing socialism, and potentially democratic socialism. Katznelson, a social democrat and Marxist of sorts, was exploring whether the Czech dissidents, unlike their Polish colleagues, sought a better socialism, rather than capitalism, as an alternative to their present miseries. For some in Czech dissident circles, Katznelson's concerns made sense. But for Jan, Ira's frame of reference was a major problem within which there were no solutions. Since I'd been having such discussions with Ira for years, I especially appreciated Jan making my points with his distinctive clarity.

Urban is a Czechoslovak patriot, but an antinationalist. Nationalism too is one of the "isms" he rejects. He is very rational about his politics. He wants to help create a tolerant democracy. Ethnic and national sentiments, he fears, only block the way: when people consume themselves with concern about ethnic hatreds and suspicions, they ignore the practical work that has to be done to solve pressing problems. And Havel, in his view, is not beyond reproach. Havel concerns himself too much with lofty symbolisms and, writer that he is, thinks that a subtle turn of phrase can defuse complicated political tensions. Urban, in general a strong supporter of Havel, has been critical of his president when he hasn't taken a strong anti-nationalist stand and has wavered in his commitment to radical economic reform.

When Urban visited The New School for four months in the fall of 1990, we talked about these issues in great detail, and much of the analysis on these pages has been informed by our discussions. But sometimes it seemed that there was something missing in his message. He so much wants a "normal politics" and is so intently in search of realistic solutions to problems that he seems too quickly to disregard the irrational motivations and fears of those he judges to be acting unwisely. To put it another way, like others who seek normality and an escape from ideology, he overlooks the function of the old ideologies in bringing enchanted enthusiasm and meaning into the hard and difficult world of politics. As an old Marxist might say, it is not an accident that many of the ultranationalists in Slovakia, and extreme anticommunists in Czechoslovakia, have communist backgrounds. Many turn toward the mysteries of the nation and its past to avoid the political and economic complexities of the present. Urban sometimes seems to want to ignore this tendency, or just argue against it; but not always. For, like Adam Michnik, a man he greatly admires, he actually does present two highly meaningful and attractive ideals as alternatives to nationalistic and internationalistic irrationalities: the value of civil society, and the value of a pluralistic Europe.

Urban is not a political theorist, but as a political agent, his actions sometimes speak as loudly as his words. A free, vigorous press, as he knows and records, is as important as wise political leadership. This Jeffersonian principle of democracy animates Urban's actions. And many others in the new Central Europe are making similar decisions. They appreciate that democracy depends crucially on social as well as political reconstitution.

For many people, this ideal of civil society is difficult to understand. It becomes appealing when it is linked with the ideal of Europe in a very positive sense. The German ideal of Mitteleuropa supported a form of continental imperialism, distinguishing the German nation from its Western European neighbors so that it could dominate those in the center and east. The Eastern Europeans similarly used an ideal of "Central Europe" to distinguish themselves from Russia and Soviet domination. After the fall, the undesirable implications of formulations such as Kundera's, and those of my academic acquaintance too, have become clear. When pressed to give his principled alternative, Urban has depicted a very attractive political vision.

As a journalist, Urban addresses himself mostly to everyday politics. When he visited New York, he wrote an editorial for Western readers, clearly articulating a practical connection between the ideal of Central Europe and democratic reconstruction. He explained that the area's history teaches that democracy requires "a certain level of prosperity." But to his mind, the prosperity must be regional. Political nationalism will lead to competition among governments, and "we have known since the 1970s that a well-tested technique for losing money while solving nothing is to pump financial aid into the governments." Instead, Urban proposes aid for regional development projects, especially those which improve international infrastructures. The people in Central Europe, "where nearly a dozen nations are crammed together in a relatively small area," can work to help themselves, and then become part of Europe. His sense is that nationalism threatens both political democracy and economic growth. If the West continues its policy of supporting individual nations, it will increase their isolation from one another, which could lead to collapsing national economies, a sellout to foreign capital (mostly German), and, in reaction, a resurgence of antidemocratic nationalisms. Western support of regional cooperation, and integration into Europe as a whole, is the positive and democratic alternative.

Two versions of this editorial were published, one in the United States (in the *New York Times*) and one in Germany. Urban clearly feels that the West has a major role to play in supporting an international framework, in order to avoid the problems of nationalism. In a speech delivered in Hannover, Germany, on May 9, 1990, he presented the theoretical background of his practical proposals. His was a self-consciously antidogmatic European tale. He depicted an ongoing tension between primeval claims to belong to a familiar place, and competing desires to escape the confines of visible borders. His reflections were obviously stimulated by the recent past. He told of a meeting in March 1977 between the world-renowned Czech philosopher Jan Patočka, the first spokesman of Charter 77, and the Dutch Foreign Minister Max van der Stoel, the first European official to meet with an open opponent of the Husák regime: "The philosopher met with the statesman, and for us, the posthumous children of Stalin, Europe opened up. The formerly impenetrable border was crossed."

Urban views such border crossing as the fundamental structure of the European experience, as promise. Those who lived on the European continent were freed from "hundreds of deep cults connected to and connecting one place, one area" by Christian universalism, though over and over again primordial particularities prevailed, often using Christian rhetorics. Europeanism covered the continent with networks of monasteries, helping the development of "commerce, crafts and education"; it developed "Renaissance humanism, book printing, overseas exploration and the Reformation," and "universal belief was confronted with science and art, which it itself had helped to renew." With the Reformation and Counter-Reformation, "[t]housands of letters began to crisscross Europe, along with hundreds of books in which the wisest of the contemporaries attempted to comprehend and explain the changes taking place around them." But these changes and more recent "great spiritual discoveries paved the way for bloodshed, and again the educated men and businessmen of Europe had to retreat from soldiers and ideological simplifications."

Urban views the two world wars and the barbarism of this century as the culmination of the limiting forces, and for the countries of Central Europe, it was only with the fall of the Berlin Wall that World War II began to end. Only now can the citizens of these countries again join Europe.

No doubt the most immediate attraction of joining Europe is Western prosperity and consumerism. The way East Germans were overwhelmed by the deutsche mark, and thus by West German politics, exemplifies this situation most tragically. But in countries with more autonomous political destinies, the accomplishment of freedom and the battle for the universality of human dignity are viewed as an important part of European identity. The developing democracies are taking part in a great European tradition, which is linked with potential prosperity. As Urban elegantly put it in Hannover,

Socrates, Kant, Masaryk and Sakharov . . . are anti-ideological missionaries asserting that there is something beyond faith, beyond ter-

restrial ideology, there is a moral law which we believe in regardless
of borders and states. Humanism spread its wings and was forced
back down. But dozens of universities kept on working, even if
with an ideological constraint, and the idea of parliamentarianism
emerged again and again and was strengthened. Commerce
renewed itself over and over again, and created links between economic centers.

Urban's is a distinct historical interpretation, most definitely
molded by his recent past. But this interpretive schema is not simply
idiosyncratic, and it is certainly not ideological. It expresses an important undercurrent of contemporary Central European common sense:
a desire for prosperity and democracy, with an expectation of limits.
Fanatics can be observed in the public arena, but the people of the
region may have experienced too much misery from the ideological
left and right to succumb to xenophobic or utopian redemptive temp-
tations. They see the Europe that is waiting across the old geopolitical
borders, and they want to take part in it, not only for consumer goods
but also for the goods of tolerance. Despite old hatreds and suspicions, the appeal of such a good life may very well prevail. It is certainly meaningful.

When he speaks and writes about the present situation and the
immediate future (like his democratic colleagues Fedor Gal, Adam
Michnik, Janos Kis, among many others), Urban often expresses deep
concern that a great civilizing opportunity is being lost. But he knows—
and we should remember—that the democratic accomplishments and
relative social peace of postwar Western Europe stand as a significant
ideal that works to control nationalistic outbursts and modify less-than-
ideal international imaginations, such as those of Kundera and the
Prague senior scholar. The "really existing Europe," despite all of its
flaws, is a very important factor in avoiding the mistakes of the past. In
the long history of humanity, and particularly of this region, democracy
is unlikely. Yet Europe, in Urban's sense, increases the odds in its favor.
The problems are great but should not be exaggerated. Both within
and outside Russia, Germany, and the nations of Central and Eastern
Europe, there is a commitment to participation in a European community of nations. The democratic alternative depends on the quality of
democratic constitution and the quality of international relations.

The idea of Central Europe, as opposed to Eastern Europe, now presents some serious dangers. Before, the idea strategically underscored that there was nothing natural or necessary about Soviet domination of Eastern Europe. "Eastern Europe" was understood as a term that implied an acceptance of Soviet domination, which the term "Central Europe" symbolically rejected. But without the threat of Soviet domination, "Central Europe" could come to refer to the supposedly natural superiorities of the more Western of the nations that used to be Eastern. On these grounds, they might compete for Western cultural contacts, political agreements, and financial investments and aid. Old stereotypes and prejudices might rule the day. This possibility first emerges within each polity. Throughout the region, parties of national nostalgia are being formed. People such as the Czechs could fall into old ideological ways of thinking.

But these ways of thinking and acting politically may well remain in the background; a Europe in Urban's sense may come to the fore. A hopeful sign that they will be permanently marginalized is that political leaders seem to appreciate the dangers. When Havel addressed a joint session of the Polish Sejm and Senate just after the fall, on January 21, 1990, he declared,

> During the process that we both call the return to Europe, coordination of policy ought ultimately to grow into authentic friendship, which is based on an understanding of our destinies, into which we have been jointly forced, on the common guidance that friendship gave us, and mainly, on the common ideals that unite us. Here we should coordinate our efforts as closely as possible also with Hungary, where, in fact, I am going tomorrow with my associates—again this is no coincidence—and with other nations in our part of Europe.
>
> We should not mutually compete with each other about who is surpassing whom, and who first wins his way into this or that European institution; on the contrary we ought to help each other in the spirit of the same solidarity with which you during your worst periods protested against our persecution and we against yours.
>
> It is difficult at this moment to foresee the institutional forms which our East European or Central European coordination will create. Western Europe is substantially further in the process of integration, and if we return to Europe each on our own, it will be

substantially more complicated than if we enter into a mutual agreement. It is not only a matter of economics, it is a matter of everything, including disarmament negotiations.

The cynically inclined might question these noble words, and point out that even while they were being spoken, significant national tensions were appearing in Eastern and Central Europe, both within and between nation-states. There did exist, in fact, an inevitable competition for Western investment and aid; and within Czechoslovakia itself, submerged problems of Slovak national pride were reemerging. But a clear public articulation of the commonality of political ideals and interests is an important control on nationalistic conflicts, keeping alive a positive idea of Europe.

When a respected leader underscores mutual indebtedness and common interest, nationalism is moved in an undestructive and even productive direction. While nationalism is not denied, as it was by the ideologists of international proletarian solidarity, it is being articulated without reference to the mutual suspicions and hatreds of the interwar period. Although Havel indicated that the exact institutional arrangements of international cooperation and coordination needed to be worked out, he most likely had in mind arrangements extending from parallel structures of the Common Market to a loose confederation of nations. If tolerance is at the center of these arrangements, there is hope; but then intolerance is the central problem. With this in mind, we should consider the continuing complexities of belief, both their promise and their problems.

IV

RELIGION

CHAPTER 11

The Church Against the State

In the early 1970s in Poland, they used to tell a joke about Cardinal Wyszyński conducting a Mass. One man is standing when he should be kneeling. Someone tugs at his sleeve. "Kneel down; why are you standing?" "It's all right, I'm Jewish." "Then what are you doing in church?" "I too am against the authorities."

In those days, the Polish church was the locus for civil resistance. It provided a widespread institutional alternative to communism; the church's struggle for independence during the communist period was the most sustained and effective resistance to the dictates of the party-state. Two great and powerful systems of authority battled against each other, but neither won. The church never defeated the communists outright. (As Stalin once cynically observed, it could not do so without any military divisions.) But the party-state did not win either. To buy some legitimacy in 1956, to give some substance to a more nationalistic notion of a distinctively Polish road to socialism, the communists retreated from the direct attacks on religious practice that had characterized the Stalinist period (from 1948 to 1956). Cardinal Wyszyński was freed from prison, and a tense modus vivendi was established in which the state and the church agreed to respect each other's authority in their own institutional domains. Although it was far from clear at the time, this arrangement severely weakened the Communist Party and helped revitalize the Polish church and civil society; and this revitalized combination significantly contributed to the ultimate defeat of communism.

The visit of the Polish pope to Poland in 1979 was a crucial precondition for the development of Solidarity. The Poles publicly acted apart from party-state control. They saw themselves in the millions as independent moral agents and citizens, not as subjects of the ideological order. While during times of repression the politically independent found sanctuary within specific parish churches, at the Masses conducted by Pope John Paul II, society itself became a sanctuary. With the establishment of Solidarity, this society, in effect, declared war on the party-state.

In a similar but less dramatic fashion, one year before the Velvet Revolution, a nationwide campaign led hundreds of thousands of Czechs and Slovaks to sign a letter of protest demanding freedom of religion. Under a regime in which even attending church could affect one's job prospects, people mobilized their opposition to the totalitarian state on the basis of their religious convictions. And in the German Democratic Republic, the small dissident and peace movements that eventually led a mass revolt against the communists existed within the sanctuary of Protestant churches. The struggle for religious freedom in each of these cases was a vital social base for open opposition to the totalitarian order.

In the early 1970s, when I lived in Poland, I learned to appreciate the positive role religion was able to play in the antitotalitarian struggle. I saw that the Polish church—despite its significant authoritarian and xenophobic traditions, many of which were far from eradicated— was a force for progressive democratic change. Anticommunism, of course, had always come easily to the church, but now something more was involved. Its strength as an institution, coupled with a tradition of sanctuary, had turned the church into a patron of societal pluralism. Furthermore, at a time when the public media were dominated by a simpleminded secularism, the richness and complexities of the alternative religious worldviews found in the church made it intellectually appealing. At times, the sanctuary role of the church seemed to be of the greatest political significance. At other times, particularly during the eighties, the church's theological mission seemed most important. Two friends whose names I've changed at their request exemplified this fluctuation for me.

Irena Walter and her husband Paweł Singer were an unusual but revealing Polish couple. I had come to know them in the early seventies when they were both students at the university, though they were not together at that time. In 1975 Paweł signed a letter protesting a proposed change in the Polish constitution. He was expelled from the university and forced to end his formal academic studies. When we met again in 1978, he was working as a clerk in the Warsaw branch of the Catholic Intellectuals Club. It was not really a bad position; it was something like a junior fellowship in the democratic opposition. Singer's late father had been a poet with a communist and Jewish background. His mother, a renowned poet, was a Catholic. His "fellowship" helped him to explore his own pluralistic roots.

Like all those with even a partial Jewish background, Paweł had personally felt the brunt of Poland's 1968 anti-Semitic campaign. Up to that point he had been in no normal sense Jewish (except, as Adam Michnik puts it, according to the Nuremberg Laws). But after the fact he embarked on a course of self-education, studying Jewish history and culture in general, and the Jewish experience in Poland in particular. When he married Irena, the child of a Zionist father and a Jewish communist mother, and when I met them as a couple in the late seventies and early eighties, their home (actually Irena's father's apartment) was a Jewish household, not in an orthodox religious sense but in the sense that Jewish artifacts adorned the walls and shelves, and some Jewish customs structured their weekly schedule.

At work, Paweł combined his Jewish self-education with his Catholic affiliation. He began to write for the Catholic weekly *Tygodnik Powszechny*, including essays on social and political thought and on the Polish Jewish experience. At the time, the communist press was *Judenrein*. While there was no longer the overt anti-Semitism of the late sixties, in the seventies Jewish issues were completely absent from the Polish popular media. There was no discussion of the Holocaust, of the Polish pogrom that followed World War II in Kielce, of the anti-Semitic campaign of 1968, or of Jewish history in a country that, before Hitler did his work, had been 10 percent Jewish. Even when the word "Jew" was spoken in imported films, it was dropped from the subtitles. But a few Catholic journals did reflect some discussion of Jewish issues, and a group of young Catholics centered in the Catholic Intellectuals Club attempted to preserve monuments of the Jewish presence.

On June 27, 1978, Paweł and I went to a Warsaw Jewish cemetery, the second largest cemetery in Warsaw, where members of the Catholic club were attempting to preserve a particularly historic section. The vast grounds were devastated. Untended, most of the cemetery was becoming a forest. The marble of the gravestones had been stolen. The grounds were unpoliced—absolutely exceptional in a totalitarian country—and young hooligans and juvenile delinquents were using it as a free zone. While the earnest young Catholics were tending the historic section, I saw a group of young teenagers setting fires, for the fun of it, off in the distance.

This visit was very depressing. But it did show the positive role people affiliated with the church were playing in remembering the Jewish contribution to a more pluralistic Poland. While it was (and is) true that the church had far from eliminated anti-Semitism from its ranks, people affiliated with the church were using its moral vision and institutional autonomy to address this delicate political issue.

When we were walking from the cemetery toward the trolley, under the shadow of the Stalinesque Palace of Culture, Paweł made two suggestions. The first was that we go to a large private apartment later that day for an illegal poetry reading. (There I met Adam Michnik for the first time.) The second was that the next day I meet a right-wing nationalist oppositionist at the Catholic Intellectuals Club.

Thanks to his affiliation with the club, Paweł was well informed about the opposition political scene of both the right and the left, and even about Jewish issues. Others, of course, were equally well informed, although because of the clandestine nature of some of these activities and their dependence on informal interpersonal contacts, being located at the Catholic Intellectuals Club provided access to activities and information not broadly known. Through Paweł, I came to understand that the church supported pluralism not only in its direct conflict with the party-state but also by overtly and covertly shielding a broad range of unofficial and antitotalitarian religious activity. In the late seventies and throughout the eighties I came across many of these activities, from Jacek Kaczmarski's satirical song concerts in a church basement, to a full-scale avant-garde theatrical extravaganza of Teatr Ósmego Dnia (which I had known in the early 1970s as a legal theater), to classes on Polish society and history given by such scholars as Jan Strzelecki and Jadwiga Staniszkis, to well-organized networks supporting political prisoners.

While Paweł introduced me to such "profane" contributions of the church in the 1970s, Irena Walter revealed to me the dimensions and limits of a religious renaissance in the eighties. Irena's mother had been a Stalinist, an orthodox communist official in the postwar era, whose political career had ended when Władysław Gomułka and the more nationalistically oriented communists—from her point of view, revisionists—took power in 1956. Irena's father had been a Labor Zionist who for a long time headed a state-supported Jewish cultural agency, a much-neglected archive of the Jewish past. Unlike many Polish Jewish survivors who chose to remain in Poland after the war, Irena's parents did not cover up their heritage. It was not during the anti-Semitic campaign of 1968 that Irena found out she was a Jew. While she had no religious training, she is a person with acute religious sensibility and concerns.

When we first met in 1973, for Irena this meant an openness to learning about the Jewish religion. When we next met in 1978, she was married to Paweł and, with their first child, they were consciously creating a Jewish home. But when we met in the mid-eighties, things had changed radically. Irena was becoming a Catholic. I was shocked. We were in her apartment in May 1988, and I had noticed that the Hanukkah menorah and Sabbath candlesticks on the mantle had now been joined by a crucifix and Russian icon paintings. We were drinking tea and French brandy around her dinner table, where in the past we had shared a traditional Jewish Sabbath meal.

Irena attemped to explain. Communism had imposed a great moral emptiness on Polish society in general, and on her in particular. It had led to political resistance, which she had whole-heartedly supported. But not only had the resistance ended in failure and disappointment, it was not enough. It addressed the mundane, most superficial aspects of Polish problems, while the moral crisis went much deeper. For a solution, people naturally turned to the church.

I asked, "But how can you, with your strong Jewish identity, become a Catholic?"

Her response was chilling. "I have had no alternative. In Poland today, to be religious means to be a Catholic."

There was a dying elderly Jewish population in Poland, but few had religious orientations. Those who did had emigrated. A few younger Jews were trying to create a Jewish community life, but a handful of autodidacts does not make a vibrant religious community. There was no rabbi, no cantor, no religious leader.

I tried to empathize, but still I was confused. Not only did the Roman Catholic church have a tradition of anti-Semitism, but there was also a virulent variety embedded in the Polish church and Polish nationalism, especially when the nation and the religion were combined. "Good Pole, good Catholic" was and is a declaration of an intolerant Polish nationalism. I asked, "Given the Polish church's anti-Semitism, and given the longer Catholic tradition, how can you become a Catholic?"

Irena acknowledged that anti-Semitism was a part of church history, but maintained that the religious message of the church went beyond its history.

"What about the Inquisition?"

"Religious truth transcends human frailty."

She was interested in mystery and morality, wanted to explore the meaning of life and moral community; and although she admitted an ambivalence about Catholicism, she felt she had no alternative.

But when I met Irena again in March 1989, she had abandoned her Catholic quest. Her father had died, and she had found consolation only in her own traditions. Still, she faced a problem: being Jewish in a world without Judaism.

Irena's problems are not typical. Yet, ironically, thinking about her unique situation helps me confront the relationship of religion and politics after the fall of communism. The people of the old Soviet bloc, especially those who were most affected by communism, are seeking religious solace. But many of the available religious institutions are compromised. Like Irena, these people seek their own religious communities, but they have been taken away. Irena's was destroyed primarily by Hitler, but also by the secular choices of her parents: Zionism and communism.

For the people in places like Bulgaria, Romania, and Russia, the secular choice was made by the bulk of the population (though often coerced), and the religious institutions were often reduced to ideological adjuncts of the party-state apparatus. For people discovering their religious needs, established churches offered little attraction. With survival in mind, these churches had so scrupulously followed the dictates of the communist censor that they became indistinguishable from the communists. When I visited Bulgaria, Romania, and Russia, I often heard the lament, "Communism has created an ethical vacuum. Our crisis is not primarily political or economic, it is moral. A religious renewal must be our first priority."

To my secular ears, these were ominous judgments. They suggested that a religious fundamentalism might overwhelm democratic commitment. Returning to the case of Irena, I understood why people made their judgments, but I also understand that democracy and absolute beliefs do not easily mix. Irena's problem was not only about religious discovery, but about the constitution of a viable religious alternative. At the same time that church and state must be separated, I thought, both must be constituted, and this is an immense task. People with religious awe and political confusion are trying to address complicated issues, with little or no experience. And the Western secular tradition provides little guidance.

The reactionary character of the politics of Solidarity was made clear to the Western left in one specific scene: the celebration of a Sunday Mass inside the gates of the Lenin shipyard during the occupation strike of August 1980. For the orthodox communist left, there was an unambiguous script, all part of a seamless pattern. Real workers would not strike against the workers' state. When some people calling themselves workers did so, they were clearly desecrating the sacred memory of Lenin; and what better proof did one need than to see them partake in a ritual of superstition? I suppose there must have been some ideological diehards holding this position, people who *religiously* followed the party line. A more restrained orthodoxy, though, was more common. The strike revealed the contradictions of "actually existing socialism" and pointed to the need for reform or revolution (depending on one's political aesthetic). But the specific nature of the strike, crucially the presence of religion, revealed to them the "poverty of working-class consciousness." Reactionary forces were reasserting themselves on the political stage.

The presence of religious symbol and ritual even provoked discomfort in those on the left, including myself, who had followed closely the antipolitical scene of the other Europe and greeted the events in Gdańsk with unqualified enthusiasm. We viewed the establishment of an "independent self-governing trade union" as a breakthrough in council democracy, a realization of our dreams of participatory democracy. The presence of the Catholic church, though, suggested that circumstances might yet again frustrate a democratic project.

The events leading to the fall and following it have confirmed the reservations of those wedded to the old categorical thinking of the left. After all, not only was religion reasserting itself in the other Europe, but capitalism was apparently being restored. First the reactionary character of the democratic movement was discernible with the influence of religion on the workers. And then it was confirmed—finally—that the workers were being put in their place by capitalist relations. I must admit that there is consistency in this scheme. The problem is that it does not speak to history as it has been experienced by active agents such as Paweł and Irena. It is, rather, history as it is ideologically imagined.

The central problem is not capitalism or socialism. Socialism has not proved to be the systemic solution to all human problems, and it is certainly not a particularly advanced form of human evolutionary development. Yet only the blindly ideological see capitalism as an answer by itself. Economic benefits are shaped by noneconomic human commitments, and a key commitment is democracy—that is, self-governance, as opposed to various forms of restraints upon democracy. By taking part in governance, people can contribute to deliberations to determine societal priorities and ways of realizing those priorities. One form of economic relation or another may serve self-determination more or less adequately. One polity may give priority to efficiency, another to a specific notion of social justice. But no economic formula will solve all problems, as socialist and capitalist ideologists claim. And when people consider their goals, and the ways and means to achieve them, as far as democracy is concerned religion has an ambiguous role to play. The ambiguity was evident in Gdańsk, and it has become more critical not only in Warsaw and Kraków, but also in Prague, Bratislava, Berlin, Leningrad, and Moscow. It is the same ambiguity that was first clearly articulated in the First Amendment to the Constitution of the United States.

The First Amendment opens with the official American position on religion and politics: "Congress shall make no law respecting an establishment of religion, or prohibiting the free exercise thereof." The amendment firmly commits the American polity to the principle of the separation of church and state, and it also guarantees the freedom of religious life. The polity cannot determine or control religious beliefs or practices. The position seems simple and clear. But examination and historical experience reveal ambiguities and ambivalences, whether one subscribes to constitutional doctrines of original intent or of historical development.

What constitutes freedom of religion from the point of view of the more religiously oriented can appear to be an establishment of religion to the more secularly oriented. So-called creationist science, for example, should be given equal time with more conventional biology in the schools, according to some fundamentalists. To do otherwise would enshrine atheism as an official doctrine. It would confuse freedom of religion with prohibitions against religion. The secular scientist, of course, objects. Creationism is a religious doctrine, not to be confused with scientific inquiry. To mandate the teaching of creationism in public schools would amount to religious interference, in other words, the establishment of religion.

Because the dividing line between religious and other human practices is far from clear, such debate is an endemic part of American civil life. It sometimes even becomes central in political contestation, as has been the case with the abortion issue. The ongoing debate about the relationship of religion and politics, not how it is decided at any one moment, constitutes the shifting boundary between religion and politics. At times religion may appear to one constituency to be a political scourge, but at other times the same constituency may strongly support a religiously motivated politics.

For years, Protestant fundamentalists worried about the interference of the pope in political affairs. John F. Kennedy solidified his presidential prospects when he strongly and unambiguously committed himself to a separation of church and state at a Baptist convention. But now fundamentalists seem to be advocating a closer relationship for religion and politics. To argue against a close connection, they maintain, would mean a support of immorality in public life. Yet, those enlightened liberals who see in these developments a tendency toward theocracy, do themselves appreciate religiously motivated antiwar and antinuclear politics and religious rejections of poverty and social injustice. These are just some of the most recent instances of the ambivalent attitude regarding religion in a secular republican tradition, which takes as a patriotic motto "In God We Trust"; a tradition that is very remote from accounts of people's opiates.

From this republican point of view, there is nothing anomalous about workers during an occupation strike, cut off from the usual rhythms of their everyday existence, expressing an important religious part of their lives to sustain them during the course of their struggles. Religion is not imbued with negative political or theoretical significance, nor is it identified with the course of political action. The Gdańsk strike's true character was not revealed by the religious ritual. It was neither politically regressive nor theologically grounded. In fact, toward the end of the strike, Cardinal Wyszyński, in a televised broadcast, counseled moderation on the part of the workers and the party-state and called on the workers to end their strike and return to work. It was a crucial moment in the strike, before anything had been accomplished, before crucial concessions had been made by the state. The same workers who took part in the church sacraments in the shipyards steadfastly ignored the intervention of the church leader. Thus, in their actions, the workers separated the ethos and strategy of their own political actions from their religious beliefs and commitments. They sought to avoid "the establishment of religion" in their political life, at the same time that they asserted their rights to "freely exercise" their religion.

Of course, before the fall of communism, the main issue concerning religion was its free exercise. Since atheism was a key component of Marxism-Leninism, the closing of churches despite popular wishes was seen, from the official point of view, to be a sign of political progress. The struggle to maintain the right of religious activity then became a priority for institutionalized churches, and for all believers. In the course of this struggle, the political significance of antipolitics was born. The antipolitical struggle for freedom of religion became a more generalized and secularized antipolitical struggle for civil society. In terms of the traditions of politics, the Russian revolutionary tradition faced the American revolutionary tradition.

There is an ominous historical joke in all this. The Roman Catholic church has traditionally had an intimate connection with state power. Although it speaks to the otherworldly condition of the meek, it has much more frequently served and been served by the princes of European power than it has been a base to oppose the powers that be. The church and church leaders have not only reconciled themselves to tyranny of the most horrific kinds (including Nazism), many in the church have been active proponents of the worst forms of xenophobia and inhumanity. In the Russian Orthodox church things have not been any better. Today there is a religious revival in Russia. But the Russian church itself, and its relation to the state, are as much a part of the problem as a part of the solution.

In March 1990 I was in Leningrad, where I spoke to a number of people about this issue. Most interesting was Yuri Bulychev, a philosopher and historian of Russian thought. He is a graduate of the state university, but teaches in an alternative educational institution called the Leningrad Independent University. This university was set up unofficially twenty years ago as the Earth and Universe Program, a series of cultural activities and courses exploring the humanistic implications of the physical sciences. Bulychev has taught the one series of explicit humanities courses. He has also been an activist in a small political movement, the Free Russia Group. In Bulychev's political view, the major task facing Russians of independent mind is the reinvigoration of the spiritual life of Russia. Soviet life has produced a moral crisis, and any move toward democracy that does not first address this fundamental crisis would yield disaster. Russia must be reconstituted as an organic community. National traditions and customs must be recovered that are independent of totalitarian definitions. Without first addressing the moral issue, democratic reforms will not take root. Such democratic reforms without distinctive Russian coloration will not survive.

Those who want immediate democratization, Bulychev calls "naïve democrats." He believes that they favor democracy primarily for economic reasons. He admits that they are not open about this priority, but if you follow the implications of what they say, he maintains, their base motives are clear. The only way to political reform, therefore, is the spiritual renewal of the nation. He attempts to address the problem in his teaching and in his political activity. His courses at the independent university almost exclusively focus on Russian philosophy, namely, the study of thinkers who have reflected on the philosophic implications of Russian orthodoxy. The political movement in which he is active takes its primary project to be the development of an "intellectual aristocracy" to mediate between "the banalities of liberalism and nationalism." They promote the spiritual renewal of Russian orthodoxy and try to introduce a revitalized spirituality into contemporary political life. They prepare position papers for other political organizations, attend other political meetings to seek acceptance for their ideas, and advise some liberal political activists. They have had some success with elements of this democratic movement, no success with other nationalists.

Bulychev's Free Russia movement is minuscule, with only a few dozen members. While it is not important as a political force, it does represent a significant antipolitical impulse—the substitution of the spiritual for the political. In the Free Russia Group, the substitution seems to have a kind of Leninist formation. The intellectual aristocracy, instead of the workers' vanguard, will prepare the nation and infiltrate other political movements, utilizing the teachings of the true church, instead of the true philosophy of history. As with other antidemocratic groups in our most democratic of ages, democracy is not denounced but deferred until the nation is ready, purged of its communist sympathies and illusions (Pinochet's Chile), or sufficiently respectful of the rights of racial minorities (de Klerk's South Africa), or in touch with its true spiritual resources (in Russia and other parts of Eastern Europe). A concrete question in the new democracies, then, is: Will democracy flourish or be overwhelmed by religious commitments? In my opinion, it can flourish only if religious commitments, as well as the political revolutions, are self-limiting.

The historical reason that the revolutions of 1989 have more in common with 1789 in America than with 1789 in France has to do with the priority given to practical problems of political constitution. There is now on the eastern borders of Europe, as there was then on the eastern coast of North America, a common understanding that political transformation should not address all of the problems of the human condition. Not all social problems can or should be solved in the act of political foundation. There must now be a religious consensus as well that religion, though it can inform the actions of citizens, must establish a set of self-limitations. This restriction was more easily accomplished by eighteenth-century Americans than it is likely to be by late twentieth-century Central Europeans. The American political enlightenment blended a supportive Protestant theology with liberal and republican thought. It has yet to be seen whether democratic and religious Eastern and Central European commitments will be mutually supportive. In some places they may; in other places they may not. The example of the Free Russia Group suggests there are very serious problems ahead. Self-limitation must come in two basic forms, limitation relative to the secular realm, and interreligious self-limitation.

In the post–Vatican II era, we live in a world of accepted ecumenicalism. A religiously conservative pope praises Luther. Jewish-Christian dialogues are ongoing, fruitful affairs. Major modern theologians seek not the one and only path to God, but an appreciation of the diversity of religious traditions. Yet we also live in an age of rising religious fundamentalism. Wars in and around Lebanon, Northern Ireland, Israel, Iraq and Iran, Azerbaijan and Armenia, Croatia and Serbia, all have some grounding in religious differences and intolerances, which increasingly give them an apparently insoluble radical edge. If the democratic transformations in Europe are to succeed, there must be interreligious understanding, rather than fundamentalism. This goal will be difficult to achieve, given the experience of the recent and not-so-recent past. A Polish version of the Jewish question comes to mind, arising from recent incidents in the city of modern horror, Auschwitz.

CHAPTER 12

The Jewish Question

In a building where Zyklon B gas for the gas chambers was stored by the Nazis, Carmelite nuns built a convent in 1984. The international Jewish community protested in 1985, and in 1987 an agreement was reached between representatives of Western European Jewish organizations and the church in Geneva. The Catholic delegation, including the cardinal of Kraków, Franciszek Macharski, agreed to move the convent to a new interfaith center near but not on the grounds of the concentration camp. The church agreed to build the center in two years, then asked for a six-month extension; but by the summer of 1989, not only had construction not begun, the church had not even acquired land to build on. In protest against this situation, an American rabbi, Avi Weiss, led a small group in protest. They scaled the walls surrounding the convent and staged a sit-in. A group of Polish workers, shouting anti-Semitic slogans, beat the protestors and ejected them from the convent grounds.

Macharski, one month later, used these incidents to renege on the Geneva agreements. Then in late August, in support of the Kraków cardinal, Józef Cardinal Glemp, the Polish primate, delivered an infamous speech purportedly defending the Polish position. He denounced Jews for "speaking from the position of a nation elevated above all others," for infringing on Polish sovereignty, for provoking "anti-Polonism" in the international media ("easily at the Jews' disposal"), and stated, "if there were no anti-Polonism, there would be no anti-Semitism." Instead of denouncing the workers' anti-Semitic outrages, Glemp praised them. Weiss's actions had "not [led] to the murder of nuns in the convent or the wrecking of the convent, for the attackers were held at bay."

This Auschwitz controversy reveals a significant problem in religious self-limitation. Some of the problem, if not most of it, can be explained as a particular Polish-Jewish one. The history of Polish-Jewish relations is long and sad. But important issues of more general significance can also be discerned.

The Polish Catholics and the American Jews who met on the convent grounds had little or no understanding of each other's religious or political positions. For Weiss and associates, the matter was simple: the presence of the convent and the cross on the site of the mass extermination of their Jewish brethren was an affront to the memory of the Shoah. The history of European Jewry is a history of Christian persecution and intolerance. The convent symbolized a continuation of this sad tradition. For the Polish Catholics, the nuns were engaged in a simple act of prayer. Forced entry onto their holy grounds was an affront of the highest order. From the viewpoint of Weiss and associates, they were simply engaging in an American political tradition of passive resistance. From the viewpoint of Glemp and the Polish workers, Weiss's actions exemplified Jewish aggression.

I do not personally believe that these two positions have equal moral claim. In my judgment, the only just resolution of the problem, ultimately endorsed by the Vatican, is the enforcement of the Geneva agreement. Nonetheless, for democratic prospects, the conflict and its outcome are not the most troubling aspects. Rather, the issue is the way the conflict unfolded, and how the conflicting parties confronted each other.

For all intents and purposes, there are no longer any Jews in Poland. Hitler's solution was finalized on Polish soil after the Holocaust by the persistence of a native anti-Semitism, the Zionist appeal in the forties and fifties, and an official anti-Semitic campaign in the late sixties. Where there were three million Jews during the interwar period, now there are only a few thousand people who acknowledge Jewish ancestry, and of these, only dozens—not even hundreds—are practicing Jews. For this reason, there was no Polish Jewish position on the convent controversy. Although one prominent self-identified Jewish voice was published in Poland on the affair—Kostek Gebert (Dawid Warszawski)—he was clearly speaking more as a critical individual than as a representative of a communal position. He did not justify or support Weiss. But he did savagely criticize the Polish Catholic response, and with pointed understatement he declared that he felt "a little less comfortable, a little less at home in Poland." There is actually no Jewish problem in Poland; the problem is rather a Polish Catholic one.

Polish Catholics, despite years of Christian-Jewish meetings organized by the church, have not gone beyond their own parochialism. They have not attempted in a concerted fashion to appreciate other religious points of view. To be sure, among the intellectual elite, Catholics have worked to preserve Jewish monuments and to examine anti-Semitism, prominently in the previously mentioned nationwide network of Catholic Intellectuals Club and in the Catholic weekly *Tygodnik Powszechny*. And Catholic theologians such as Józef Tischner have examined the common grounds of Judaism and Catholicism. But at the very heights of the church hierarchy, the old religious bigotry of anti-Semitism is clearly ascendant. Before the fall of communism, Catholic liberalism seemed to be most important. After the fall, unfortunately, fundamentalist illiberalism of the worst sort seems to be most prominent.

Professor Maciej Giertych, according to many accounts a man close to primate Glemp, is an active proponent of the revival of the highly nationalistic and anti-Semitic interwar National Democratic Party, and for many Polish priests and parishioners, this position, more than the intellectualized philo-Semitism, represents the Polish Catholic view. At the grassroots level, the Catholic intellectuals may be more or less beside the point. They speak a different, cosmopolitan language and seem to be happy to operate among themselves. This situation was most evident during the course of the Auschwitz controversy. In discussing with me the problem of anti-Semitism, Jan Józef Szczepański criticized his Catholic colleagues for avoiding an important public responsibility. During the controversy, no one objectively published an account of the Jewish position on the convent. For this reason, he maintained, for the average Pole the events had a clear and simple meaning: Jews were trying to stop nuns from praying.

Such oversimplification has potentially explosive political consequences. Some anti-Semites raise very modern or postmodern versions of the Jewish question in surges of anarchistic despair, emulating Western skinheads. Others raise the Jewish question in the old way, apparently because they cannot make political sense of their situation without reference to old demons. The extreme views of these marginal groups could become central in the context of political and economic despair. They represent a flight from the responsibilities of political freedom. Before, the communists were in fact to blame for just about all that was wrong in society. After the fall, especially if the reforms do not work well, the (in reality nonexistent) Jews may be blamed, the very Jews who would trespass on the sacred holy grounds of a convent.

That an ecclesiastically sanctioned anti-Semitism still lives in that part of the world is an abomination. Yet, with the exception of Soviet Russia, it would be a serious mistake to overemphasize the political significance of contemporary anti-Semitism. The problem of sacralized politics has less to do with the way that others are treated, and more to do with the way that nations of Eastern and Central Europe do or do not learn how to govern themselves. Will they learn that self-governance requires both the freedom of religion from state interference, and the autonomy of politics?

The ecclesiastically "correct" position, obviously, is not always the democratically derived one. Religious belief should not be a precondition for political citizenship. The rules of politics are very different from the rules of religion. Differences of opinion are important in democracy, as are shared values concerning the rules of the political game. In religion, absolute truths are of central importance. Religion and politics make for strained bedfellows.

In fact, the relations between the church and the political opposition of the other Europe have always gone in more than one direction. There was the church of the Solidarity priests, who often defied not only state authority but also the church hierarchy in their chosen religious mission. There were the churches that sought primarily to sustain their institutions. They compromised as much as necessary with party-state authorities all over the Soviet bloc. And there were even church authorities who aggressively denounced political opposition. In the mid-eighties, Glemp used official anti-Semitic Newspeak when he criticized Solidarity leaders for following Trotskyist infiltrators. In Solidarity circles, he was thereafter commonly referred to as Comrade Glemp. In a democratic polity, such different church-based positions, along with other political differences, must be articulated. Within political institutions, the challenge is whether they will function with sufficient independence from the church. While the experience leading up to the fall should remind us that religious freedom and civil freedoms are intimately connected, the political activist of the other Europe should learn that religion and politics cannot be conflated in a democracy.

Following the guarantee of religious freedom, our First Amendment adds, "or abridging the freedom of speech or of the press; or of the right of the people peaceably to assemble, and to petition the Government for a redress of grievances." In their practical actions in the other Europe, citizens have forged the link between religious freedoms and the fundamental freedoms of a civil and democratic society. But, of course, the free practice of religion is far from guaranteeing political or civil freedoms. Before totalitarianism existed as a distinctively modern form of tyranny, ecclesiastically sanctioned tyranny was a well-known human experience. This older tradition is again observable after the fall of communism.

Liberals are prone to reject totalitarian atheistic policy primarily on the grounds of individual religious conscience. It is clear—individuals should be free to practice their religious beliefs without state interference. For the more secularly oriented, the respect for freedom of conscience may be viewed as a freedom of the ignorant to engage in an obsolete practice. For the religious, profound truths are involved. But both secular and religious liberals focus on the centrality of individual conscience. From the political point of view, though, individual religious liberty may not be the most crucial issue. Religious freedom is a communal matter as well as an individual one, and this presents complications, especially in societies in which civic identities have been identified with religious ones.

Today, the world views Polish Catholicism as a vibrant religious community. But in the nineteenth century it was different. From the point of view of religious purists, Catholicism was so connected with national longings for independence that there was little room in it for religion. The political functions of the church undermined its religious calling. The present Polish pope seems to worry about this issue as it is linked with liberation theology, especially in Latin America. Yet, clearly, the complex relationship of religion and democratic practice is a significant threat not only to the religious calling but also to democratic polities. The political function of the church may be transformed from sanctuary to hierarchy; an old-fashioned structure of authority may replace a modern tyranny.

The issues are familiar enough to us. American political life, with its two hundred-year tradition of grappling with the relations between church and state, is still quite vulnerable to sacralized politics. Some of those whose religious convictions tell them that abortion is the murder of the unborn cannot compromise with those who hold alternative views. Freedom of speech, religion, or choice, for them, is not the issue. Murder is. Yet, viewed from a comparative and historical perspective, the remarkable aspect of our political contestation is that it has remained, for the most part, within the bonds of legality, and that the legal system holds. The legitimacy of the political structure facilitates the civil articulation of harsh, absolute, theologically motivated differences of opinion. In the emerging democracies of Europe, such legitimacy did not exist.

Before the fall, religion was able to facilitate a democratic antipolitics; after the fall, the antipolitical potential of religion is a significant problem, not an advantage. Religious identity may replace citizenship; religious dogma may replace public deliberation and representation; religious authority may make impossible the constitution of an independent civil society and a democratic political order. While these problems can be observed elsewhere—for example, in Iran—they have a particularly tragic quality in Central Europe. If the polity becomes closely identified with the church, the fact that the Jew in the aforementioned 1970s Polish joke is standing, not kneeling, may become more important in the 1990s than the opposition to totalitarianism that brought him to the Mass in the first place.

Unlike the joke of the seventies, a 1990 Polish political joke has ominous implications: "The Hungarians have two political parties in their parliament, the Jews and the Reds; while we Poles do not have Reds." I heard this joke, apparently one of an anti-Semitic series, when speaking to two formerly communist Poles about the open anti-Semitic graffiti I had observed in Budapest, on posters for the Hungarian parliamentary elections, and in Warsaw. In reply they told the joke, to underscore the prevalence of a serious national pathology. Such graffiti, jokes, and discussions have a multiplicity of meanings. They unintentionally point to the infantilizing impact of totalitarianism on political culture. They show that traditional xenophobia has persisted in the shadows (anti-Semitism is nothing new in Hungary or Poland, or in Russia, for that matter). They represent an instance of the flight from freedom (now that the communists cannot be blamed for the condition of the nation, the Jews can be, even if there are few remaining). They also indicate a deep suspicion of modern secular liberal democracy, which anti-Semites believe the Jew represents.

For public discourse and foreign consumption, the Hungarian parliamentary election of March 1990 was a contest between the more-right-than-center Democratic Forum and the more-center-than-right Free Democrats. The political and economic programs of the parties were practically indistinguishable. The Forum was more nationalistic, the Democrats more cosmopolitan. Privately, among "true Hungarians," the Democrats were the Jews, the Forum the Hungarians. In Russia too, the conflict between "Russians" and liberal democrats is reduced by the more nationalistic to a battle against cosmopolitan, alien, Jewish influences. For the chauvinistically minded, such as the Russian scientist, former human-rights activist, and author of *Russophobia* Igor Shafarevich, the same alien forces that brought Russia communism (particularly Jewish Zionists) now want to impose the alien politics of liberal democracy. And in Poland, at a Congress of the Right held in

Warsaw, Polish priests denounced the "communist" idea of separation of church and state. A religiously sanctioned anticommunism, anti-Semitism, and antisecularism make up an all-too-familiar right-wing brew. How can this be, after the horrors of the twentieth century? Although there are many explanations, they should not be confused with justification.

It is true that because a disproportionate number of people with Jewish ancestors were active in the Polish and Hungarian democratic oppositions (in relation to their numbers in the general population), after the fall there were some highly visible Jews in public life. For those who have not confronted the legacies of anti-Semitism and the Holocaust, this situation may be proof that an alien force is again dominating the nation. The imposed mythologies and censorship of communism, and the official use of anti-Semitism to legitimate a so-called progressive political order, facilitated such reprehensible views. The continued confusion between religious and political identity made matters worse, suggesting very serious political difficulties.

Who is a Pole, a Hungarian, a Russian? For a significant segment of the population, the answer was to be found in religion. In 1966 the Polish church and state struggled over the millennial celebration of the Polish nation. The church, on solid grounds, maintained that the celebration commemorated the conversion to Christianity. Its criticisms of the communist state broadened political discourse. But for many, with the fall of communism, Christianity should politically prevail. Abortion should be made illegal. There should be religious instruction in the schools (not just prayer). Polish Catholicism should be the basis for Polish political identity. Vernacular speech represented this view as a popular common sense. In Poland, there were not Catholic Poles and Jewish Poles, secular Poles and so on, but just Poles and Jews. Likewise, in Hungary, there were Jews and Hungarians, and in not-so-Soviet Russia, there were Russians and Jews. There are two sides to the problem. The Jews in question had little or no religious identity, but they were excluded from full citizenship on the basis of that identity. Those who are not Jewish could relate national identity to religious background and religious identity.

It is not a coincidence that the Jews are again at the center of such controversy. In *The Origins of Totalitarianism*, Hannah Arendt argued that the centrality of anti-Semitism to European totalitarianism could not be adequately explained as traditional anti-Semitism, or even as a universal mechanism of scapegoating. After totalitarianism, conventional explanations were not sufficient either. Totalitarian practice, Arendt showed, was predicated on the expendability of human beings, who lost their human rights because they were understood as being outside the political community. The racist practices of anti-Semitism and imperialism were preconditions for totalitarianism. Jews, as aliens in the midst of national and transnational solidarities, were attacked by nationalists as well as Pan-Slavic and Pan-Germanic movements. After the fall, the new nationalists found the same Jews in their midst, at least in their imaginations, ready to undermine the appropriate moral (that is, religious) grounding of political life. Jews were not Poles, Slovaks, Hungarians, or Russians. They were something else: an alien force, again threatening the moral order.

And the people of the other Europe are desperately seeking moral order. They were held together by totalitarian terrors and dreams. Now, not surprisingly, some dream of national and religious community of a fundamental sort is forming. Anti-Semitism is once again an expression of the underside of the vision, of Eastern and Central Europe's terrors. Yet, as we have observed, the search for a moral community does not simply result in abominations, and does not only emanate from bad faith. When secularized Westerners viewed the Mass at the Lenin shipyard in August 1980, they saw an anomaly, a genuine workers' movement motivated by "superstition." But critical people from such places as Romania, Bulgaria, and Russia saw something more. Like the Westerners, they appreciated the democratic impulse, but they further understood that the constituted pluralism of the Polish workers' movement was based on a moral community, a legitimate and genuine religious belief. When such a belief is coupled with tolerance, it is a strong support for democracy; but only when coupled with tolerance.

For some of the countries of the new Europe, tolerance is the primary problem. For others, the more fundamental task is the formation of a semblance of a moral community, without which tolerance can hardly be said to exist. On a trip to Sofia, Bulgaria, the important contrast was pointed out to me. A Bulgarian sociologist there came up to talk to me after I had given a lecture on recent developments in American social science. (Although this man understood English, he spoke it poorly, but he had gathered from my talk that I spoke Polish, and so after struggling with English, to my astonishment he switched to Polish.) He wanted to underscore the vast differences between the northern and southern parts of Eastern and Central Europe.

The immediate topic was the condition of university education. He explained to me that Western study for Bulgarians was absolutely impossible. The social sciences did not exist in any real sense. There were only the history of Marxism and the study of scientific socialism. For students who sought something else, for the critically inclined, there was virtually nowhere to go. One of the very few options was study in one of the other fraternal socialist states. The especially enterprising realized that by learning Polish and gaining admission to Warsaw University throughout the sixties, seventies, and eighties, they could gain access to a real social-science education.

We began to talk further about common friends and professors, and discovered a common admiration for Solidarity and the democratic opposition of the 1970s. Although he was not a religious man, he pointed out that in his opinion, the Poles' major asset was the Catholic church. "They still have something to believe in," he said. And it was this belief, he thought, that made the democratic transition possible in Poland. He knew I had just been in Romania, and said that anomie existed there as it did in Bulgaria; a normlessness that made an independent politics very difficult.

In fact, I did find that in Bulgaria and Romania, critical activists often spoke about a sense of mutual distrust and fear. People who had worked together as anticommunist dissidents were not able to work in concert as democratic activists. The Bulgarian sociologist thought the reason was the absence of a legitimate and strong moral agency like the Polish church.

Yet the Polish church isn't what it once was, the primary anti-totalitarian, antipolitical social institution. Things have changed dramatically. Noted intellectuals like Adam Michnik, known for attempting to bridge the secular-religious divide, have been warning about the sacralization of politics, and ordinary people have been condemning the "blacks" (priests and nuns) along with the "reds."

Indeed, public opinion polls have revealed the first documented decline in the prestige of the church in the postwar period. On my visit in 1990 I heard several Poles observe that Poland was becoming a normal Catholic country like Italy, France, and Spain, with both clerical and anticlerical partisans.

Some countries of Eastern and Central Europe seem to be most strongly secular in areas where religious questions are not major issues one way or the other (for instance, Bohemia and most of urban Hungary), but other countries must contend with either strong religious traditions or the effects of strong antireligious propaganda and action. Poland, with a vital church, seems to be in a better position to normalize the relationship of church and state than those countries where religious institutions were more efficiently and brutally repressed.

It would seem that in some grand stroke of irony, this too is a result of the vibrancy of the Polish church during the communist period. In the countries that suffered the most under communism, where religious freedom was most forcefully attacked—particularly in Russia—grand nineteenth-century-type obsessions with "the national soul" (such as Solzhenitsyn's) have the greatest appeal; and this appeal may overwhelm the prospects for a democratic politics. The critical sensibility that the Polish church supported before the fall of 1989, by contrast, is being applied after the fall to the church itself, causing greater rigidity among the most dogmatic of church partisans and greater anticlericalism in the general population. This polarization will likely harness the church's political activities. The anti-abortion laws being proposed in the democratic parliaments of Poland and its neighbors may or may not pass (as in the United States), but as the church presses this and other issues of its special interest, it is likely to proceed ever more cautiously.

In 1990, a government decree mandated religious training in Polish public schools. The church strongly supported it. Only marginal libertarians, leftists, and secularists opposed such training in principle. But the whole enterprise proved to be unpopular. Parents knew the schools were mediocre and didn't want their children confined in them any longer than was necessary. Many who gladly sent their children to church for religious education were against training in the schools. And to make matters worse, the religious classes were being held in the middle of the school day. Originally, since formally the classes were optional, they were supposed to be held at the very beginning or end of the day, so that those who didn't attend would not be stigmatized. But the church scheduled its classes in the middle of the day to minimize truancy.

This situation excited great local concern, which supported a healthy public controversy. At this writing, whether such controversy will be strong enough to balance the immense powers of the church is an open question. Nonetheless, it breaks down unanimity, and this breakdown could successfully promote tolerance, making socially acceptable a variety of beliefs or disbeliefs.

Such tolerance is present in the everyday life of the democratizing Europe, along with a pluralistic commitment to the nation and the balancing of a general political consensus about the political rules of the game with an acceptance of political differences of opinion. Many people desperately seek democracy and understand the challenges they face. But people are also terribly frightened, and fear leads to antidemocratic developments: the turn to a charismatic leader with simplistic solutions to their problems, the rise of xenophobic nationalism, and religious fundamentalism. The collapse of the statist economy and the dismal economic prospects are primary sources of fear.

V

THE ECONOMY

CHAPTER 13

Anti-Economic
Practices

Looking at the socialist economies was like seeing reflections in a carnival mirror. Although in some ways these economies resembled our own, they seemed to have been ordered by an alien sensibility. They included elements that looked something like their nonsovietized counterparts: large-scale enterprises, factories, banks, stores, and trade unions. The same sorts of people as ourselves seemed to be in them, apparently engaged in the activities to which we are accustomed. But it was not so.

As a political-economic system, socialism of the Soviet type was strong on politics and very short on economics. It was not simply that political collectivistic exhortation replaced individual economic initiative. A great deal of initiative was actually necessary for survival. Rather, to a large extent, ideological political logic replaced economics. Although grand designs were drawn and realized, industrial output was increased, and an unsurpassed military was constructed, these achievements were more the result of political will than economic coordination.

Official trade unions, for example, were unlike any non-Soviet institution. Broadly speaking, in our world we recognize two different sorts of unions: those formed by workers to defend their interests (however they may be defined), and those formed by companies to undermine the activities of the unions of the first type ("company unions"). A convenient way of thinking about Soviet unions is as party-state company unions. Yet, even though these unions functioned to control workers' actions, enforcing the company's (that is to say, the party-state's) interests and ideology, distributing scarce goods such as vacations, scholarships, and even food and housing according to the company plan, they were much more than Western company unions. These Western unions are meant to disarm, to allow the capitalist firms to get on with their business. The unions of the Soviet type commanded, as an integral part of political, economic, and cultural life.

The Soviet Writers Union was archetypical, and since the fall of 1989 it has been a significant base for totalitarian restoration. This union has had little in common with any cultural institution outside the old Soviet bloc. Unlike legitimate labor unions, the Writers Union has been an instrument not of its membership but of the ultimate communist authority. Yet it was also not like company unions, because it served its membership with immense financial benefits as long as the Communist Party line was toed. The Soviet Writers Union was and is about the Party line. When it was not followed by individuals, the union was a primary agency of political repression.

The line was formulated by Lenin in his call for a party-spirited literature in 1905. In the 1930s, when the Writers Union was founded, this meant the promotion of socialist realism, and arrest and sometimes death for writers who did not comply. Between 1936 and 1939 one-third of the union's members were arrested, with their fates determined by the union's leaders.

But it was really after the Stalinist terror that the union came into its own. It became a leading agency of a soft, bureaucratic kind of totalitarianism. The union organized literary life through its control of publishing and social benefits to writers. It, in turn, was controlled from within by party ideologists and agents of the KGB.

With a few notable exceptions, the system worked. Ideologically sanitized writing was produced in great bulk. Dissident literature was invisible to the general public. Only a few well-known cases—most notably those of Boris Pasternak, of Andrei Sinyavsky and Yuri Daniel, and of Aleksandr Solzhenitsyn—challenged the happy, if not exactly creative, Leninist relations between party politics and party literature.

Although the system worked bureaucratically, even on its own terms it never worked culturally or economically. The union promoted and published a vast literature that the public refused to read. Russian and foreign classics and foreign contemporary literature were in great demand but scant supply. Instead, the union presented such literary gems as the collected writings of Leonid Brezhnev and the practically unreadable fictions of the union's apparatus. These books were produced to be pulped. No wonder the union has become a primary base of reactionary opposition to Mikhail Gorbachev and his democratic critics. It was a political product of the old order, created to support that order; and with the order's transformation, the Writers Union became, not surprisingly, a base of nationalistic authoritarianism. When a group of liberal writers met to assess the writers' situation under *glasnost*, union-supported anti-Semitic authors violently attacked them in defense of the "purity" of Russian letters.

The political economy of other workers' unions is essentially the same as that of "literary workers." As with the writing of books, the union organization is geared to politically correct production. Heroes of labor are glorified. Dedication to the Five-Year Plan is a commitment of the first order. Overfulfilling the production quotas of the plan is the primary group goal. The unions play a key role in industry for industry's sake. They maintain discipline, perhaps not quite so brutally as the Soviet Writers Union of the thirties, and dispense scarce goods, perhaps not quite so lavishly as the privileged Writers Union did in the sixties and seventies. They were primary agencies linking workers to the existing order. Play the game with the union and the worker survives; act against the union and essential goods and services become unavailable. Unions have special access to goods and special commissaries, and a great deal is distributed through their intervention.

Thus official trade unions of the Soviet type have been an integral part of political economy in ways unknown in Western experience. They are essentially a cross between company unions and a political machine of the old Chicago or Tammany Hall variety. They are not unions in any sense with which we are familiar.

Banks, factories, and retail stores as well are both more and less than they appear to Western eyes. Credit is dispersed primarily on political grounds. Large-scale unproductive enterprises are kept alive out of political necessity. For an American, it might be useful to imagine financial resources being distributed societywide in the way that we open and close military bases. Grandiose industrial projects are constructed more to show the might of socialism than to serve specific economic needs. Once established, they function as ends in themselves, often producing unusable goods and services. The major sectors of industry make up powerful interest groups, which are both politically and financially supported. The rationale for economic planning covers the dispersal of financial and economic favors for crystallized interest groups.

Grand politics of revolutionary transformation and socialist revolution mix with the petty politics of interest groups to form a fundamentally irrational economic policy. Steel is produced according to the same logic that leads to the publication of hundreds of thousands of volumes of the collected works of Leonid Brezhnev, Edward Gierek, and Janos Kadar. Banks are institutions that specialize in facilitating this sort of activity. Economic judgment has less to do with creditworthiness than political clout. Retail stores are also mythic economic entities. Many scarce goods are distributed outside these stores, and even when supplies appear to be plentiful, they may very well not be. In the store windows of furniture and appliance shops, for example, there may be displayed a wide range of products, but frequently they are unavailable. The stores function as museums, offering colorful consumer potential, beautifying the urban landscape. Someday the exotic goods may be accessible, if one waits months or years or has the right political connections. Meeting consumer needs is not the central retail task; as with unions, factories, and banks, politics of a special variety is.

One of the great ironies of history and social theory is the fact that the self-defined "progressive" political economy of socialism has proved itself to be not only regressive but archaic and brittle. The irony perplexes those wedded to conventional understanding, both on the left and on the right. Progress has long been defined by a teleology of class struggle. The ascendant class of history—the working class—was seen as forging a new progressive order, socialism, and it was expected to bring social justice. The experience of the new order, however, has revealed to ordinary people, particularly workers, the lie in this utopian script. According to the official ideology they were "the new ruling class," but they knew from every aspect of their daily lives that it was just not so. They worked in factories under primitive and life-threatening conditions not unlike those in the nineteenth-century English factories described by Marx in *Das Kapital*, the major difference being that the capitalist factories of the past produced might and wealth, while the socialist economies enervated and impoverished.

Socialist rhetoric promised more and more and better and better; such was a propaganda slogan plastered all over Poland in the early seventies, when the Polish population was said to be building the Second Poland. But the economic reality was of an ever-deepening economic crisis, which finally in the eighties led to a blocwide breakdown. Along with their fellow citizens, workers could see, feel, and even smell the breakdown coming. All day long the workers in the famous Lenin shipyard in Gdańsk subjected their bodies to abuse, many building ships in shoulder-deep water, ships for which there was no demand on the open market. The steel mills and chemical plants in and around Kraków, Prague, and Leipzig not only destroyed the natural environment, but significantly lowered life expectancy and public health. These and other industrial works made the eastern part of Europe one of the world's major ecological disaster zones. Now the water in the region is unfit for drinking, the air is unfit for breathing, and its forests either have been killed or are dying. The living standards are low not only in comparison to their wealthy capitalist European neighbors, but in comparison to these nations' own economic past. The environment has been devastated with little economic gain. Just after the fall, the average Polish worker made less than eighty dollars a month. His Czech and Hungarian neighbors made a bit more. His Soviet neighbors made much less.

We now know that communist economic policies end in bankruptcy. This fact has led many, with their feet firmly planted in the ideologized terrain of the Cold War, to deduce that the polar opposite of communist policy leads to affluence. The freer the market, the more productive the economy and the more creatively entrepreneurial the economic actors. Yet economic activity, both in the West and in the East, belies this ideo-logic. Nations with governments that actively "interfere" with the free workings of private enterprise are now flourishing. Germany, not Great Britain, is the economic powerhouse of Western Europe. Japan, not the United States, appears to be the ascending economic actor on the international stage.

Economies flourish or flounder for very specific reasons. The truth of this proposition reveals itself in daily economic life. The failure of the statist economy has often been explained with reference to its concrete irrationalities. Bread is fed to livestock because it is cheaper than grain. Factories and entire industries produce goods for decades that no one wants or can use: steel that is unusable, ships that have no purpose. Just about everyone observing Eastern and Central Europe agrees, therefore, that radical economic reform is a necessity. They also tend to agree (with a few exceptions) that the end of reform must be a market economy.

Yet the road to the market is not clearly marked. There is much debate about it, and a great deal of concern about how ordinary people will fare during the journey. Industrial workers in big cities, farmers in the countryside, intellectuals inside and outside official cultural institutions, and new business classes, among others, must realize the economic reforms as producers and consumers. And at the same time, as citizens they are seeking to constitute a new democratic order. Although these economic and political activities do come into conflict, they are also both mutually supportive and directly emergent from the most fundamental weakness of socialist political economy.

Changing the economics must necessarily start with the politics. Most significantly, this link is what gave the opposition unions their special character. Such unions emerged all around the bloc. They played a central role, particularly in the Polish transformation, and in my judgment they may very well do the same in the Soviet Union. When the independent trade unions formed in Poland in 1980, they were difficult to characterize, not only for outside observers but also for inside observers and activists. The languages of politics and social science, both those of the totalitarian regimes and those of the West, were not adequate for this new social development. The unions opposed their official counterparts. The workers wanted to form organizations that would defend their interests. But just as the official unions were not merely Western company unions, the organization of independent unions that eventually came together as Solidarity was not simply a Polish AFL or CIO. It would take a long time for them to reach such "normality," and they might never do it. Indeed, there is nothing necessary or natural about the process. Radical changes in the connections between politics and economics will occur, and the new connections will define the character of the various economic units and their relationships, from trade unions to banks to retail stores. Although it is agreed that the market should replace the plan, the social and political contracts supporting the market are now vital matters of contestation. The experience of Solidarity reveals the central issues.

Solidarity began as an antipolitical organization, and the change in the politics must take into account the imperatives of economic change emerging from a collective action directed against the odd political economy of the workers' daily lives. By the time of Solidarity's founding in 1980, Poland had a long tradition of antipolitical postwar labor action. Worker strikes in 1956, 1970, and 1976 determined the twists and turns of communist Poland. In 1956, responding to price increases and labor shortages, a Poznań workers' strike led to the ascendance of Władysław Gomułka and his more anti-Stalinist wing of the Polish Communist Party. They promised a Polish road to socialism, which at first enjoyed broad popular support. But throughout the sixties the socioeconomic road was rocky, and when drastic food price increases were announced in December 1970, the workers again staged mass protests and strikes, this time most prominently in the mining region around Katowice and in the northern ports of Szczecin and Gdańsk. The price increases were rescinded. Gomułka fell officially because of an "illness of the eyes." In 1976, the strikes centered in and around the cities of Warsaw and Radom. Again, food price increases sparked the strikes. But a new pattern was set. The regime of Edward Gierek did not fall. Although the government did back down from the price increases one day after the strike (officially after "consultations with the nation"), when the active strikers were repressed, they were aided by intellectuals of the newly formed Committee for Worker Defense. The committee set up an information network to publicize the cases of repression and an informal welfare network to support the families of the imprisoned and those forced into unemployment because of their strike activities. The pattern of the bread strikes of 1956 and 1970—which were settled by a change in the regime's leadership, economic concessions, and a reestablished stability—gave way to political and economic activity in which the demands for more bread and more freedom were closely linked, and were directed at the constitution of the regime itself. A way to address the peculiar political economy of actually existing socialism was developed in the context of an ongoing political struggle.

In the late seventies, the intellectuals' support of workers blossomed into the formation of an underground opposition movement. Intellectuals constructed a nationwide system of underground publishing and lectures, and workers, particularly in the Gdańsk region, began forming illegal independent labor unions on a small scale. Two distinctive features of these activities were the systematic bridging of the gulf between the workers and the intellectuals, and the simultaneous addressing of economic and political questions. The slogan was, "No bread without freedom." It suggests a new question for the nineties: Can there be freedom without bread?

The crucial moment in the Gdańsk strikes of August 1980 came when the workers refused to end their strike until those members of the Committee for Worker Defense who had been arrested in the beginning were released from jail. All of the other issues, including their economic demands and their right to strike, had been resolved. But the workers felt that they could not "abandon their friends," as Wałęsa put it. The strikers' own sense of integrity required this resolute action. They probably did not realize—neither they nor anyone else could have realized—the importance of this final stand. They made visible to themselves, their compatriots, and the whole world the distinctive features of their previously underground activity. They affirmed that theirs was not simply a movement of workers pursuing their economic and class interests. They understood that freedom was a crucial part of their struggle and that their struggle was not a class struggle defined by economic relations, but an antipolitical struggle defined by the opposition to a totalitarian power. No one was then able to imagine that the totalitarian power could be overthrown, so the primary goal was to disengage as much of social life as possible from party-state control. Solidarity sought evolutionary change from below, following the strategy of societal transformation first envisioned by Adam Michnik in 1976.

For the Solidarity activists, this process meant the repeated assertion that they were simple trade unionists seeking better working conditions and defending their right to strike, while respecting the "leading role of the Polish United Workers Party," in other words, the Communist Party dictatorship. There was, of course, significant irony in their political minimalism. In a political-economic system in which all aspects of human existence are theoretically subjected to ideological interpretation and totalitarian control, to assert the right of autonomous self-defense is a major political act that fundamentally undermines the dictatorship. By creating a union outside the logic of the totalitarian system, they were, in effect, embarking on the constitution of a competing political economy, one in which the distortions of ideology did not define the economic units and their activities.

The vision and ethos of the Solidarity activists were not utopian. There was no clear ideology at work. They sought to improve their situation one step at a time, without a vision of where the steps would end or an exact idea of how the journey would be accomplished. They did not foresee the winding path that would eventually lead from their heroic actions in the Lenin shipyard to the desacralization of Lenin and his isms from Berlin to Beijing. And certainly they were not prepared for what proved to be a futile and highly expensive last-ditch defense by the communists of their power and privileges—the war against Solidarity as an underground movement. But from its beginnings to its existence as an underground movement to its open status both as a new government and as a force in opposition to the new government, the "normalizing" of the political economy has been an underlying theme of Solidarity's politics. Now the variations on and complications of the theme are of crucial importance in Poland and throughout Eastern and Central Europe.

In the "other Europe," there is a desire for what is called a normal society. People want their political, cultural, and economic institutions without ideology: trade unions that represent the economic interests of workers; banks that offer credit on the grounds of sound economic calculation; political parties that compete and do not command; and schools, publishing houses, newspapers, and theaters that educate, entertain, and inform but do not propagandize. For those of a liberal laissez-faire conviction, these norms can all be achieved directly and efficiently through the rapid introduction of the free market. Others with more social-democratic convictions have principled doubts about the classically liberal position. They are especially concerned about issues of justice. Still others more pragmatically realize that even if a market economy is desirable, its constitution presents political challenges that must be addressed strategically, with a balancing of the social costs and economic gains, one step at a time.

Despite the variety of opinions about how to constitute a market and how freely it should be run, all of the political parties in all of the nations of Eastern and Central Europe have as one of their primary political goals the replacement of the command economy by a market economy. All agree that the unions, banks, and industrial enterprises of the old variety must be fundamentally changed. But when the politics of economics is viewed in this way, the real problems of the transition become most apparent. Some institutions simply cannot be transformed. Unions do have an important role to play in a market economy. They defend the collective interests of workers, qualifying the freedom of entrepreneurial and managerial decision. But the old Soviet-type unions will not readily take on this role. As we have already observed, they are primarily systems of patronage with ideological justification. Even if the Party ideologists and KGB watchdogs were to withdraw from the Soviet Writers Union, the leaders and the active membership would attempt to persist in the old way of doing things. These people have made their careers upon, indeed, have dedicated their lives to the literary politics of the old order. Take the totalitarian ideology and privilege out of the union and their professional lives will end. They fight, therefore, for ideological politics and literary life. The content of the ideology seems to be of minimal importance. The most Stalinist and internationalist comfortably adapt to extreme anticommunism and ultranationalism.

In industries in which ideological production is not the only product, nevertheless it has often been an important major product. The old unions are among the last strongholds of ideological resistance. The strongest antimarket rhetoric in Poland comes from Alfred Miodowicz, the leader of the old Party-founded union federation that competed with Solidarity. Indeed, the communist regime's last attempt to maintain the old order was in a televised debate between Wałęsa and Miodowicz in December 1988. Faced with a need to engage in radical economic changes, with at least minimal popular support, the regime hoped that their well-informed union ideologist would reveal Wałęsa to be a man of the past, ill-informed about economic realities and out of touch with the Polish population. After Wałęsa ran circles around Miodowicz, the regime faced the political facts and in effect conceded that it had lost its war against the Polish nation. Then began the roundtable talks that eventually led to the Solidarity government.

The economic and ideological interests embedded in the old order, which people like Miodowicz continue to respect, must be taken into account in facilitating the creation of a new economic system. Even though the unproductive industries were created for ideological purposes, they do, however inadequately, serve the economic needs of their workers and those of the cities and regions in which the workers are located. It may be that in the long run everyone will be better off if steel works close when they are not competitive on the world market. But for the people employed in these factories, the long run—as we know from our own experience in the so-called rustbelt—is not the primary consideration. In such situations, real tensions and paradoxes emerge in the relation between democratic aspirations and economic transformation.

While the plants and their official unions were ideological creations, the independent unions, where they have existed, and the new government are anti-ideological. There is a limited convergence of interests between the newly democratic governments and independent workers' associations and unions. Only in Poland have such unions engaged in prolonged struggles, but everywhere just before or after the fall, similar organizations have emerged. The starting position of these unions is a rejection of the way things used to be done. They want managers of their enterprises to be competent in production, commerce, and finance. They want a real chance to be productive themselves. They want better living conditions, of course, but their experience tells them that the way to achieve an improved standard of living is to depoliticize their workplaces, not only by taking the Party out of production, but by freeing economic life from state control. The unions, like the new governments, initially assume that enterprises will be more productive, delivering more benefits for the nation and the workers alike, if the state withdraws from direct economic responsibility.

There is a fundamental problem with this position, and it is utilized in a dangerous rearguard politics by the ideologues of the old order. Since many if not most of the economic enterprises of the old order are ideological creations, the direct application of economic rationality demands the widespread closure of enterprises. While this might be in the interests of the nation as a whole, it is certainly not in the best interests of workers in the enterprises. By defending the old way of doing things, the old unions and managers can claim that only they defend the real interests of the workers. They can reveal that the new government and unions are working against the interests of ordinary people, at the same time that the alternative they present is more of the same old thing.

There are dangers and opportunities here. The politics of economics lies between two poles. On one side is radical liberalization, epitomized by the Polish shock therapy. On the other is gradualism, the extreme being the Bulgarian communists, who now call themselves socialists. The name change of the Bulgarian party is not just a cynical manipulation. The transformed communists do seem to recognize the dimensions of the communist economic crisis and, like their more explicitly anticommunist political neighbors, promise a market economy and a multiparty system, a turn toward Europe. Nonetheless, considering the dimensions of the economic crisis, along with revelations that the political repressions of the Bulgarian communist order involved its own gulag, with thousands murdered, it may at first be hard to comprehend why the Bulgarian population actually freely chose continuity with the old order by electing the socialists in Bulgaria's first free elections.

There are a variety of reasons for the Bulgarian exception; in fact, a similar situation can be observed in Serbia and Albania. The opposition was well organized only in the cities, primarily among intellectuals. Rural people and urban laborers were beholden to local party bosses at state farms, in factories, and in unions for their very existence. And most significantly, this existence was understood to be a genuine improvement over the precommunist standard. Further, the Communist Party of Bulgaria boasted of being the oldest in Europe, claiming and receiving a legitimacy unknown in the rest of Europe. After the fall, this less illegitimate party emphasized that it would promote the transition to a rational economics with a minimal amount of pain. The Socialist Party maintained that it understood the need for change, but assured the population that it also understood their needs for security and general well-being. Fearful of the unknown, the conservative populace made the conservative choice.

That such a conservative choice would not lead to fundamental change did become clear to the Bulgarians. When the majority did not face up to the need for radical change, the old ideological interests predictably dug in, as they are doing in the Soviet Union, and economic transformation was found not to be workable. Union officials, plant managers, and financial officers who held their positions more because of political loyalty than because of ability were encouraged by the Bulgarian popular caution and had a real opportunity to fortify their positions. When the Bulgarians saw this outcome, the popularity of the socialists plummeted.

Elsewhere in Eastern and Central Europe, the old guard is under more sustained attack. In Romania, the National Salvation Front has faced fundamental criticism for attempting to engineer economic and political reforms by using the personnel of the communist elite as leadership and the privileged working class as political storm troopers. In Poland the radical monetarism of the finance minister, Leszek Balcerowicz, aims to do away with the old patronage system completely and rapidly. In Czechoslovakia and Hungary there is more caution. The Hungarian electorate chose the political party that promised a more gradual transition. The Democratic Forum is not against a free market, but maintains that for the market to work, its institutional context must be properly constituted. Since the economic crisis did not seem to be as severe in Czechoslovakia as in Poland, the new state authorities there too wanted to manage the economic change more deliberately, advocating a "soft landing." They wanted to avoid "the Polish situation," a euphemism for economic collapse. Only in East Germany was the economic crisis directly and harshly addressed. The population unambiguously opted out of the socialist system. Although there were real fears concerning personal fates, the East Germans chose the Western political economy over the Eastern, first with their feet and then with their ballots. For them, the economic transition will be relatively straightforward, even if painful. They will be part of the strongest national economy of Europe, one of the strongest in the world. In Germany, the old managers and workers will either meet international standards or they will be fired.

The leaders of the East German democratic opposition were disappointed by the people's choice. While the leaders of the New Forum were severe critics of the former system, as radical intellectuals with their roots in the leftist tradition and as activists with connections to the West German cultural and political left, they did not want to substitute the American-style commercialism of West Germany for the Soviet-style totalitarianism of East Germany. Their goal was to create a humane and democratic socialist alternative, a so-called "third way."

But theirs was a position destined from the beginning for the historical dustbin. This was not because of an absence of sincerity, or even because they did not understand the concerns of their compatriots. It was because the concerns of their compatriots for a prosperous life with security—perhaps even, as the critics understood it, without the cruelties of the West—were overwhelmed by the sheer economic and political strength of the West. East Germans quite rationally did harbor some fears about unification. As citizens of the most prosperous of the Soviet-style socialist nation-states, they had much to lose in the transition, not the least of which were subsidized food and shelter, medical care, education, vacations, and so forth. But the claims by the New Forum intellectuals and semidissident academics that the

humane values of the German Democratic Republic should be pre-
served along with democraticization seemed to ordinary citizens to be
a pipe dream masked in an oppositional Newspeak. The choice was
clear: the "normalization" of the West, or a continued second-class
citizenship. Given a choice, when emigration was open to all, there
was no choice.

With a normalized economic order, the particular interests of
workers were defended in the Western way. New unions were formed
and merged with West German unions; a battle was fought concerning who would bear the costs of transition. A laissez-faire approach
was taken: East Germans would continue to have a lower standard of
living (approximately one-third of West Germany's), and its workers,
particularly those in large, outmoded industrial complexes, would suffer mass layoffs and unemployment. New investments, coupled with a
rising productivity, would eventually lead to economic parity with the
West (at the time of economic reunification, labor productivity, like
salaries, was one-third of West Germany's).

East and West German workers proposed a more social-democratic
transition. IG Metall, West Germany's largest union, which the newly
formed independent metal workers of East Germany joined,
demanded a two-year freeze on layoffs. The union proposed that the
two-thirds of their salaries they would have received as unemployment
benefits be paid to the workers as they continued to work and retrain.
The state, and thus in effect the citizens of West and East Germany
alike, would pay the costs of the transition, not just East Germans,
and particularly East German workers, as would be the case following
the laissez-faire plan.

The East German citizenry, along with their fellow Eastern and
Central Europeans, knew that they were abandoning a marginally
comfortable economic mediocrity for a challenging and perhaps difficult new economic order. They abandoned illusions of a low-cost, relatively painless "third way." Significantly, this common sense of
ordinary East Germans demonstrates a greater cogency than was
shown by their more sophisticated intellectual elite. All around the old
Soviet empire, the same joke was told about the political economy of
everyday life: "We pretend to work and they [those in the party-state]
pretend to pay us." Now, in the new democracies, people are attempt-

ing to transform the economic jokes into real economies.

Moving from economic pretense to economic reality involves danger, pain, and fear, all of which have profound public and personal implications. These were revealed to me in a conversation I had with an old friend, Jan Lityński, then a Polish member of Parliament and assistant secretary of labor in charge of labor-union affairs.

CHAPTER 14

On the Road to Capitalism?

J an Lityński knows the problem of economic transformation from the bottom up. He is a veteran of the long struggles of the Polish democratic opposition. As a student in the late 1960s he was a Marxist of sorts, a Marxist-humanist opponent of the stagnating Gomułka regime. For him, in retrospect, those were times of naïveté and ignorance. He and his friends were labeled Trotskyists both by their supporters in the West and by their enemies at home (the communist authorities), though he actually knew very little about Trotsky or the situation of the "masses" in Poland. He and his friends knew only, in the international spirit of 1968, that things were fundamentally wrong and needed radical reformation. They used the moral ideals of their political parents to reject the Marxist realities of their lives.

Like many others, such as his lifelong friend Adam Michnik, Lityński paid dearly for his youthful rebellion. He was not able to pursue his academic ambitions in mathematics or to hold a real job in any significant sense until the fall of 1989. He became a professional dissident, without a university degree, cut off from the normalities of an official existence. He was not then and never became an opposition political leader. Because his forte was not political theory or writing, as was the case with Michnik, he was not then and never became a leading dissident intellectual. Instead he was an organizer. He wrote primarily about pressing political challenges and acted politically to address them.

In the late seventies, when the workers in Gdańsk started to form an independent union, Jan Lityński became a contributor to the independent newspaper *Robotnik* (The Worker). After Solidarity was legalized, Lityński spent much of his time with the miners in and around the provincial town of Świdnica on the Czechoslovak border. He stayed with such people when he was part of the underground, evading arrest, and now he is their representative in Parliament, and in a way their advocate in the government.

As a professional revolutionary in a political movement that was deeply skeptical about revolutions and their professionals, Lityński is a man who appreciates the ironies of his situation. But because of his abiding respect for the people he has led, his dilemmas are not unbearable. When he helped publish *Robotnik* he did not put words into workers' mouths, but simply helped them articulate what they had to say. When he assisted those workers who were far out of the limelight of Polish political life, it was clear to them and to him that he was learning as much as teaching. Among his close friends in Warsaw were the leaders of Solidarity, Poland's leading intellectuals and dissidents; but the workers of Świdnica knew him as Janek, a small, quiet, even diffident friend, who gave them necessary information and offered sound advice. Lityński, as a high government official, makes the six-hour drive from Warsaw to Świdnica once every two weeks to meet with his constituents. During these trips, the cultural and political obstacles to political and economic reform and freedom become most apparent.

For the new political leaders in Warsaw and for similar ruling circles in the other new democracies, economic reform was evolving into a matter of large-scale strategy. The economic generals were planning a most difficult and unprecedented campaign: the dismantling of a political-economic system based on grand ideology and the exchange of petty favors, and the construction of a rational, modern economic system. The broad approach of the quick fix seemed to be rational: control hyperinflation through radical monetary reform; balance the budget; let prices rise to international levels, but control wages; force the bankruptcy of unproductive enterprises; improve foreign trade; understand that there will be an induced depression of economic activity, but once the unproductive is washed out, the depression will be followed by a sound economic upturn.

In the provinces and the major cities, in the trenches, places like the mines of Swidnica, the reforms looked quite different. With the monetary reforms, basic necessities like food and shelter, as well as luxuries like newspapers and clothing, seemed to be getting beyond the means of many. Employment was suddenly uncertain. Some, the winners in the lottery, were about to find themselves employed in plants and mines that could make a go of it, but others, no matter how hard they worked, were going to be laid off. No one knew who would be weeded out. All sensed doom on the horizon. Even productive private industrial entrepreneurs were going through a very tough time. Dependent as they were on orders from state enterprises, which were now cutting back on production, the capitalists who had flourished in the last decade of communist reform were being severely challenged by the market reforms. On the grounds that financial help would feed inflation, the planners in Warsaw were offering no special help to the very firms that would have to replace the large-scale socialist industrial works. These firms, therefore, like the small farmers, were moving more quickly toward bankruptcy than the large firms that continued to draw upon the state budget.

On March 31, 1990, I joined Lityński on one of his fortnightly trips. When he arrived that Friday evening, he was greeted as the greatest of VIPs. A rock concert was being held to raise funds for the Solidarity local; and because Lityński was a bit late, the concert had already started. He was seated in the first row during the opening act. When the performing group finished, the emcee announced his arrival and Lityński was greeted by the audience as a leading star, a more important celebrity than the nationally famous musical groups.

After the rock concert, people in small groups expressed their consternation in Lityński's presence. To be sure, there was an exhilaration, because they were able to take responsibility. But there was also desperation. They did not know which way to go. Lityński went to talk with them, to explain Warsaw policies and reasoning and to get a clearer sense of how government actions were affecting the lives of his constituents. He met his constituents individually and in groups. The general theme was that so far the new order had led to a new type of suffering while the irrationalities of the old order still prevailed. Individuals complained to him about specific problems. A much-needed new school had been planned for years, and people saw materials on the projected building site, but no one seemed to be able to get the building built. Health-care costs were going up without improvements in delivery. The old *nomenklatura* still used special privileges. The organization of work in a firm continued to follow old patterns. On a collective farm, one of the party bosses built himself a private farm using collective resources. Farmers desperately needed financial credit so that they could plant their crops. If it was not immediately forthcoming, not only would farmers face serious problems, but there would be a shortage of food.

Lityński responded to the individual complaints with respect, but also with some impatience. They had come to him with a set of grievances that they hoped he would alleviate. He was their political patron, elected by them in order to provide them with help. Before, the reds had controlled everything. Now, with people like Janek in authority, things would be set straight. To a limited extent Lityński accepted this role. He listened to grievances, inquired about the details, and, after consultation with his local political associates, tried to resolve pressing problems. Yet, even more often Lityński had to turn the issues back on his constituents. He reminded them over and over again that now they were responsible for their situation. The state did not control everything, and therefore central authority could not settle all issues. If an old party hack in a factory was resolutely holding onto power and privilege, the workers should organize and oppose him. It did not require ministerial intervention. Popular opinion and political power were now on their side, but they had to act. If no one was taking responsibility for building the needed school, people should become active in the local elections (scheduled for May) and get firm assurances from the local candidates that that particular issue would be resolved.

At a gathering in City Hall, Lityński met the public along with the mayor of Świdnica, a competent communist whose days, I thought, were clearly numbered. Lityński began the meeting with a brief overview of the general economic situation. He pointed out the accomplishments of Balcerowicz's program. The style of life had improved. Goods were available in stores, though at very high prices. People did not wait in lines any more, which saved people, particularly women, about three hours a day. He explained that the program had led to a downturn in the economy, which he understood directly affected their standard of living. He maintained that the present hard time was necessary so that a more productive economy could be born.

Earlier, on the road to Świdnica, Lityński had told me that he expected the recession to last for about two years, much longer than people were prepared for. And he conceded that what would happen after two years was not certain. He said he felt comfortable, however, with the government's economic policy, because it was being formulated in a democratic context. If the public perceived that the present policies were not working, alternatives should be proposed by competing political groups, and the people could choose among them. Indeed, he hoped that sound alternatives would be presented in the very near future, so that a reasonable debate could ensue. But such debate must be predicated on an understanding that the political-economic world was changing.

That understanding was not in evidence at the Świdnica City Hall. The first question was the most telling, because of what the questioner inadvertently communicated. He reminded Lityński that society's situation was extremely difficult, and people were losing patience. He asked whether Lityński thought the government was still popular. Lityński conceded that with increasing economic difficulties, the government's popularity was waning. The questioner then wanted inside information. "Are the rumors true that an increase in prices is being planned for May?" Lityński responded with an elementary discourse on the logic of supply and demand. He explained that if prices went up, it would be the result of the workings of autonomous economic forces, not because of a direct decision by the authorities. The question assumed statism, and Lityński answered using market logic.

The ensuing discussion covered many topics, including geopolitics (Świdnica was once German territory, and still had Soviet forces stationed in its region), but it kept returning to the first query. The citizens of Świdnica were not thinking in terms of the new political-economic realities. They were approaching the present using the dichotomies of the past. The authorities had governed, and the people had either reluctantly accepted their lot or protested against it. They could not conceive that their economic and political fates were both, to a great extent, now in their own hands. If they engaged in productive enterprise, they would flourish. If they chose responsible political leadership, politicians both local and national would attempt to act in ways that served their needs. As activists in the Solidarity movement, they had made it impossible for the communists to govern. Now they must not simply veto the authorities, they must act themselves to create a productive economy and a responsible politics. The step had to be made from participant in a democratic social resistance to citizen of a democratic polity and productive agent in a free economy.

Some hesitate to make this step. They are so accustomed to blaming "them" that they look for new all-powerful authorities who are "ruining their lives." If things are not going well, some dark force must be the cause. I overheard one of the local activists speaking to a pair of British diplomats, friends of Lityński. She asked them a rather horrific question: How did people in England deal with their "Jewish problem"? The embarrassed diplomats quickly but gently tried to answer. They celebrated British pluralism, then admitted that prejudice and discrimination were a part of the British past, but emphasized that they were trying to overcome them and hoped the Poles would do the same. The woman was not satisfied, but understood that further conversation would not be helpful.

Lityński, in the meantime, was being interviewed by a journalist from a local newspaper. The journalist was remarkably ill-informed, clearly an old professional accustomed to filling his paper with Communist Party handouts. He asked whether Lityński was or had been a member of the Confederation for an Independent Poland (a right-wing ultranationalistic group) when, in fact, Lityński was a long-time opponent of the group. The journalist was seeking answers to questions that were already part of the public record. When Lityński added something new, such as a justification for the continued presence of Soviet troops as a way of maintaining good relations with Moscow, so that Poland could help more effectively in the crisis of Lithuania, the journalist did not take note. When it was clear that the interview was over, the journalist insisted on asking just one additional "important" question. He asked if it were true that the government leadership, with the exception of Mazowiecki, was made up of Jews. Lityński answered, "Yes, Jews, Germans, and Bolsheviks," and then sardonically added that he thought the Poles were too smart for such thinking. With the journalist expressing his doubts to Lityński, a man with Jewish heritage, the interview ended.

Nevertheless, in Świdnica, a town particularly prone to nationalistic rhetoric because it feels vulnerable to German claims and is still oppressed by the Soviet presence, ultranationalism and xenophobia have not overwhelmed politics. The people of the district elected Lityński. They are struggling with the difficult problem of ridding their politics and economics of totalitarianism. Some, of course, do look for easy solutions to the remarkably difficult problems about them. Some cannot seem to understand the full implications of their new democratic and free situation. But others do understand. They search for solutions to their own immediate situations, attempting to act democratically. One of the constituents who met Lityński was a farmer from outside Świdnica. Like the others, he had particular complaints and wanted to express them. But that was not his major concern: he wanted to make clear to his representative that there was a major flaw in the government's policies. The economic program must be amended, he told Lityński, to allow farmers to raise their crops. The laws of supply and demand were all well and good, but some minimal price had to be guaranteed to the farmers. They were currently receiving old-order prices for their produce, but they had to pay new-order prices for fertilizers and machinery. Farmers were being forced out of business, and it meant that there would be food shortages in the near future.

Lityński agreed that some exceptions had to be made to the government's economic policies. But he reminded the farmer that a first priority had to be fighting hyperinflation and establishing a new economic order. Lityński recognized, of course, that here was a legitimate ground for passionately held differences of opinion. Political contestation on this issue would improve, rather than undermine, economic reform.

The government's policies were based on economic theories developed from Western experience and the experiences of the Third World. Jeffrey Sachs, who has been an important adviser to Solidarity on economic affairs, and the IMF, which is overseeing the economic reforms, have no real theory of or extensive empirical evidence on "detotalitarianization." Sachs has proposed transplanting to Eastern Europe policies developed for countries like Bolivia. For these or any other policies to work, they must be adapted to the particular circumstances of specific economic agents such as farmers.

While one way of knowing the circumstances is through expert knowledge based on research and technical opinion, the politically effective way is through democratic contestation. If this farmer and other farmers do not get satisfaction from representatives such as Lityński, they will—and should—seek other representatives. After Lityński's visit to Świdnica, there were nationwide protests against the government's agricultural policies. In that these kinds of actions force the economic generals to take into account the economic footsoldiers, the end result may be politics attuned to the specific conditions of the transition.

It is an article of democratic faith that competition and compromise yield a more just and effective result than monolithic "true" solutions to societal problems. Technocrats of one variety or another argue against this faith. They maintain that the immediate pursuit of group interests could undermine economic rationalization. Yet they overlook the functional contributions of open democratic practice. If democratic contestation is viewed as legitimate, policies that are not completely in the interest of particular groups will be more easily accepted. The time required for austerity measures to have their effects will then be more fully utilized. And if such legitimate democratic contestation is open to a plurality of points of view, then insights like those of Lityński's farmer constituent may be incorporated into the shaping of economic policy. Only in this way will the fundamental problem of communist political economics be overcome.

The old systems were based on secrets, rather than on the open exchange of information. Democracy is the cure. Theorists of laissez-faire capitalism as well as communist ideologists need to be informed about, and indeed instructed by, the experience of the citizenry. Mikhail Gorbachev wanted to use limited dosages of freedom and democracy to buy legitimacy and to gain some of the advantages the free flow of information can provide in a democracy. He wanted to do this without completely dismantling the Soviet political economy. But the experience of Eastern Europe suggests that a dismantling of both the totalitarian economy and the totalitarian polity is necessary, and the process requires democracy.

But what is the democracy about? Not only economics, to be sure, even though different views of the transformation of the economy are central. There exists one set of choices between something like European social democracy and European liberalism (American laissez-faire conservatism). And since everyone agrees that privatizing the economy is imperative, any step-by-step approach does offer these two alternatives. But the choices available are not only the most dramatic ones: Polish-style shock treatment versus Bulgarian gradualism. Once a decision is made to restructure an economy fundamentally, the actual, less dramatic process of instituting changes involves choices too. Edward Szywala knows this well.

Edward Szywala is someone I encountered in Świdnica. He is a relatively wealthy producer of industrial equipment who now faces bankruptcy because of the shock-treatment reforms. A politically active man in the Polish provinces, he joined the Communist Party at the wrong time, in 1979. He was active in a communist reform movement, the horizontal structure movement, which failed and is now long forgotten. He is marked as an ex-communist, and he is doubly damned because he is wealthy. He would like to pursue a political career, but feels that egalitarian resentment and reflexive anti-communism preclude it.

Nonetheless, his ideas about the political divisions in Poland are

quite important. In intellectual circles in Warsaw and Kraków, the first
Solidarity government is identified as being of the left. Its most vocal
opponents remember that such major figures as Bronisław Geremek,
Jacek Kuroń, Jan Lityński, and Adam Michnik had communist pasts
or were children of communists. They were and are secular in orientation and suspicious of nationalism. But for Szywala, this past history is
not important. He is most concerned with present policy, particularly
its approach to productive enterprise. He does not want the government to continue to support large-scale socialist enterprises, but he
does think that the state must actively help nurture productive alternatives, by helping industries to retool, by retraining workers, and by
developing favorable tax policies and government supports so that
independent entrepreneurs may get returns on their investments. The
government's right-wing laissez-faire approach, to Szywala's way of
thinking, will simply lead to economic failures. A more active cooperation among state, industry, and agriculture, he believes, is the only
way to get results. In pursuit of such results, he is helping to found a
local Chamber of Commerce and Industry.

The laissez-faire liberals believe that the social-democratic positions
of people like Szywala and the Polish farmers will stall the transformation. The reforms, for them, have a clear end point, an unfettered capitalism, and the only means to that end is the end itself—removing
government hands from economics as quickly as possible. In the economic and political trenches, this transformation is much harder than
they anticipate, and it may not lead to the happiest of results. Rational
alternatives are being articulated. In Hungary and Czechoslovakia
more cautious transformations are being instituted, and in Poland
alternatives to the government programs are welcomed even by those
in the government. As Lityński put it in an interview with Western
journalists:

> I know we don't possess all the political wisdom, and that others
> can, if nothing else, give us something to think about. [Other]
> movements . . . influence our political views by the very fact that
> they exist. If there is another organization to compete with, you are
> more democratic, that is obvious.

One can expect, or at least hope for, a continuation of the step-by-
step anti-ideological approach pioneered by Solidarity and the demo-

cratic oppositions of Eastern and Central Europe in the 1970s and 1980s. This process will lead to different results in different places. Just as there are great differences among the economics of Great Britain, West Germany, Sweden, and Italy, there will be analogous differences in Eastern and Central Europe.

CHAPTER 15

History and Class Consciousness

My trip to Świdnica left me much to ponder. Many ordinary people, I thought, were either uncomprehending of the dimensions of the economic transformation, or else hysterical about them. My old friend Lityński, on the other hand, seemed a bit too sanguine. Further, I didn't think he realized that common ignorance and fear represented a profound problem both for economic reform and for democracy, a problem that had to be addressed politically. He seemed to think that the government's reform package would prevail because it was rational, a kind of enlightenment prejudice. It also appeared that he and the first Solidarity government were overlooking the emergence of a new class structure and class consciousness in democratizing Poland. They were simply ignoring the crystallization of distinct and competing interests in the society they were transforming.

Class conflict was becoming a normal part of societal life in Poland,

and those who had been taught to disdain the notion in a school of hard knocks were, understandably, not seeing a very important part of society's new experiences. At the root of the problem was the difficulty of "normalizing" the politics of antitotalitarian opposition. Viewed from the West, the unity of intellectuals and workers was one of the most admirable characteristics of Solidarity. Workers and highly educated and privileged intellectuals had been able to work in concert in a relatively nonhierarchical fashion. The intellectuals did not bring the truth of an opaque theory to the workers; they were only advisers. The workers maintained their democratic dignity, not through political or philosophical metaphysics, but as a result of the bravery and astuteness of their actions.

The relationships between intellectuals and workers came naturally. They were the outgrowth of a genuine mutuality of interests. The party-state was the universal employer and political power. Workers and intellectuals shared a common interest in opposing this universality. That they acted on this mutual interest with mutual respect was the good news of the Solidarity movement, and it suggested a new type of social movement to such observers as the French postindustrial theorist Alain Touraine. Tied not simply to a nineteenth-century sort of class interest, the movement addressed itself to broad social and moral concerns, political and civil liberties, decentralized social and individual autonomy, self-determination.

Yet after the communists left the political stage, conflicts suddenly emerged in the mass movement. With the demise of the universal exploiter, political and social divisions became manifest. The workers found that the democratic movement that they had created had in a real sense turned against them.

Imagine the changing situation of a typical worker, a composite whom I will call "Jan Kowalik." He is a steelworker in a large state industrial works in the town of Ursus, twenty kilometers outside of Warsaw. In December 1970, as an eighteen-year-old, he experienced his first strike against communist power. Party Chief Władysław Gomułka had just imposed a 60 percent increase in the price of food. Outraged, Jan, though he had no family to support, went on strike with his older fellow workers, who had suddenly seen Christmas celebrations become an impossibility. They and he had a fundamental distrust of the authorities; few among them took seriously the idea that "People's Poland" was actually a workers' state. But that the supposed "workers' vanguard" would act so flagrantly against real workers' immediate interests was insupportable.

Jan knew that some of his older friends had taken part in the "anti-Zionist and antiliberal" crackdowns in 1968. Although they were no communists, they had been willing to support the authorities against "alien cosmopolitan influences." But now these same authorities were turning against them, making even a minimally acceptable life impossible. It was one thing to know that drudgery and bare sustenance were one's fate in life, in the purported workers' state. But it was something else to face the fact that in the name of building a disbelieved socialist paradise, one's living standard was to be consistently undermined.

Jan's outrage followed the workers' strikes in the northern ports and the southern mines. A broad nationwide industrial working-class strike threatened the communist order. After some hesitation, Comrade Gomułka, the more "nationalist" socialist, once quite popular as the herald of "the Polish road to socialism," resigned his post as party chief, officially because of an illness of the eyes. What he did not see, as an austere ascetic communist, was that ordinary people were not willing to put up endlessly with poor working and living conditions in pursuit of an abstract ideal tied to a complicated ideology, neither of which they could understand.

After attacks on the Party headquarters in Gdańsk, ending with dozens if not hundreds of deaths, the Party finally noticed. The new party chief, Edward Gierek, promised ongoing consultations with the workers and improved living conditions. Jan was skeptical. But the price hikes were rescinded, and promises were made to build a "Second (more prosperous) Poland."

And at first Gierek seemed to work a miracle. A good life was promised and, in some significant ways, delivered. With the help of his factory union, in 1972 Jan and his wife Jolanta and their child, Romek, got a decent modern apartment and no longer had to live in one room in the three-room flat of his in-laws. His new apartment, in fact, was larger than theirs. Jan was able to buy a refrigerator, tape recorder, radio, and television, was able occasionally to eat peanuts and bananas, and go to a local movie theater where they showed relatively recent American and French films. By 1975, as part of the Gierek regime's push for "motorizing Poland," Jan and Jolanta were able to buy a small Polish Fiat and travel around the city and into the countryside. They fully shared in the apparent prosperity of the Gierek era. They knew they didn't live as well as their counterparts in Western Europe, but they did appreciate their newly acquired comforts.

They also feared, however, that their prosperous bubble might burst. Rumors were beginning to circulate about an impending economic catastrophe. For sober economists at universities and research institutes in Warsaw, Kraków, and Poznań, the economic crisis was expressed in cold facts. Poland had borrowed heavily in the West with the aim of updating technology, in order to produce more and better goods that, when sold, would allow the nation to pay back its debts. But it did not happen. The goods produced were not of sufficiently high quality to be marketed in the West. Too many foreign bank loans and grants were used to subsidize food prices or to flood the market with Western-made consumer goods, buying some political legitimacy for Gierek's regime. Also, too many members of the regime were opportunistically buying themselves villas and cars, purchasing a life-style they felt to be their due as the guardians of history's vanguard, or at least as society's managerial elite.

While to Jan this situation was only vaguely discernible, more serious rumors circulated as well. Food prices were going to be doubled, while consumer goods, affordable housing, cars, and the like, were becoming less available. Meanwhile the regime's propaganda continued to chug along, promising, in its leading slogan, "More and more, better and better" in the "Second Poland." When the inevitable happened, and the rumors became reality, Jan and his friends protested vehemently, expressing their pent-up anger. They did not understand the details of the economic problems, but they knew they had been lied to.

In June 1976, when food price increases were instituted, the workers in Jan's factory did not simply go out on strike. They ripped up the train tracks linking the Soviet Union to East Germany and the

West. Farther to the south, in the city of Radom, there was a riot, and the Party headquarters was burned to the ground. But despite these events and more, Gierek held power by making a strategic retreat. The day after the protests, Gierek's premier, Jaroszewicz, announced that after "consultation with the nation," the price increases were being rescinded.

Soon afterward, workers who had been prominently involved in the strikes and disruption of the transportation system, including some of Jan's friends, were brought up on charges. Their trial proved to be a turning point in the history of communism. In a certain sense, the trial marked the beginning of communism's fall—a process that was completed (at least for Eastern and Central Europe) in the fall of 1989. Because when Jan and his friends went to the courthouse to observe the events, they came into contact with a section of Polish society they had not known before. Secret-police officials, Party and official-trade-union apparatchiks were familiar parts of their lives. But their friends' lawyers were an alien species. These people were not just "going along with the system," trying to cut the best deal for their clients, as almost all professionals seemed to do. Like the workers, but in a different way, they were attacking the communist authorities and their actions *based on the laws and documentation of officialdom itself.*

Odder still were the known and previously unknown "antisocialist elements" (Lityński among them), who were not only observing the trial but distributing aid to the families of workers arrested for political offenses. They spoke to Jan and his friends about working conditions in their factory, and they documented abuses in the factories and at the trial in an illegal "Bulletin of Information." They were members of the now-famous Committee for Worker Defense (known by the Polish acronym KOR). Their cooperation with Jan and his friends was the beginning of the much admired "class alliance" in Solidarity.

While the distance between Jan Kowalik's town of Ursus and the center of Warsaw is less than twenty kilometers, the sociological distance is much greater. Like the other previously existing socialist societies, Poland has a highly crystallized hierarchical social order. The middle class in the interwar period was underdeveloped (in comparison to the Western European experience), and even then Jews and Germans, who for obvious reasons are no longer part of the Polish scene, played major intermediary roles. Strangely enough, the communist system reinforced the old polarized hierarchies. To be sure, while differences in wealth and salary were minimized, stratification of social status was maintained. The workplace became the site of distribution of fundamental goods and services. Typically, factories, universities, and police units had their own commissaries and cafeterias, and apartment complexes were "cooperatively owned" by official-union work units, as were vacation resorts and retreats.

These structures fitted a socialist ethic; work was valorized. But they also led to societal atomization. From cradle to grave, people tended to associate with their own kind. Apart from official propaganda and ideological institutions, Warsaw intellectuals and workers, like those all over the bloc, had very little to do with one another. The intellectuals in KOR were an even more segregated group. Political repression tended to leave many of them unemployed (and thus without workplace interconnections), and the illegal oppositional nature of their activity cut them off from most people, who ordinarily played by the official rules. From this point of view, KOR's activity showed Jan and his friends that their outburst of dissatisfaction with communist price policies had a direct connection with the sustained dissident activity of the KOR intellectuals. At the same time, the workers showed KOR members and other intellectuals that the communists could be challenged frontally.

The dissatisfaction of the intellectuals primarily had to do with political and cultural freedom. The first concern of workers like Jan, however, was economic need. The cooperation at the trials demonstrated to both strata that their primary concerns were intimately connected. The underground publishing of the "Bulletin of Information" was at first a very practical activity, but it became a vehicle for somewhat broader political expression; and when it wasn't repressed, other political and cultural reviews were published illegally. Even before the emergence of Solidarity in August 1980, unofficial publishing, "the secondary publishing network," rivaled the primary official network in political and cultural impact, and sometimes in publishing reach.

Along with the bulletin, some of the illegal publications were directed to and created by workers (at least in part). The link was thus clearly made between freedom of expression and the dissemination of information on one hand, and economic well-being on the other. Instead of the blatantly false slogan "More and more, better and better," the opposition press asserted the more profound "No bread without freedom." This understanding gave the strike of August 1980 its special character.

A distinct working-class interest did not seem to be as important as the broader-based interest in "normalizing" social life—in other words, freeing it from totalitarian controls. This was the wisdom that led Jan's factory colleague Zbigniew Bujak, leader in the eighties of the Solidarity underground, to promote cultural oppositional life instead of frontal political resistance during the long period of martial law. His reasoning, by then well understood by workers like Jan, dated back to the 1976 alliances and understandings. A free public zone, a "civil society as if," would allow for the pursuit of political and economic goals. Without it, the authorities would prevail. So in the eighties, Jan and Jolanta regularly attended lectures at their local church on current politics and economics, and although they became quite discouraged, and when things got very tough in 1986 and 1987 they stopped paying their union dues, they passed on their insights to their children and younger colleagues.

By the late eighties, Jan and Jolanta were privileged. Younger workers in plants and factories could only dream of achieving their material success. Waiting lists for apartments extended for ten, twenty, and even fifty years. Some families lived in separate worker hostels. Consumer goods were no longer available. Food had become a major struggle. The Jaruzelski regime's experiment in economic reforms without political reforms had ended in failure. Solidarity, then, became the main political force. But in significant ways, the new Solidarity did not include Jan and his friends.

Lech Wałęsa, for years the figure Jan Kowalik most admired, first negotiated the transfer of power from communism to democracy in the roundtable talks of 1989, then, in the same year, appointed the first Solidarity government, then became the Solidarity government's most substantial critic, and then won Poland's first completely free presidential election in 1990. After the election, Jan and his family and friends were bewildered, somewhat hopeful but also disillusioned. At a union fund-raiser for Solidarity in March 1990, I met a person who could have been one of Jan's friends, a Solidarity shop steward. Although we were not previously acquainted, the shop steward knew that I was a longtime observer of Polish affairs, and he was interested to hear what I thought about the present Polish situation.

I didn't know how to answer. During my visits to Poland, people had often asked me how I liked the country, and I had faced a similar dilemma. I could have referred to the ghosts of my ancestors, the bitter experiences of Polish-Jewish relations and Nazi Germany's final solution. Or I could have referred to the sovietized political order and its degradation of human and natural resources. But I could also have responded bearing in mind the persistent resistance to political repression. In the event the question was posed as more than a simple pleasantry, I explained my complex feelings and judgments. If not, I simply responded by mentioning my friendships with many Polish people whom I had come to know, admire, and (in some cases) love. The shop steward's question at the fund-raiser didn't have a simple answer either. I needed time to evaluate the situation.

Mostly, I realized, I wanted to find out what he thought. This was my first visit to postcommunist Poland. So even though I knew the political and economic going was tough, I first talked about the great political accomplishment and the justice of the situation. I said that it was great to see Poland right side up, with its real political leaders in a position to address pressing problems, instead of in jail or under the control of a police state. It was great to see ordinary Polish people free. It was also good to see decent meat, fruit, and vegetables readily available all over the country.

I had put a happy spin on my reactions. In contrast, the veteran Solidarity activist responded gloomily. "The boys are getting restless. They can't make ends meet. They can't feed their families. It's worse than before the change. Something has to be done and done quickly."

This exchange took place soon after my arrival. But during my two-week stay, I was to hear versions of the conversation again and again. People appreciated the signs of general economic health: the new stores, the plentiful goods. They were ready to believe in the fundamental goodwill of the government. But many sensed that they were being left out, and they didn't know what to do. Macroeconomic statistics pointed in both hopeful and disheartening directions. But lived economic experience was presenting a new class structural challenge.

Polish and foreign policymakers, expert advisers, and foreign observers debate the Polish performance. The Harvard economist Jeffrey Sachs, for example, has been a self-appointed close adviser to Polish economists and the first Solidarity government, and chief salesman for radical economic reforms. In 1989, like many foreign economists, Sachs advised and exchanged views with Polish colleagues concerning the problems and prospects of a "market transformation." But unlike most such views, Sachs's were well packaged and sold. *Gazeta Wyborcza* (at that time the Solidarity daily) promoted his ideas in a dozen articles. Sachs's nationally televised speech before the Polish parliament was highly persuasive. With American academic self-assurance, he urged his Polish audience to "seize the day." Fundamental action must be taken, he warned, or success would elude them. But by acting decisively, Western aid would be forthcoming.

Sachs's call for radical action was taken seriously by Leszek Balcerowicz, the newly appointed minister of finance. The minister knew he had two primary problems to address: inflation, which was running at 30 percent to 40 percent *monthly*, and the transformation of a dysfunctional and collapsing state-commanded economy into a market economy, which Polish economists and politicians believed could only be accomplished through privatization. Sachs's ideas more or less represented the conventional wisdom of the IMF, and Balcerowicz accepted it. But he and his governmental colleagues were challenged to apply this commonsense solution to uncommon circumstances: tough monetary reforms in the context of the dismantlement of a totalitarian economy, and the movement from an antieconomy to a normal one.

In an article in *Foreign Affairs*, written during the initial phase of the reform, Sachs summarized the Polish economic strategy. A ballooning budget deficit and easy-credit policies, according to this article, had to be ended as the basis for eliminating shortages and halting rampant inflation. Prices had to be decontrolled and subsidies eliminated in order to establish a supply-and-demand system of price determination. A regime of free trade with the West had to be established by creating a convertible currency at the outset of the program and by eliminating almost all restrictions on international trade, thus allowing Poland to "import" a realistic price structure. Restrictions on the private sector had to be done away with as soon as possible, and specific sectors targeted for rapid demonopolization. Privatization had to proceed as rapidly as possible, though he recognized that it would be a long process, involving many or most of the seventy-eight hundred industrial enterprises under state control.

The strategy yielded controversial results. One year after the reforms, Sachs and some other foreign observers accentuated the positive. The increase in unemployment, they pointed out, which was reported to be somewhere between six hundred thousand and one million, sounded a lot bigger than it was. In fact, it stood somewhere between 3.5 percent and 4 percent of the population—actually much lower than in the United States and much of the West. With the cost of living moving up to international levels, and wages and salaries tightly controlled, living standards were reported to have dropped by 40 percent; but according to Sachs, this was an exaggeration. The 1989 prices were often those of unavailable goods, and thus not real prices. And moreover, when these goods were available, consuming them often meant waiting in line for hours. With such waiting eliminated as a part of daily life, leisure time had increased exponentially. Third, one year after the fall, food consumption seemed to be down by 5 percent; but this drop was a small price to pay for systemic transformation.

Perhaps more ominous was the fact of a severe downturn in industrial production, officially measured at 28 percent. Sachs believed that this figure overstated the case. "The index covers only state production, completely ignoring the private sector, which is small but growing. Moreover, some of the production decline reflects a rise, not fall, of economic welfare." For instance, cutbacks in the workweek and the closing of inefficient or polluting plants could be understood as contributing to the commonweal. Sachs pointed out that the decline had to be understood as being as much a function of the economic collapse that preceded the economic reforms, and the loss of Soviet business, as a consequence of the reforms themselves. He argued forcefully "not to blame the cure for the disease." And indeed, from a macroeconomic point of view, his arguments were quite persuasive. There was a sense among enlightened policymakers in Poland and its neighbors that at least Poland was embarking on substantial economic changes during the course of the "transition."

Other countries were having much greater difficulty. Take the Soviet Union. Just as it reached the point of embarking on the genuine construction of a new market system, through the proposed "five hundred-day program," Gorbachev blinked, hesitated, and sought refuge in the support of the military-industrial complex and the police. The old economic order was half dismantled and falling apart when this opportunity for replacement came along. But then the leader of the former superpower tried to put it back together again. His fate is likely to be that of Humpty Dumpty.

Elsewhere in Eastern and Central Europe, economic reforms were being attempted more soberly, but the political will and legitimacy needed to embark on Polish-style radical reforms were difficult to maintain. Czechoslovakia's Havel spoke about a "soft landing." In Romania and Bulgaria, there was still talk about a "third way." In Hungary, conflict between political parties left the competing political elites without broad societal support for meaningful change. Throughout the region, there was a sense that domestic economic changes were necessary, but there was little practical understanding about how to achieve them. Among reformers, the hope seemed to be for Poland to succeed, because such a success would give them a chance to take the deep plunge as well.

It is not surprising, therefore, that Poland's efforts received broad acclaim in international circles, from the IMF to government leaders to the editorial pages of such newspapers as the *New York Times*. To be sure, some economists warned about the limits of the Polish approach, pointing out that huge problems still lay ahead. Privatizing some large industrial complexes and closing others required more than the aggressive monetary policies that characterized the reforms of the first year after the fall of 1989. Social welfare and social class had to be addressed. The problems would multiply as unemployment rose and whole regions went into sharp decline. Privatization might not be enough. Intelligent state action with a long-term and disciplined industrial policy along the lines of the economic approach of the Pacific rim (Japan, Korea, Taiwan, and Malaysia) might be required, or at least such an approach might be desirable. And the real problems and promise of "the Polish model" might be most evident and pressing not to experts, either foreign or native, but to ordinary people such as the Kowaliks.

Jolanta Kowalik, of course, was grateful that she did not spend three hours a day waiting in line for food and other necessities. But Jan was not sure whether his plant would remain open and whether, if he was laid off in the name of greater labor efficiency, he would find employment somewhere else. At forty, he felt obsolete. Their son, Romek, hoped to avoid such a condition by going to an engineering school, but he wasn't sure if the school would remain open, given cutbacks in state expenditures. And even if it did stay open, he realized that the faculty was not very well qualified to teach the state-of-the-art technologies on which his future depended.

All of the talk in the newspapers during the course of the presidential campaign seemed strange and beside the political point to the Kowalik family. Life had grown hard and uncertain, so naturally people wanted to "throw the bums out"—a good, healthy democratic response. Lech seemed to talk sense. Accelerate change, get rid of all communist remnants, and consider those who suffered so much both during the martial-law decade and the first postcommunist year. But Wałęsa's action in keeping in office the director of the economic change, Leszek Balcerowicz, was upsetting to the Kowaliks. Most people like them had voted for Wasłęsa, hoping for lighter personal burdens and improved personal situations. But many others had voted for Tymiński, a Canadian businessman who had promised them everything, although any person who thought, even for a second, had realized he would deliver nothing. Among the young and the most alienated and disoriented, Tymiński was a way to reject "them all." The Tymiński vote represented a continuation of the "them against us" mentality, which made sense during the communist era but no sense after the fall. It seemed like an early "escape from freedom"—unless class was considered. Because there was an irony in the fact that Lech Wałęsa, the leader of an industrial union, was being forced to administer a deindustrialization policy.

It is true that the carnivalesque economy had to be dismantled in Poland, and perhaps it was fitting that the work was being done by an industrial trade-unionist. But such poetry must be deconstructed. Note, first, the odd power base of Lech Wałęsa. He was really a leader of striking workers only once. To be sure, his tough and articulate leadership of the Gdańsk shipyard strike in August 1980 provided the fundamental grounds for all of his subsequent powers. But after that strike, his political power accumulated through his ability not to wage strikes but to end them. During the first Solidarity period of 1980–1981, when Wałęsa was not negotiating with the communist authorities, he was traveling around the country mediating between wildcat strikers and local Party authorities, trying to maintain order so as to avoid a repressive crackdown or even a Soviet invasion. Later in the decade, during the time of martial law, young workers, including "Romek Kowalik," were striking in attempts to better their economic and political positions against the counsel of their older, more experienced union colleagues, including Wałęsa. He negotiated an end to these strikes as a prelude to his negotiations with Jaruzelski's junta.

Significantly, from 1981 until the formation of the Solidarity government, Wałęsa's power derived from his ability to quell workers' unrest, not for defending or at least representing workers' interests. During the first Solidarity government, he did the same. Mazowiecki and Balcerowicz pursued a policy that most directly hurt Solidarity's main constituency—industrial workers. Wałęsa convinced them to endure the suffering, promising them only that things would have a chance to get better.

Mazowiecki and his associates did not do a good job of relating their understanding of the economic situation to the Polish population. Also, early on, a conflict developed between Wałęsa and the government. Strikes erupted, not to the point of economic breakdown, but sufficiently widespread to raise the question of whether the social order necessary for economic transformation could be maintained. Wałęsa became the candidate who promised justice to workers, so that they would support order and transformation. It succeeded neatly as an electoral strategy. But the fundamental contradictions in his political position, and in Solidarity as a labor movement, probably cannot be maintained.

The worker-intellectual coalition is now breaking down. The interests of industrial workers and the pursued goals of a democratic state cannot be identical. As the head of state, Wałęsa must pay attention to the directions of the IMF, the advice of international investors and lenders, and the expert opinions of Balcerowicz and other Polish economists. It is clearly in the interests of the society as a whole to develop sound economic institutions and practices. By contrast, the industrial workers, along with peasant farmers, must pay attention to their own immediate needs and look for public policies that will take those needs into account. Understandably, the government is establishing policies that will promote the rise of a new entrepreneurial class and attract foreign investment. Workers wisely support this policy in general. But their patience became short when it turned out that the new middle class was none other than the old *nomenklatura*. Mazowiecki's party claimed it was the party of the yet-to-emerge middle class. Wałęsa still spoke in the name of ordinary working people, but he too wanted to promote sound entrepreneurial interests.

The problem is that the group most capable of fulfilling such a role is the old privileged elite. In the words of David Ost, an American political scientist and longtime observer of the Polish opposition,

> The problem, in other words—and this is one more legacy from the old regime—is that the one group most likely to take advantage of the new possibilities that come with liberalization and marketization is the one group with the least legitimacy to do so. Throughout Eastern Europe, there are stories of managers and directors and old party officials using their connections and their capital to lease firms, set up new companies, and otherwise provide for themselves in the new economic environment.

Western observers, then, and informed Poles who know the ways of the parliamentary West, recognize a need for a grand political realignment. They speculate that perhaps there ought to be a normal left and right: a social democratic party that addresses equity issues (a decent treatment of those who most suffer from the transitions and supervision of those who most benefit, making sure that they are not the henchmen of old), and a conservative free-market party that addresses productivity issues (establishing state policies that promote capital growth and investment, and putting in place a legal system that holds responsible a handful of the former communists, so that the vast number of old opportunists can become the new capitalists). Such a political ordering makes both economic and political sense. Coherent and competing programs of reconstruction could be formulated. The interests of both the ambitious and the frightened could be articulated in political programs and policies. Two sources of antidemocratic action would be contained. The populist search for easy solutions of a Tymiński sort would be democratically represented if the party of the left addressed the confused and frightened. The ambitions of the new emerging economic elite would be encouraged if the party of the right promoted an ordered policy of privatization. A Pinochetesque dictator would be understood to be unnecessary.

Yet, understandably, political and economic confusion reigns. Like the Czechoslovak minister of the interior, Jan Langoš, the people of the region are reluctant to identify with anything that is leftist. Anticommunism is confused with antileftism. The openly leftist former communist parties are the only ones with political salience, still receiving significant support based on the maintenance of privileges (between 10 and 20 percent support throughout the region), but other leftists are far out on the margins. The self-identified right (or at least the pragmatic nonleft) is torn between anticommunism and laissez-faire economics. The Wałęsa problem arose from this situation: he had to present himself as offering a set of mutually exclusive policies. He would simultaneously get rid of the communists, he declared, and rapidly promote a market economy, taking care both that the disadvantaged were treated fairly and that the formerly advantaged were treated justly.

So as a political leader, Wałęsa had to make choices, and these choices will almost certainly crystallize class conflict. If priority is given to the generally accepted end of the transformation—the establishment of a free-market economy—working-class grievances will develop, because this class is overwhelmingly employed in inefficient and often useless enterprises. If a political party or parties fail to articulate the interests of these people, there is a great danger that political and social demagogues will ascend.

On the other hand, if Wałęsa's government is truer to its working-class roots, giving top priority to the immediate concerns of people like the ones I have called the Kowaliks, the modernizing elites within and outside the government and nation, with and without communist pasts, will be dissatisfied. And again, dissatisfaction may either be expressed democratically within political parties, or else against parties in the name of technical necessity.

In important ways, therefore, the legacies of both communism and anticommunism undermine the prospects for a democratic resolution of these political and economic dilemmas. Add in the confusion over national and religious issues, and it becomes clear that a somber pessimism is in order, not only with regard to Poland, but with regard to the whole region.

Nonetheless, despite the fact that democratic prospects for the transition seem dim from almost every point of view, considering it in terms of political issues, leadership, nation, religion, and economics, I can't help but be cautiously optimistic. I know that the people of Eastern, Central, and even Western Europe are much better off after the fall of communism than they were before. And many of them are aware of the immense problems they face, which leads me to think they may find solutions that are perhaps not optimal, but workable. European imagination and creativity, arts and letters, political theory and science, suggest hope for the future. It may be reasonable to judge that the postscript to totalitarianism (modern tyranny) is likely to be one sort of authoritarianism or other (traditional tyranny), but it is foolish to believe that this outcome is a historical necessity.

VI

CULTURE

CHAPTER 16

Against Despair

Viewed from a distance, the case against hope is overwhelming. If we look more closely, pessimism must be tempered. The sad facts are economic, political, and cultural. The positive rebuttal is marvelously individualistic and pluralistic, linked to the ideals of Europe and the constitution of civil society, but ultimately tied to individual human capacity and inventiveness.

Take Bulgaria. When I visited there in November 1990, the country was in the depths of its post-totalitarian crisis. The electricity was periodically turned off for hours at a time. A Soviet model nuclear power plant was down because of what was reported to be a minor mishap. Soviet oil deliveries were becoming irregular and, within two months, fuel supplies would be set at astronomically high international prices. For the first time since the war, food supplies were erratic. Political and social tensions were at a boiling point. During my three days in the country I saw two major political demonstrations and, more disturbingly, I saw a gypsy boy beaten up in a busy public square with no one intervening. When I expressed dismay to my host, I was told, "He was probably a pickpocket." I had the sense of a society falling apart. The old ways of doing things were no longer working, but no new ways had come into being.

At first it seemed that the Bulgarian population wanted to continue the old order. The renamed Communist Party—the Bulgarian Socialist Party—won with by far the largest percentage of the first free vote (48 percent), and in a second round won a parliamentary majority. Having the oldest Communist Party in Europe, one with genuine popular legitimacy in the postwar era, the electorate chose the safety of a purportedly reforming socialism over a clean break with the past. But then, as was happening elsewhere, free public discussion and information revealed the sorry state of Bulgarian affairs. The revelations of past abuses could be explained away in typical communist fashion. With Todor Zhivkov, the longtime Party leader, replaced by Peter T. Mladenov, all past problems were supposedly overcome. Yet less than one month after the parliamentary elections, Mladenov was forced to resign over charges that in December 1989 he had ordered the use of force against demonstrators. Promises were made regarding fundamental economic reforms. But although some fifty bills were introduced into parliament aimed at turning the command system into a market economy, people observed only the breakdown of the former, with few or no signs of the latter.

Knowing well the changes in Poland, and even in Hungary and Czechoslovakia, I had the sense in Sofia that I was still in a communist country (I had the same feeling in Leningrad and Bucharest). This feeling was especially acute at the university. I was in Bulgaria for a quick visit, the purpose of which was to make contact with Bulgarian social scientists and arrange to introduce them to colleagues in the West and other countries of Eastern and Central Europe. I had prepared a lecture on recent developments in the sociology of culture and their relations to political developments in the former Soviet bloc. I wanted to show how the emerging focus of critical American sociologists on the limits of liberalism and individualism, without dependence on warmed-over Marxist ideology, pointed in the same political direction as some of the antitotalitarian struggles in Eastern and

Central Europe: both Western scholarship and some Eastern politics pointed in the direction of a civil society. In the written paper, I maintained that one of the great achievements of democratic oppositions to the totalitarian powers, such as KOR and Solidarity in Poland and Charter 77 in Czechoslovakia, was that they actively constituted autonomous political, cultural, and social life through an aggregate of individual actions. The great cogency and appeal of these activities, I believe, was their immediate practicality, combined with their broad future and international implications.

We in the West paid special attention to such activities, and not only because of their immediate political significance and heroic qualities. We saw and admired the bravery and creativity vis-á-vis the *ancien régime*. But some of us realized something else, that contrary to the prevailing orthodoxies of laissez-faire liberalism and social-democratic statism, many significant social problems had to be addressed through the bonds of friendship, family, and community, in the sort of voluntary associations celebrated by Alexis de Tocqueville in *Democracy in America*.

There was a rebirth of civil society as an object of investigation in the West, and in fact it had been stimulated by the political practice of the East. A new reflective sociology, therefore, should raise critical questions and quiet those in both the East and the West who aggressively proposed new ideological "magical solutions" involving the market or the state. This is the very practical implication of the new reflective sociology of political culture being practiced by researchers like Alan Wolfe and Robert Bellah and his colleagues. Their work was reminding us of the centrality of studies of community and family structures and processes, and of the importance of social psychology, socialization, and education.

In broad outlines, I spoke with my Bulgarian colleagues about the convergence of intellectual currents in American scholarship and Eastern and Central European politics. But in very preliminary introductory remarks and exchanges, I realized that I couldn't present my position in any great detail. They were too poorly informed about developments in Western social science and Central European politics. Many of the people in the audience had held social-science positions for many years. They were professors, instructors, and researchers in the history of Marxism, or the discipline of scientific socialism. Until recently, for them, classical political theory and contemporary social science were either pre-science, transcended by the development of Marxism, or contemporary antiscience, that is, theories other than Marxism. Some were actually committed to this position. Disoriented, they were reluctantly rethinking their previous ideological stances. Others knew the absurdity of the previously prevailing ideologies, but it was my first impression that they were still remarkably ill-informed about much that went on beyond the official borders of the previously existing socialist bloc. Of course they had heard about Solidarity and Charter 77, knew about and in recent meetings had met some leading democratic figures, and even realized the importance of "civil society" in the democratic project; but their familiarity with the constitution of alternative democratic and oppositional politics was quite superficial. One of the most informed among them didn't know the identity of Milan Kundera, the world-renowned Czech emigré novelist and political commentator. When I mentioned the names of prominent American sociologists whose work formed the basis of my prepared paper, I observed either blank faces or the barest signs of recognition. I thus decided to explain more concretely my view of American social science, reviewing my past research projects on Eastern Europe and discussing how such inquiries could be theoretically linked to their practical circumstances.

I met significant bad faith during my visit. I knew that highly incompetent academics hoped to use me and my colleagues as a sort of Berlitz program to academic legitimacy. They had learned by rote a Marxist catechism, which was a key to their professional careers. Now they sought easy lessons in liberalism. We were proposing something much more ambitious. We wanted to help those who genuinely wanted to constitute independent social sciences. In my mind, my goal was clear: find real colleagues, regardless of academic standing, and get to know what they had been doing and what they thought they needed. But because of the country's tradition of centralization, I found myself talking not only to academics but to the communist-appointed minister of education, Ilia Konev.

I met the minister early on Sunday morning, November 4, 1990, in a shabby café in what used to be a luxury hotel. The minister, also a

respected authority on early Slavonic literature, arrived with an assistant who made all of the arrangements, including large glasses of
cognac for himself, me, the minister, and my two guides (a Bulgarian
political theorist, Rumyana Kolarova, and an American lawyer on
leave from Helsinki Watch in New York, Ted Zang, who was lecturing
on human rights). This was a meeting in the old-fashioned style.
Formal introductions were made. And then the minister went into a
long-winded explanation about the present situation of Bulgarian
higher education. He spoke about the different types of universities,
the laws that applied to their governance, and the need to engage in
systematic change. It was with regard to the proposed changes that he
wanted to talk to me. He had been told that I was visiting Bulgaria to
assist in the development of social sciences. Konev obviously thought
that he was the man I should talk to.

He worked with a conventional model of centralized education
and research. As a professor with sound scholarly achievements, he
strongly supported the depoliticization of the university. Yet he still
believed that the universities' autonomy should be limited by the ministry. Universities, he maintained, should have the freedom to make
pedagogic judgments; their academic councils should discuss and propose curriculum innovations; but the minister insisted that it was the
ministry's responsibility to confirm curriculum changes in order to
assure the legitimacy of academic degrees. He was clearly defending
his turf. Though favorably disposed to Western aid for Bulgarian education, he was committed to the idea that it could only be truly helpful if it passed through his institution.

The minister's assistant stepped in. He explained that they had
resources to make the most of scholarly exchange. They could provide
free housing and transportation to academic visitors and distribute
donated books and journals in an equitable manner. They had long-
standing experience in such arrangements. With that, we reached a
point of embarrassment. Without stating it explicitly, everyone at the
table except the assistant, who was a holdover from the previous
regime, realized it was exactly the long-standing experience that had
to be avoided.

The minister, an intelligent man, shifted gears. He was interested
to know how curriculum judgments were made in the United States

without central control. To my astonishment, he knew nothing about normal American academic practices. When I talked to him about professors deciding course readings, the credit system, university majors and minors, the debates over the core curriculum and "the canon," he looked at me as if I were from another planet.

Zang joined the discussion, and together he and I explained how peer reviews worked, along with state, regional, and professional certification processes. The minister furiously took notes. I explained that the variety of course offerings and approaches to higher education was readily discernible in college and university catalogs. Zang explained the statutory framework of accreditation. We were far from proselytizing, and he was far from converted. Most striking was the fact that the chief administrator of Bulgarian higher education seemed to be completely ignorant of educational systems that did not follow the centralized model. This, no doubt, was both a communist and a precommunist legacy, but it was parochial nonetheless.

We ended our meeting with a practical discussion of possible exchange arrangements. The minister spoke about housing and transportation resources, emphasizing that academic exchanges should not be confined to any one university. I had been prepared for this subject by an earlier discussion with Rumyana Kolarova, and asked whether the central library of the Bulgarian Socialist Party (previously the Communist Party) would be open to non-Party academics. I had been told, I said, it was the most complete collection of previously restricted books, and it would be foolish to spend a great deal of money for journals and books that were already in the country. The minister denied that such bibliographic riches existed under lock and key. On that note of bad faith, our meeting wound down.

The meeting with the minister, along with my general meeting with the Bulgarian social scientists, suggested to me that the problems in Bulgarian cultural life were very much like the problems of the economy, and were even interconnected with them. The overcentralized command educational system was not only unproductive, it was counterproductive. It propagated ideology, conflated ideology with science, and controlled rather than facilitated the exchange of information. This approach, in fact, was a major source of economic crisis in the Soviet bloc. Although the economic breakdown of the Soviet Union and its fraternal allies was not as sudden as it sometimes seemed, something very basic was manifested that has to do with information, secrecy, and publicity—the exact realm the Bulgarian minister was refusing to confront. A lack of information in the West about the state of the Soviet economy had led to an overly rosy estimate of its condition. The same lack of information in the East was a key to its economic weakness.

We live in a postindustrial economic order. Primary bases of wealth in this order are information and data processing. Before the Industrial Revolution, agricultural and natural wealth, along with trading capacity, were at the center of economic activity. With the Industrial Revolution, the key to economic strength was the capacity to mass-produce steel, industrial machines, railroads, modern armaments, and consumer goods. More recently, the ability to coordinate the complexity of political, economic, and technological exchanges is of crucial economic importance. Some suggest, in fact, that we live in an information society, with class structure, power, and privilege determined by knowledge. Once, the vast majority of the population dedicated their lives to hunting, gathering, and producing food. Then industrial production became a primary occupation. Now the so-called service sector and its hierarchy define social order and change. The computer has apparently replaced the industrial machine and factory as the primary engine of gross national products.

Such imagery has to be handled with care. Agriculture and industry are still important for a healthy economy. The willful destruction of either in favor of the glamors of high technology would be a mistaken economic policy. Nonetheless, while the computer has not replaced industry and agriculture, and the intelligent use of information has always been a major economic factor, there are now economic facts of life with which Soviet-type economies are incapable of dealing. Open and rapid information exchange is vital to contemporary economic life, while secrecy has been at the very center of the Soviet-type political economy. This is a major political, economic, and cultural contradiction of so-called "actually existing socialism." No minor reforms can overcome it. While there are idealistic reasons to favor the free exchange of ideas and goods and fight for the human dignity that a democratic system brings to ordinary people, the most recent political and economic events suggest that there are practical reasons as well. Economic and cultural liberalism and democracy foster national wealth. Repressive political, economic, and cultural policies yield inefficiency and backwardness.

In the long run, the absence of free information exchange fatally weakened the communist political and economic elites. The necessary sophisticated, detailed political and economic coordination became impossible. Grand industrial projects were imagined and implemented, from the making of new cities to *Sputnik* and weapons of immense destructive capability, but coordinating the anticipated and unanticipated implications of such primary production was a failure. The economic and ecological landscapes of the Soviet bloc were littered with the ruins of half-realized economic activities. Goods were produced that no one needed, because there was no way to know what the needs were. This kind of information is articulated by an open market and an open political system. The Soviet-type economy, like all economies, requires both, or their functional equivalents, but to introduce both means doing away with the distribution system of "actually existing socialism." This problem is most evident in the natural development of Mikhail Gorbachev's economic policies.

Gorbachev started as a trusted communist, a product of the Brezhnev system of bureaucratic socialism, chosen as Party leader by a conservative Party elite. As soon as he was appointed, it was clear that he wanted to invest his youth and vigor in the obviously stagnating system. His first move involved a neo-Stalinist strategy: an anticorruption, anti-alcoholism campaign. More discipline, with less graft and vodka, he seemed to assume, would solve the economic malaise. When the desired effects did not result, he started to act more fundamentally. He wanted to make the radical connection between freedom and economic performance, though very much within restricted boundaries. He wanted to add innovative thinking and the support of the intellectual class to a more disciplined work force in revitalizing socialism. Give the intellectuals freedom of speech and start telling Soviet history more honestly, or at least permit its honest telling, and the intellectuals would move from cynicism to active support of the Party. Old Bolsheviks were rehabilitated and the enormity of Stalin's crimes was revealed, as were the official corruption of the Brezhnev era and persistent social problems. The literature, history, and art of the dissident and innovative were made available and even celebrated. For all this activity, Gorbachev gained personal popularity both at home and abroad; at least at first.

But there were major problems. The economy continued to stagnate and, with *glasnost*, the population became acutely aware of it. At first Gorbachev sought intelligent socialist planning, but when this proved impossible, he took the next step: instituting what he and his advisers called a controlled market. The owning of private property he initially viewed with suspicion, but soon he promoted it. The initial steps he took were for socialism and against capitalism. He and his associates then came to support innovations against backwardness, and anything that would bring positive change. They no longer made great efforts to promote their policies as socialist. Yet the major problems with his reforms were still strikingly evident, and not easily remedied.

The policies of *glasnost* and *perestroika* tore apart the bureaucratic system of state patronage and its ineffectiveness, but did not replace it with a workable system. The half-measures required by politics, which did brilliantly disarm political opponents on the left and right, and in the Russian center and non-Russian peripheries, made little economic sense. At first Soviet citizens greeted the turmoil with excitement and, for the most part, with support. Knowing the distortion of their pseudo-political economy as a matter of their daily lives, a reordering of the system suggested to them changes for the better. But when they continued to go from bad to worse, blaming the situation on the legacies of the Brezhnev stagnation and the Stalinist tyranny began to wear thin. People saw the system breaking down around them, and they also saw real changes occurring in Eastern and Central Europe. The choices ahead became clear and polar: either the complete political and economic reversal of the democratizing Europe, or a new forceful tyranny. Either choice could be made, with or without Gorbachev.

Political, cultural, and economic freedom cannot be used simply to buy greater political support, as Gorbachev tried to do. In order to have its effect, it must be applied to actual political and economic practice. But this is not easily accomplished. Freedom is not a com-

modity one chooses and then uses. It must be constructed. The actual
constitution of freedom is a greater challenge than the choice to seek
it. This is the present experience of Eastern and Central Europe and
the Soviet Union. It is a challenge both for the economic, political,
and cultural elites, and for ordinary people.

This point connects most dramatically to the theme of the paper I had
planned to deliver to my Bulgarian colleagues, along with a number
of their individual responses. Viewed from a distance, the situation in
Bulgaria does seem hopeless, a small replication of the situation in the
Soviet Union. Up close, even during my short visit, I saw a breakdown of order in the streets and cultural breakdown in the universities
and scientific institutions and the Ministry of Education; but when I
stayed around a little longer, metaphorically speaking, there was real
evidence of hope. After I had finished my presentation to the
Bulgarian social scientists, a number of people came up to me to
introduce themselves and ask questions. One man, whose name I
have forgotten, was well informed about sociology and Eastern
European politics. While we were conversing, two other people joined
us. One, a researcher on authoritarian and democratic child-rearing
practices, was particularly challenging. I learned that they had studied
social sciences at Warsaw University, as an alternative to Bulgarian
Marxist-Leninism and scientific socialism. Sustained study in the West
was prohibited in hard-line Bulgaria to all but the most politically
trustworthy, so a practical if not ideal solution was to study in a more
liberal socialist country, where some of Bulgaria's young and ambitious students could benefit from the expanding cultural autonomy.
      During my stay in Bulgaria, my closest colleague was Rumyana
Kolarova. A woman in her early thirties, she has an approach to ideological repression that is individual and intense. We began our collaboration when I was still in New York, with the help of Ted Zang of
Helsinki Watch. In New York, despite the unreliability of Bulgarian
international communications, I found her to be an earnest and
dependable associate. But after a few hours with her in Sofia, I truly
realized her accomplishments. She is a well-informed political theorist.
In her recently completed dissertation, she critically examines Anglo-
Saxon liberal political theory, drawing on such contemporary figures

as John Rawls, Robert Nozick, and Michael Walzer (a theorist whose work we both especially appreciated). Our conversation about shared interests had a normality that I did not immediately apprehend. It could just as well have taken place in Berkeley, New York, or Cambridge. It would not have been terribly unusual in Budapest or Warsaw. But in Sofia, it was noteworthy.

Particularly after I had met her colleagues, a pressing question was: How did Rumyana do it? How did she penetrate the barriers of ignorance that seemed to surround Bulgarian academic life? I decided that the answer had to do with a combination of individual drive and fortuitous circumstance. Her drive I cannot explain, of course, not knowing her well. The fortuitous circumstance was a five-month stay in England a few years ago. She was based in London but went to a number of universities, knocked on the doors of prominent political theorists and historians, explained that she was an ill-informed student from Bulgaria, collected bibliographies, bought, borrowed, and read books, went back to talk to her teachers, and by November 1990, when we met, had become very much their colleague. And now she herself is doing the same for young and ambitious students (and professors) in Sofia. She has an impressive collection of social-science books and journals in her office, which she actively circulates among her colleagues.

I observed her dissemination activities with a number of books, including my own *Beyond Glasnost: The Post-Totalitarian Mind*. After my talk, we went to her office, and she proudly showed me her "lending library." She bumped into a senior colleague, a professor of the history of Marxism. They talked about my visit and my work. She lent him my book, and I felt uncomfortable, wondering about his reaction to my writing, which treated his subject matter as a huge and horrific mistake. Would he, as an opportunist, learn a new "sacred language" and pursue his career? Or would he, as a last-ditch defender of the old order, dismiss my work as just another piece of anticommunist drivel?

When I expressed these thoughts to Rumyana, she displayed a respect for her colleague that exposed the limits of my political imagination. "He's a real scholar," she said, "a committed Marxist. He will read your book and seriously think about your ideas. He's probably too old and set in his ways to change his mind. But I respect him for that. Others who change more quickly are more distasteful."

I was being forewarned about the strange Bulgarian political landscape, strange for me both as an American and as an expert in the
more northerly parts of Eastern and Central Europe. Genuine, believing Marxists actually exist, and the communist rule was viewed by the
general population as a legitimate regime. Those who are now confused, or who are trying to remain steadfast, in a way have more
integrity than those who are not. For a principled liberal such as
Kolarova, easy liberal talk from the mouths of those who had recently
questioned her political reliability on very illiberal grounds is a source
of deep consternation. The problems are cynicism and opportunism,
rather than communism and Marxism.

Kolarova wanted to see a free university, and a free polity for that
matter, emerge from free, principled discussion. That somehow she
managed to educate herself and is now engaged in the reconstitution
of higher education along with her Polish-speaking colleagues and
others, suggests that even in the most unlikely places, resources for
democratic constitution can be found. Such people were educated
despite overwhelming odds. Now they must use the same determination and sophistication to constitute independent social and cultural
institutions. Kolarova seemed to understand naturally that this work
begins with respect for the genuine diversity of independent opinion.
Such opinion is not widespread in places like Bulgaria, where
autonomous cultural life was least developed and most repressed, but
even there (and more so elsewhere, in the more liberal zones of the
old bloc), it supports the development of an independent public life
and a civil society.

CHAPTER 17

The Institutionalization of Cultural Imagination

I believe it is a mistake to write off hope for a democratic alternative to totalitarianism of the left and the right. Antitotalitarianism has been a long-time component of cultural life in East-Central Europe, clearly in Poland and Hungary, but also elsewhere in the region. And such activity has been produced and reproduced within the very structures it opposed. In film, music, theater and literature, in the social sciences and the humanities, in the universities and in unofficial seminars, alternative understandings of art and science, politics and religion, society and history and their relationships, were formulated and made public. While a totalitarian culture organized public life, an antitotalitarian culture emerged and developed against totalitarian domination. Embedded within existing totalitarian arrangements were the cultural seeds of their own destruction.

The central point is this: While much of the pre-Sovietized political culture in East Europe, and all of the totalitarian culture, may have

227

misinformed and enervated, nevertheless, democratic cultural alternatives have been developing there over a long period of time, supporting the heroic activity of individuals like Kolarova in the worst of places, as well as broad social movements like Polish Solidarity. The cultural alternatives were, and continue to be, significant available resources for democratic transformation. The contributions of the autonomous arts and sciences to political culture, in the face of the very difficult obstacles of totalitarian controls, may have given Eastern and Central European people a means for democratic enrichment. At the time of oppression, this was accomplished particularly by supporting the development of an embedded autonomous social and political life. An independent civil society emerged from within the very structures of totalitarian domination.

For its own purposes, Soviet totalitarianism allowed, and even encouraged, the national development of the arts and sciences, drawing on past national accomplishments. The new revolutionary Soviet order claimed the best of the national literature, from Tolstoy to Dostoevsky and even to Pasternak. In the late 1950s in Poland, the reclaiming of the nineteenth-century Polish romantic poets Mickiewicz, Krasiński, and Norwid, along with the symbolist dramatist Wyśpiański and the avant-gardists Witkiewicz and Gombrowicz, marked the post-Stalinist regime as nationally aware, tolerant of the different and challenging, and progressive. The regime wanted to identify its own qualities with the best of the national inheritance and the claim that it fulfilled the nation's past promise. In so doing, it made available to the public a rich culture of critique that went well beyond any purpose the regime may have intended. Brecht may have returned to the German Democratic Republic and expressed allegiance to the communist overlords, but his theater produced works with a critical sensibility that easily led to unorthodoxy and even "antisocialist" ideas.

In *The Captive Mind*, a classic study of the totalitarian temptation in Central Europe, Czesław Miłosz showed how all sorts of people, from the religious to the deeply skeptical, from the cynical to the highly principled, from leftists to rightists, committed themselves to communism once it was in power and then were used by the new regime in the consolidation of its power. This situation proved to have volatile consequences for the new tyrants. Cultural literacy among the totalitarian subjects included significant resources for the development of alternative sensibilities to the officially prescribed ones. Not only did the broad availability of Marxism open the regime to Marxist critique, the incorporation of the national inheritance as a support for communist hegemony assured that the critique would eventually move beyond Marxism and the syntax of official propaganda. Marxist along with non- and anti-Marxist critiques were supported by the very social institutions created by the totalitarians to produce and perpetuate their political culture. Significantly, a crucial challenge in the new democracies is to contrive to support the development of cultural resources while dismantling the cultural institutions of the old regime.

In the old regime, the political administration of cultural life led to the intended result: the propagation of a culture that supported the communist order. But it also led to a crucial unintended consequence: the support of a critical culture. Now that the old order is being dismantled, the application of market principles to cultural affairs may also lead to both intended and unintended results. The pernicious aspects of official cultural life, such as the work supported by the Soviet Writers Union, will be eliminated. But the supports for a critical culture may also be undermined.

There was a fundamental contradiction in the political administration of cultural life in totalitarian orders. The creation of an official culture was predicated on the idea of an official truth, which was supposed to organize all aspects of social and cultural life. Marxism and the "Party spirit" were culturally imperialistic. They denied all truth claims based on other theoretical systems and practical activities. There was a self-conscious attempt to simplify the complexity of modern societies. Modern existence depends on different sorts of people, doing different sorts of things, following a variety of principles, viewpoints, and expertise. The communists wanted the expertise and the resulting technological and economic development, without the different principles and viewpoints. They wanted the arts and sciences to develop and reflect the grandeur of the new order without, at least at first, permitting the independence of the artist and the scientist to develop their crafts and disciplines according to their inherent logic. They wanted the unitary ideas of ideology and propaganda to inspire work in politics

and in education, in science and in agriculture, in the arts and in industry. But they also wanted education, science, agriculture, the arts, and
industry to function. This unrealistic goal led to conflicts that were
everyday articulations of major societal contradictions.

Because the cultural commissars wanted culture to flourish, they
supported, rather lavishly, the arts and sciences. Because they wanted
the arts and sciences to follow an ideologized script, the support was
contingent on passing ideological muster and accepting official censorship. In extreme circumstances the ideological reins were held
tightly, and the support was distributed narrowly. Only nine plays
were performed during the Cultural Revolution in China, when
Madame Mao ruled the theatrical day. The same was true in the sciences. Genetics, according to the crackpot "Marxist-Leninist" theory
of T. D. Lysenko, was a bourgeois science, forbidden in the Soviet
Union of Stalin and Khrushchev as well as in Mao's China. Yet these
extreme examples were in many ways the exceptions rather than the
rule, particularly in Eastern and Central Europe. More common was a
volatile compromise, with an underlying tension between the principles of cultural practice and ideological mandate. The authorities'
framework was set by official ideology, but within this framework they
attempted to act in a reasonable fashion.

Industry may have been nationalized and agriculture collectivized,
but the functional needs of the enterprises as understood by experts
and managers, not only by ideologues, were given attention.
Although the attention was far from sufficient, it is important to recognize that ideological fantasies were limited by practical imperatives.
Engineers, mechanics, farmers, and teachers did have a say about what
was necessary to get their jobs done. If they did not, no work was
accomplished. This tempering of ideology had central political implications in the case of the arts and sciences.

During the Stalinist period painters may have been compelled to
produce socialist-realist works—positive heroic images of workers and
peasants happily building the happy future—but even then, art classes
and discussions among artists still had to pay most of their attention
to color and form, and more attention to the history of artistic work
than to the history of class struggles. If these cultural elements were
ignored or minimized, only ideology would remain without art. To

be sure, such was at times the outcome. Ideological practice seriously compromised Russian painting, literature, and theater for decades. But the artists persistently resisted it, and the resistance sometimes prevailed. From the individual heroics of people like Kazimir Malevich, Boris Pasternak, and Vladimir Vysotsky to the more sustained, organized, and officially accepted accomplishments of Russian poetry, Hungarian film, Czech jazz, and Polish theater of the 1960s and 1970s, these artists and their works were often censored, sometimes even harassed; but at other times they were supported with political justification.

From the official point of view, independent, innovative, and even critical art was at a certain point understood to be a political asset, as long as it passed through official channels. Within the traditional pattern of patronage, the hope was that the glories of the supported art would be viewed as a reflection on its patron, the party-state. The quality of Polish, Czech, and Hungarian film, when the regimes were liberal, indicated not only that the cultural revisionists were an advance over the Stalinists, it also suggested that socialism might be preferable to Western consumerism and mass culture. It was possible to explore artistic traditions and problems under existing socialism, which the demands of the market in the West would not permit.

A comparative pattern was apparently set: in the West, the individual artist was free to pursue an artistic or intellectual project, but reaching an audience through the market was the problem. Commercial considerations about marketing a cultural product could lead artists to produce works that satisfied consumer demand more than the imperative of artistic practice. In contrast, in the political East, the individual artist had to worry about the political correctness of artistic work. Even the proverbial "works for the drawer," which were not meant for public distribution, could lead to political troubles during harsh times. Yet, reaching the audience through the administered distribution of works was no problem, once the political criteria were met or circumvented.

The politics of cultural practice in the West is about using the market for artistic purposes, avoiding mass-market demands by creating specialized markets or nonmarket supports through state, foundation, corporate, or individual patronage. The politics of culture in the East was about using or avoiding the party-state for artistic purposes. If cultural work closely followed the demands of the party-state, it was heavily subsidized—artists were lavishly supported in their union, institutes, and workshops, and access to the art, for example through cheap ticket prices and low book prices, was heavily supported. Under these circumstances, a great deal of tendentious mediocrity was produced and distributed, but works of significant value as well were created and made public. Gaming with the censor became part of the cultural world. As Western artists are forced to work or subvert the market, the artists of the socialist bloc worked or subverted the administered art world. They pretended to do what they never intended, to build a socialist culture. They found zones in which censorship was lax, for example in student cultural institutions, and they used elliptical language and other techniques of formal disguise. In this way, as in the case of artists in the West who must play with and against the market to get on with their work, the artists in the socialist world got on with their work by playing with and against the party-state.

A great deal was accomplished. Although many individuals suffered, and some artistic forms such as Russian theater were extinguished, significant cultural traditions stayed alive and developed. Polish theater, for example, was one of the most politically and culturally challenging in the world. The literary works of the region, epitomized by the writing of Milan Kundera and the political essays and dramas of now-President Václav Havel of Czechoslovakia, were not only reflections on the abnormalities, ironies, and complexities of totalitarian existence, they spoke directly to the human condition in the late twentieth century. It is important to remember that the accomplishments began from within the system, and then turned against it. They started from within a zone of socialist tolerance, and then struggled toward a principled pluralistic tolerance that would no longer be qualified with the adjective "socialist."

A crucial aspect of the transformation of Eastern and Central Europe was the establishment of an independent cultural sphere when writers, scholars, and artists decided to turn off the internal censors, to stop working with the constraints of the party-state in mind, and to work instead as if they lived in a free society. This change led to the constitution of alternative cultural worlds, from the simple harassed

networks of *samizdat* in the Soviet Union to the full-fledged oppositional cultural systems of Hungary, Czechoslovakia, and (in their most
developed form) Poland. The elliptical metaphors of struggle to
maintain cultural identities under official constraints gave way to
antimetaphoric bluntness. The gentle, positive criticism of Marxist-
humanism was abandoned. The stark imagery of truth-telling, from
Solzhenitsyn's reports from the gulag to Havel's political and dramatic phenomenology, became the order of the day; and this order
changed politics and culture, moving them in the direction of democracy both as a social form and as a cultural one.

When the decision was made to stop playing with the party-state,
there were two sociological transformations. The cultural system
moved away from administration and toward self-organization, and
the primary political dialogue was conducted between citizens rather
than between the authorities and their subjects. From the Western
viewpoint, it is hard to imagine how significant these changes were,
because their goal is taken for granted as part of our social reality, a
"normal" civil society. Especially in the United States, where just
about all social intercourse, no matter how vile and objectionable,
proceeds apart from the state, the idea that people writing essays and
distributing them on their own is a revolutionary act may be hard to
understand.

Even harder to understand is that the political significance of the
work probably had more to do with the way it was distributed than
with what it expressed. The fundamental contours and conditions of
social, political, and cultural life were set and enforced by the party-
state. When those involved in independent culture refused the setup,
when people stopped acting as subjects of a system and started acting
as active agents (citizens) constituting a part of their social world, the
political order was fundamentally challenged. The importance of the
authorities receded; people learned that they could speak to each
other independently of authoritative commands, and that they were
responsible for what they said. The seed of a democratic practice of
self-determination was planted, and it bore significant fruit. Alongside
the official cultural network, an independent cultural market was
established. The demand for the challenging, innovative, and independent was great, so the work was self-sustaining.

In Poland, such an arrangement existed under a variety of conditions: in the 1970s, before Solidarity; during the 1980–1981 Solidarity period; and during martial law. Indeed, a major decision was even made by the Solidarity underground leadership not to establish an underground political authority, but to direct most of its energies to the support of independent cultural and social activities. The strategy was that of constituting an alternative society.

Under much more difficult political conditions, and with narrower social supports, the same activities were created during the twenty-one years between the Prague Spring and the Velvet Revolution in Czechoslovakia. In the cities of the Czech lands and in Slovakia, independent seminars functioned in defiance of the communists. Philosophy, history, linguistics, and theater were subjects, not necessarily politics. But the alternative culture had broad political importance. In fact, in Slovakia, unlike Bohemia, the leadership of the Velvet Revolution was not primarily political and human-rights activists, but those most active in the alternative society of independent culture.

Such activity existed elsewhere as well. In the Soviet Union, it was long the case that weekly gatherings of friends and colleagues who worked in the disciplines of the sciences and humanities allowed for a freer discussion of scholarly issues than happened in official gatherings. Were they parties or seminars? The answer is in the eye of the beholder.

Much more formal independent activity existed in Hungary. Especially in Budapest, in the late seventies and throughout the eighties there functioned an independent cultural system. Because it was not linked with a mass social movement, it did not penetrate the society as deeply as Poland's oppositional culture, but it was an extensive exercise in the civil constitution of social and cultural institutions.

The accomplishments and themes of the independent culture were rich, and they are difficult to characterize simply. Simultaneous with mild, practical analyses of pressing policy questions, particularly concerning the economic crisis, were wild calls for national independence and impassioned accusations of all who would settle for anything short of complete national sovereignty. There were careful exercises in philosophical reflection, detailed histories of the most recent communist past, and avant-garde poetry, literature, and even video art. The left and the right were represented, but most significantly at the time, a special sort of center was constituted. It had little to do with the distinction between left and right. It was, rather, an antitotalitarian consensus. It was anti-ideological, but politically principled. It involved a commitment to pluralism rather than to absolute truth in politics, and it was against the clichés of official rhetoric, preferring the vernacular of daily life. This center self-consciously rejected totalitarian culture, and all those who made the rejection agreed that their shared action was more important than any differences.

Thus, former communists and longtime anticommunists worked together in Charter 77. Secular and Catholic intellectuals contributed to the ethos of Solidarity, and Russian nationalists and westernizers worked together in the dissident human-rights circles of the Soviet Union. As we have observed, after the fall the differences among these and other groups took on increasing importance. But the contribution of the past consensus, where it existed and where it endured, should not be minimized. It culturally supported and was supported by the self-constituted (in other words, democratically formed) zones of autonomy within totalitarian controls, and now it is an important cultural base upon which to create sustained post-totalitarian democracies.

Such a post-totalitarian culture faces two fundamental problems: with the fall of the communists a common enemy has been lost; and the transformation of the political-economic system, from the coordination of a party-state apparatus to the coordination of the market, presents new challenges for cultural life. The first problem is much commented upon. There was a common enemy among people with differences. Now that the common enemy is gone, the differences are of primary importance. This state of affairs is to be expected, though it may not feel very good; the warm feelings of solidarity are naturally preferred to often petty contention. Civility is the challenge for post-totalitarian culture at this time. The conservative and the liberal, the nationalist and the cosmopolitan, the religious and the secular, and the left and the right must face each other with the mutual respect and deference that they displayed when they had a common enemy.

This cultural challenge is particularly severe because the institutions of culture, from the universities to the book publishers to the theaters, are in a particularly beleaguered condition. The goal of the most independent-minded was to free cultural life from party-state interference. Now that the interference has come to a complete end, there is little financial support for cultural life.

Can the new regimes afford the Academies of Sciences, which were very expensive to maintain, produced very little work of immediate practical importance, and did not even educate as in the case of universities? Only 20 percent of the expenses of theater were covered by ticket prices. Will the new democratic states continue subsidies when ordinary people in the countryside and cities are having problems with the most basic necessities? Suddenly there is little or no money to support the film industry, which had produced works of sustained artistic import and political challenge in the most democratic of art forms. There is a real chance that the autonomy carved out in the cultural world, which led to a democratic politics and a normal marketization of economic life, may now lead to its own self-destruction.

In terms of a comparative framework, the artists and scholars of the old political East are westernizing. They must learn to play the market as well as they played the party-state apparatus. But there is a special problem. In the Western democracies, the market is strong, and alternatives to the market have developed, or have always existed: state and foundation support, private and corporate patronage. In the democratizing East, neither of these conditions exists, though they are being fought for. Advocates for the universities and higher education, the arts and humanities, book publishing and film are arguing for public policies that will promote the depoliticization of culture while keeping a continued viable financial base of support for it: special tax policies and exemptions, legal statutes that promote philanthropy and recognize the importance of a vibrant culture for the social and political transformation.

There are important differences of opinion on these issues, as there are in the United States; but generally, both those who promote special state supports for the arts and sciences and those who argue that such special supports, while justified like many others, would compromise the process of marketization, make their arguments with a respect for those who hold contrary opinions. Different kinds of compromises can be expected throughout the region.

● ● ●

There are no signposts, ideological or otherwise, to guide such institutional compromise. Just as with the path to the depoliticization of economic institutions, like large, polluting steel plants, the path to the depoliticization of culture is unprecedented. The problem is of special societal importance because cultural institutions must play a central role in the democratic transformations of Eastern and Central Europe. Not only must a great variety of educational institutions provide the needed skills and knowledge for constructing a social and economic system and constituting a democratic polity, an independent and civilized cultural life must also present and represent the civil ideal of Europe—a tolerant Europe, as a significant alternative to fundamentalism and xenophobia.

How does one learn to act democratically? Be economically efficient and effective? To a certain extent, of course, one must learn in a school of hard knocks. Enterprises must form, fail, or flourish. Democratic institutions and laws must be constituted, and if they don't work, they must be reformed. And the nation-states of Eastern and Central Europe must take part in continental affairs and try to hold their own. It's a matter of trial and error. But schools, books, theaters, art, and scholarship can help, and they must be made available to a broad public. Reach the Kowaliks of Warsaw, the physics graduate student of Bratislava, the confused citizens of the town of Świdnica, and the ethnic Romanians and Hungarians attacking each other. Consider the Poles who voted for Tymiński. These people obviously need a free, flourishing press, greatly improved schools, and books that make modern politics and economic and social problems understandable and that consolidate the accomplishments of the independent critical culture of the region. The privatization of cultural institutions alone cannot possibly accomplish this task, any more than an almost exclusively state administration of cultural life could.

This privatization under the harsh conditions of economic reform will bankrupt the great bulk of cultural endeavors. Continued state administration of cultural life, on the other hand, will probably institutionalize inherited mediocrity—people like the Bulgarian scriveners of the history of Marxist-Leninism and scientific socialism. The struggle is to sustain cultural life with a combination of state and market support without exclusively depending on either form of support. It is a struggle for a free culture in a civil society.

Toward a New
Civilized Social Order

W hen I first traveled to Poland
in June 1973, I believed the world of communism to be a fairly stable
alternative modern order. I knew it wasn't a good order, or in particularly good order, but I assumed its permanence. I was not unusual.
Everyone then recognized a bipolar world consisting of the two
superpowers. Some accepted the polarity as inevitable, while others
imagined there would someday be a convergence of one sort or
another. Still others imagined a cold- or hot-war victory; but even
among these, few really expected the final showdown to happen in
our times. Indeed, by the late seventies, with the oil shock and stagfla-
tion, it was not unreasonable to assume that the ascendant superpower was the Soviet Union. Henry Kissinger's realpolitik seemed to
be based on such a vision, as did Ronald Reagan's anticommunist cru-
sade. Obviously, we now live in a transformed geopolitical world.

Yet while the old order has disappeared, the new order has not yet fully formed. It would be foolish to predict with any pretense of certainty what will happen during this time of global change. Too many problems remain unresolved. As we have seen, political constitution and leadership, nation and religion, the political economy and culture —all present both democratic opportunities and prospects for fundamental failure. Even the idea of "Europe" is not without its downside.

But simply to declare that "only time will tell" is not appropriate either. Our present actions are necessarily based on mediations between our understanding of the past and our imaginations of the future. In less dynamic times, such mediations were facilitated by traditional beliefs and authority. In the late nineteenth and most of the twentieth centuries, on the other hand, ideologies supplied absolute guidance based on scientistic certainty. Now, without the help of either tradition or ideology, we must think consciously and steadfastly about "the chasm between past and future," to use Hannah Arendt's phrase. We must imagine what a desirable and possible future might be, remembering past accomplishments and problems, so that we may plot a sound course of action in the present. To do this, as I have attempted to reveal in these reflections, we must both avoid unfounded euphoria and the promises it suggests, and overcome despair and the resignation it demands. I believe this is both a practical necessity and a realistic strategy.

So what is likely to emerge after the fall of communism? We should first note that it is unlikely to be just one thing, or even to go in just one direction, whether dictatorship or democracy, presidential or parliamentary system, nationalism and fundamentalism or tolerance, economic breakdown or a robust economy, cultural repression or cultural freedom. It follows that we in the West, as well as the citizens of the old bloc, must be open to variations on democratic and not-so-democratic themes and be ready to improvise appropriately on these variations.

In assessing the situations of the previously existing socialist societies, we have observed some geopolitical regularities. The situation of Eastern and Central Europe is different from that of the Soviet Union, and in Eastern and Central Europe, there are important differences between the northern and southern areas. Roughly speaking, in terms of the extremes along a post-totalitarian continuum, democratic prospects are brightest in the northwestern sector of the old bloc and dimmest in the southeastern zone. Poland, Hungary, and Czechoslovakia have the strongest grounds for hope, while Georgia and Azerbaijan, along with Serbia, Bulgaria, and Romania, provide ample grounds for pessimism. Yet things are not so bad in the southeast that the problems cannot be overcome, nor are they so good in the northwest that the new governments cannot fail. Further, because of the growing interdependence of Europe, failure in one place increases the likelihood of failure elsewhere, and success as well may be contagious.

The looming danger facing the newly independent countries of Eastern and Central Europe is still the Soviet Union. Before it was a matter of domination, political infiltration, and military occupation. Now, economic collapse, political disintegration, and military dictatorship are the primary dangers it poses. The problems are immense, and the capacity of the citizenry and leadership to address them is not very great. The Bolshevik experience amounted to seventy-five years of miseducation for the tasks at hand. I believe that the consistency of Gorbachev most adequately reveals this difficulty.

A great deal has been written about the image and identity of Mikhail Gorbachev. No other leader of the Soviet Union has evoked so much admiring attention from the West. He has played a significant if not a key role in bringing the Cold War to an end and provoking the fall of communism in the former satellite countries. But the latter accomplishment, it seems to me, was inadvertent. Gorbachev has steadily asserted his identity as a communist. There is no evidence to suggest that it was ever his intention to oversee either the communist collapse or the dismantling of the Soviet empire. He wanted to restructure (through *perestroika*) and open (through *glasnost*) the political and economic orders so as to revitalize them, not destroy them. As a believing communist, Gorbachev seemed to expect reform of the Soviet empire to empower it. As a realist, he was able to accept the loss of Eastern Europe. But as a communist, and perhaps as a Great Russian, he was much more reluctant to accept similar losses within the Soviet boundaries.

Gorbachev's way of thinking has interfered with his way of acting.

He has dealt with the subtle issues of political constitution and federation with a crudeness that has led to armed aggression against those seeking a greater degree of independence. His compromises with nationalist opinion have offered too little too late. His desire to revitalize socialism through a so-called "socialist market" has meant little more than hesitating to engage in necessary economic reforms. In the name of socialism as an ideology, the interests of the Party apparatus, and the police, military and industrial elites have been supported. Gorbachev wanted reform, but at a crucial point he appeared to realize that if reform proceeded, the ideologically conceived edifice called the Soviet Union would disappear. And this he apparently could not accept.

Nevertheless, although I realize that Gorbachev is a key political figure, in that his actions have triggered global and societal transformations that are impossible to reverse or repress, I believe it is not particularly helpful to indulge in endless speculation about what is or has been on his mind. The important fact is that because of his actions, along with the actions of many others, communism fell, despite his subsequent last-ditch attempts to shore it up. People in Eastern and Central Europe now realize that they needn't worry about a new Gorbachev Doctrine to replace the old Brezhnev Doctrine. Their concern is primarily with chaos and breakdown, and possible responsive authoritarian remedies. Their own problems in Central Europe are difficult enough to resolve without the possibility of mass hunger migrations from the east, or civil war, or an ascendance of the Soviet military elite and the KGB wielding aggressive ideologies against Russophobia. Invasion as such is a very remote possibility. At the same time, an unsettled European house (to use Gorbachev's rhetoric) is quite likely.

This is not really a prediction. It is a simple observation. Within the old Soviet entity, in Estonia, Latvia, and Lithuania, in Georgia, Armenia, and Azerbaijan, and even in the Ukraine, Byelorussia, and Russia, nationalist conflicts are proceeding. As Soviet republics clamor for independence from central authority, inter- and intra-republic nationalist tensions become political facts of life. Indecisive and contradictory economic reforms have effectively undermined the command economy without market replacement. Industrial strikes have spread widely. And many people among both the leadership and the general population, lacking both long democratic traditions and recent experience with democratic opposition, seek easy solutions— often authoritarian ones. Those who want to be democratic are discovering the complexities of democratic deliberations and decision making. The ineffectiveness of the democrats and the impatience of the authoritarians make a volatile mixture. Added to the tensions and uncertainties of Eastern and Central Europe, this mixture constitutes a prescription for postcommunist despair.

Yet I do not think this response is appropriate to the present situation. Civility may be more infectious than chaos. Those factors which led to the fall of 1989 were, and continue to be, very powerful. The dream of a "normal Europe" may prevail.

I suspect that people will muddle their way along the path to democracy in the nations of Central Europe. The tensions of nationalism, economic weakness, emerging class conflicts, and problems of political constitution and leadership will not be definitively resolved in an unambiguously democratic or authoritarian direction. But I think the general situation will eventually be a democratic one, even if less than ideal.

From the point of view of principled secularism, for instance, the role of the church in Polish political affairs will seem to be much too great. The church will tend to dictate its political positions on abortion and other private issues, and it will do all it can to expand its political influence. Although there are, no doubt, dangers in this tendency, realistically we might note that the church's role in Poland will probably be more like that of the church in Ireland than like that of the church in France.

In Hungary, it's likely that nationalist rhetoric will be much more widespread than confirmed cosmopolitans would like. The large Hungarian minorities in neighboring countries will keep the national question very high on the political agenda. But if we recognize that German democracy can withstand this sort of concern, and I believe that the postwar experience clearly indicates it can, there is no reason that Hungary can't withstand it as well.

The problems in Czechoslovakia seem to me much more serious.

Slovak nationalism does threaten the integrity of the multinational state. But how different is this situation from Canada's? In both cases, the odds, in my judgment, are in favor of a liberal democracy.

To be sure, the Czechs, Slovaks, Hungarians, and Poles, along with their other Eastern and Central European neighbors, find themselves in a much more vulnerable situation than do the Canadians (French and English), the Germans, and the Irish. Politically constituting a democratic order is much more difficult than politically acting within already established democratic institutions. For this reason, I believe, the accomplishments of civil society, and the idea of Europe, play such important civilizing roles.

Xenophobia and personal insecurity have become Central European facts of life. Democracy does not automatically deliver the economic, political, and cultural goods, and a market economy does not only promise riches, it also creates unfathomable problems for those who don't know how to work in it. A natural human response to such a situation is to blame someone other than oneself. We can hear such responses throughout the "other Europe." Many people in that Europe (which was named "other" by Philip Roth in a series of books highlighting the accomplishments of Central European writers) are now looking for an "other" to blame for their present predicament. For some it is the "reds," or anyone who collaborated with the former regime. For others it is the Jews, and in the grand tradition of European anti-Semitism, many identify the Jewish reds.

This on the lands of the Holocaust. I have never felt more revolted than when I observed anti-Semitic graffiti in Warsaw, heard anti-Semitic rhetoric in Bratislava, and, in the safety of my home in New York, read reports of neo-Nazi outrages in eastern Germany. Yet it is a great mistake to confuse marginal extremists with emerging political centers of gravity. Of course in times of uncertainty extremists have to be watched, but the mere existence of extremism does not define the political situation. Adam Michnik made this point graphically in a speech accepting the Shofar Award of the Central Synagogue of Manhattan in the spring of 1991. "Anti-Semitic pathology doesn't define Poland, just as Le Pen doesn't define France, the John Birch Society doesn't define America, the Black Hundreds don't define Russia, and extreme Israeli chauvinism doesn't define the State of Israel."

But how will Central Europe be centered? How can the citizens of the region act in a way to assure that the extremes will stay at the margins? I've argued here that the ideal of Europe and the practice of civil society are essential, and that this practice has broad theoretical and political significance that goes beyond the European continent in an age when ideology should end.

In the late seventies and early eighties, developments in Poland captured the world's attention. Poland was viewed by confirmed conservative and liberal anticommunists as a valiant David up against the Soviet Goliath. But for me, and for some others in the Western democratic left, something even more exciting seemed to be involved. In the politics of Solidarity, we saw more than an interesting variant on the grand geopolitical drama of the Cold War. We saw a significant alternative to Cold War politics.

Solidarity demonstrated that one could be democratic, and even of the left, and reject communism without denying its connection to the socialist tradition. Polish anti-ideological rhetoric, along with a radical commitment to self-determination on the part of ordinary people, suggested a way to seek alternatives to Western social and political practices without succumbing to the recurrent political pathologies of the Western left. The Poles didn't outline a new utopian vision, nor did they find it necessary to choose capitalism over socialism or vice versa. Instead, they struggled to take control over their lives as much as possible; they fought to establish a zone of social autonomy, requiring the party-state apparatus to recognize it and negotiate with it.

During this time, Lech Wałęsa became an international celebrity. His wit and irony had great appeal. When he stubbornly insisted on his apolitical orientation, his recognition of the Party as Poland's leading social force, and his simple identity as a trade union leader, he seemed to have his tongue firmly in his cheek and at the same time to be deeply serious. His game appeared to be one of remarkable cunning. The communist bureaucracy had finally met its match.

Yet I perceived a greater political significance. The Solidarity strategy of a "self-limiting revolution" was more than a subtle instrument for the ultimate political end of overthrowing communist oppression. *The strategy was a significant end in itself.* Like other subjects of communist orders, the Poles were tired of having their lives defined for them. They wanted to take control of their own fates. They realized that no one else could take care of them if they didn't act for themselves. They understood that their economic well-being was connected to their political freedom. They came to appreciate what Hannah Arendt called "the lost treasure of the revolutionary tradition." The Poles came together, formed a public, spoke their minds, and acted in concert. That was what it meant to act "as if" they lived in a free society. And for people outside the communist bloc, it had a lot to recommend it.

In all her writings, but especially in *On Revolution*, her study of the French and American revolutions, Hannah Arendt defined political freedom with reference to people constituting and marking out an arena in which they could come together in their plurality and speak and act in the presence of others. The experience of such an activity, she said, brings public, as distinct from private, happiness. Arendt recognized this experience in fleeting moments of revolutionary periods: in the American committees of correspondence and town meetings; in the French political clubs; and in the Russian soviets of 1905 and 1917 (but not in Bolshevik party practices). In each case, however, a lack of appreciation for free politics led to its disappearance. In one of the postscripts to *The Origins of Totalitarianism*, Arendt pointed out the same experience in the Hungarian workers' councils of 1956. As a political theorist, she made it her life's project to name this experience of public freedom so that it could be remembered and supported, so that freedom could be achieved not through a grand design but through remembrance of and appreciation of human accomplishment.

The Polish events of 1980–1981, it seemed to me, called for such Arendtian appreciation. I started working on it in *On Cultural Freedom*, and continued in *Beyond Glasnost*. In both studies, I grounded my arguments on the belief that the Polish events and subsequent Central European developments spoke to our situation in the West as well as to those in the East; not simply because of their potential for changing the sociopolitical balance, but because of the profound significance of public freedom.

Now these ruminations must be viewed in a somewhat different light. I have argued here that a central cause of the fall of communism was the struggle to achieve public freedom in a besieged civil society. Further, I have maintained that overcoming the tensions and dilemmas of the postcommunist period requires a robust civil order, one that does not succumb to either the rationales of statism or the magical promises of the market. I made these judgments with the full awareness that they moved against the grain of ideological common sense. Now I feel that such a move is absolutely necessary.

But a problem emerges. My Central European colleagues, in their anti-ideological commitments, are appropriately skeptical of utopian dreams and social and political experiments. They have lived an experimental rather than a normal social existence. Now they seek normality. They want to be realistic, to turn away from attractively packaged political slogans and toward political realism: for them, no "socialism with a human face," Marxist humanism, or so-called "third ways." Politics and the economy, then, have become operationally defined: presidential or parliamentary democracy; laissez-faire liberalism or welfare-state capitalism. This approach is certainly understandable, and even wise, but some things are being overlooked: the social and cultural bases of the normal political and economic operations; the institutions of civil society.

The voluntary associations of civil society led Alexis de Tocqueville to believe in the early nineteenth century that Americans could overcome the special problems of democratic politics, and it was this same sector in the late twentieth century that played a significant role in the downfall of communism. But there is a danger that by ignoring this sector after the revolutions of 1989, we will witness another instance of "the lost revolutionary tradition." The Central European capacity to constitute a sound new political and economic order could then be significantly undermined.

The civility of civil society is intimately connected with democratic renewal. While this has always been the case, the extreme incivility of communist practices makes the issue today much more pressing. Ironically, its distortion in Central Europe during the communist period once more revealed to the world the importance of civil society. The revelation of that truth is one thing I found so appealing in the Gdańsk shipyard. But the imaginative appeal of struggling for civil and independent society, an appeal that can be used to criticize actually existing liberal democracies as well as previously existing socialist societies, can seem impractical, even utopian. There is a real danger that emerging civil societies can be overwhelmed by rationales of state and market. This is the institutional and cultural context in which political debate occurs after the fall.

Central political questions arise. Does it make sense to contrast capitalism with socialism? What's left? What's right? Has there been a new end to ideology? Do we live in a new world order? The first four questions I posed at the beginning of these reflections, and tried to address in a variety of ways by considering the specific problems facing the new democracies. And while I was composing my questions and proposing answers, George Bush raised the fifth question in justifying American policy in the Persian Gulf, the first major international crisis after the breakdown of the bipolar geopolitical world. His question is obviously related to my inquiry.

I do not feel adequately qualified to judge the merits or demerits of the Persian Gulf war, and I don't intend to try here. Yet there is a long-term significance in the justifications of and reactions to the war that pertains directly to our inquiry. My initial reaction to the developing conflict tended to be more like that of my Eastern and Central European colleagues than like that of my compatriots on the American left: Saddam Hussein was a totalitarian dictator, and I couldn't oppose a war against him. Yet when Bush started talking about a new world order, I became very uncomfortable, again drawing on my Central European sensibilities. Not only did I recall the fact that the phrase "the new world order" was first popularized by Hitler, but I noticed that from the lips of Bush, too, it had a totalitarian ring. For my taste it was a bit too grand and vague, was more connected to military might than to reason. It was unclear to me whether the so-called new world order meant anything more than American geopolitical hegemony. Further, it was a logical conclusion drawn from what seemed to me to be a misunderstanding of the implications of the end of the Cold War.

The meaning of the Cold War's end for Bush, and other American celebrants, was clear and simple. The West won. The new world order, then, in view of the United States' preeminent military power, meant American dominance. But this view didn't take into account the way the anticommunist struggle undermined the foundations of our own political-economic house. From the Palmer raids after World War I to McCarthyism to George Bush's condemnation of Michael Dukakis as "a card-carrying member of the American Civil Liberties Union," anticommunist ideology has taken the civility out of American political discourse and life. And the long-term and huge military buildup directed against the "evil empire" has so centered our economic life on military production that the Cold War's end presents profound economic challenges to American industry and enterprise.

Bush's proclamation of a new world order seemed to be a deliberate attempt to cover up these problems. He seemed to want to keep alive the Manichaean ideological vision that came out of the Cold War even after the collapse of communism, although the enemy was a demonized Third World force. But if I am right that the fall of 1989 opens up a new political epoch, one in which ideology could end, the problem with this position becomes especially acute.

As should be clear from my arguments, I believe that the contrast between capitalism and socialism has become meaningless. There is no alternative to a market in complex economies. The terms of economic exchange, of course, vary tremendously, as do the roles of the state and other social institutions such as trade unions. But it seems to me there is no complete systemic alternative called "socialism" to what has been called "capitalism." From this perception, ideological free marketeers draw proof of their victory. But it overlooks the great variety in so-called capitalist systems, the United States versus Germany versus South Korea for example. Celebrations of capitalism will not help distinguish among the very different sorts of economic practices in these countries. They will also not help guide political and economic reform in the old political East or West. I have argued that two intellectual moves are required: a turn against ideology, and a turn toward redefined political principles.

Thus Bush's new world order fills me with dismay. It is an attempt to sustain a new ideological position in the world (however vaguely formulated), and—as was most evident in the political aftermath of the Persian Gulf war, with Saddam still in power and the mass migrations and suffering of the Kurdish population—it apparently had little to do with antitotalitarian principles or commitment to human rights. Bush's ideologically declared new world order has as little room for them as

Cold War ideologies had. When human rights and democratic principles served ideological purposes, as they did when Bush was putting together the international coalition or while the war was under way, they were recognized. But without such purposes, people who continue to adhere to them are conveniently labeled "unrealistic" by those with Manichaean minds. Events both before and after the fall in Central Europe suggest that this position is incredibly ignorant politically.

Remember, totalitarian power was brought down by so-called impractical idealists who proved to be the genuine realists; people who were willing to act as if they lived in a free society, and often suffered the consequences—because in fact they didn't. But by living according to their ideals, they turned ideal into reality. My great hope is that they and we don't lose sight of the lessons of their actions. They should continue to move against ideology—not lose sight of the political principles that brought down the empire but instead develop those principles.

It will be hard to develop those principles. Problems of political constitution and leadership, nationalism, religious intolerance, and emerging class conflicts overshadow the commitment to civil society. It is here that the idea of Europe takes on its great importance—Europe not as a specific set of national characteristics or as the home of imperialism, world wars, totalitarianism, the Holocaust, and the gulag, but the Europe of democratic ideals, political tolerance, cultural accomplishment, and economic exchange. The attractiveness of Europe, and the popularity of the slogan "going back to Europe," gives me reason to hope.

Viewed from the larger political stage, the ideal of Europe raises some anxieties. To the Third World, Eurocentrism presents real and present dangers. In an international economy of limited resources, proposed Marshall Plans for Central Europe seem to be indifferent to the much more pressing poverty and human suffering of Africa, Asia, and Central and South America. Why is there increased debt relief for Poland and not for Zambia? Why is food aid being sent to the Soviet Union, where there is no starvation, while people in Somalia go hungry? When one tries to answer these questions, the idea of Europe may seem to lose its luster.

But the Europe of the Rights of Man, of democracy, of the ideals coming out of the liberal, conservative, and indeed socialist traditions, is not really confined to one particular corner of the world. The Czech political journalist Jan Urban, as we observed, argued that these special European ideals emerged in opposition to the parochialism of specific European locations, and this opposition suggests that the notion of Europe in Europe has counterparts elsewhere. Thus in the United States a renewed appreciation of our national political culture, as it is enshrined in the Declaration of Independence and the experience of making the Constitution, has played a recurrent role in political reform and renewal—most spectacularly during the postwar period in the civil rights movement.

As I have argued here, distinctive American political experiences also speak directly to those trying to constitute the new democracies in Europe. And both European and American democratic experiences are resources that can be used far beyond the North American and European orbits. Thus, with regard to Iraq, a dissident emigré maintains with considerable cogency that the coalition's military might was ultimately directed not against the totalitarian leader and his regime but against the Iraqi people. American bombing destroyed the country's infrastructure, and the ground forces killed tens if not hundreds of thousands of ill-fed and demoralized troops; but the dictatorship was allowed to continue. Most telling, from the point of view of this inquiry, is that Samir al-Khalil strongly argues for the possibility of pluralistic democracy in Iraq. He points to traditions of more benign rule in the recent Iraqi past, and, most significantly, to the fact that the ideal of tolerance in Europe emerged after a century of religious wars. He properly considers liberal and pluralistic ideals not as the possession of a certain group of people in a certain place and time, but as a practical basis for a modern civilized social order.

The tragedy of the first international conflict after the Cold War is that those who fought in the name of civilized liberal ideals betrayed those ideals even before the battle was over. I am reminded of very sad European facts: the railroad tracks and trains leading to Auschwitz, which went untouched by Allied bombs in World War II; the Warsaw uprising, which went unaided by Allied forces; the Yalta agreements, which sealed the fate of postwar Europe, leaving the continent to exist half free and half enslaved.

But to speak of tragedy in our historical moment is to leave out a crucial part of the story. In recent years, throughout the world, principled commitments to liberal democratic practices have been gaining ever broader appeal. To be sure, with the virtual disappearance of communism, some of the most desperate have turned to one form of ideological fundamentalism or other—witness Saddam Hussein's Pan-Arabist appeal in 1991. Yet, just as striking as the Arabist example, and much more promising, is the turn of former radical critics toward democratic practice around the world. In Nicaragua, Argentina, and Kenya, as well as China and Cuba, critical intellectuals and ordinary people have been coming to realize that democratic institutions and practices are primary, significant ends in themselves, aside from immediate economic interests and political dreams. Even more: democratic institutions and practices are preconditions for the fulfillment of such individual interests and dreams.

The dawning of this realization points to the end of ideology, and it constitutes a challenge to both the left and the right. Earlier in this century, the political aspirations of the ideological and totalitarian left and right were not directed toward parliamentary institutions at all; they were directed against them. But now, in situations like those of Eastern and Central Europe, there is a general awareness that political aspirations *must* be articulated through such institutions, if we are to avoid the horrors of the recent past.

Such an awareness has led people in Central European democratic oppositions to deny the saliency of left-right distinctions. For people like Adam Michnik and Václav Havel, commitment to a free public domain has taken precedence over the specific orientations and traditions of the left and the right. Yet, at this point, the relevance of Kostek Gebert's joke should be clear. Before the fall of communism, it may have been the case in Central Europe—as Gebert's joke goes—that the difference between left and right was revealed by the leftists' insistence that there was no difference, while the rightists maintained that there was. After the fall, the differences are again appearing, not only in general, but with reference to the specific, pressing problems of the new democracies.

As we have seen, those who draw on the wisdoms of the right address the problems of politics, leadership, nation, religion, and the economy, with special concern for order and community, tradition and belief. Those who draw on the ideals of the left focus more on change and rights, equality and reason. Even socialist ideals of egalitarianism and social justice have pressing salience now. But people are aware of the need to make a strong distinction between ideological socialism and its egalitarian ethos; between system-defining orientations backed by the coercive power of the state and socialism (at least in the socialist ideal) as it can be pursued within a modern economy.

Socialism is simply not the answer to all social ills. But neither are capitalism or nationalism. If one thinks in such ideological terms, today, after the fall of communism, euphoria and despair become inevitable. On the other democratic hand, between euphoria and despair lies the possibility for the deliberative resolution of complex human problems animated by principled ideals in a civil society. This is the less than utopian basis for a new civilized social order. Ideologies have promised much more, but have given us much less.

We should, therefore, appreciate what has happened in Eastern and Central Europe, and not be overwhelmed by the problems faced by Eastern and Central Europeans. These problems are very real, but they can be addressed. We should not substitute new ideological global visions (like "a new world order") for the old visions of communism or myopic anticommunism.

History has not yet ended. But modern totalitarian ideologies may have come to an end—appropriately, on the European killing grounds. If we act wisely, and support the constitution of democratic politics, we may yet close the book on the horrors of the twentieth century.

Bibliographic Note

I n writing this book as a theoretical reflection upon the revolutionary developments coming after the fall of communism, I have drawn mostly upon what I saw and heard in the capitals of Eastern and Central Europe in 1990 and 1991. Interviews and participant observation provided my primary empirical sources. Yet, I did not go to Europe with a blank slate. I have been thinking, researching, and writing about the region for the past two decades. My books, *The Persistence of Freedom: The Sociological Implications of Polish Student Theater* (Boulder, Colo.: Westview Press, 1980), *On Cultural Freedom: An Exploration of Public Life in Poland and America* (Chicago: University of Chicago Press, 1982), and *Beyond Glasnost: The Post-Totalitarian Mind* (Chicago: University of Chicago Press, 1989), elaborate my developing position on the politics and culture of the region before the revolutionary changes of 1989 and also provide more systematic overviews of the scholarly literature on Soviet bloc affairs.

A major thesis of this book is that 1989 represents a fundamental turning point in modern history, requiring a principled rethinking of political and social theory. Hannah Arendt, in my view, more than any other modern political theorist, shows us how to begin this rethinking process. Her books and essays confront the distinctiveness of twentieth-century horrors in a way that points toward a more hopeful future, drawing upon profound reflections on past experience. *The Origins of Totalitarianism* (Cleveland: Meridian Books, 1958), *On Revolution* (New York: Viking, 1963), *Between Past and Future* (New York: Penguin Books, 1968), and *Eichmann in Jerusalem: A Report on the Banality of Evil* (New York: Penguin Books, 1977) were crucial to me in understanding the unfolding hopeful events in Europe and their theoretical significance. Her insights suggest an alternative not only to despair but also to an easy triumphalism such as those cited in the text. On the side of capitalism, see Francis Fukuyama, "The End of History," *The National Interest* (16 [Summer 1989]: 3–18), and Zbigniew Brzezinski, *The Grand Failure: The Birth and Death of Communism in the Twentieth Century* (New York: Charles Scribner's Sons, 1989). On the side of socialism, see Paul Sweezy, "Is This the End of Socialism?" *The Nation* (February 26, 1990). In the analysis of the dilemmas of the new politics, I refer to Edward Banfield's *The Democratic Muse: Visual Arts and the Public Interest* (New York: Basic Books, 1984) as an example of an approach that conflates free enterprise with cultural freedom. I drew upon Mirosława Marody's research on the human limitations on economic and political reform, reported in her paper "New Possibilities and Old Habits," presented to the International Workshop of the Democracy Seminar, The New Democracies: The Act of Foundation (Budapest: March 21–22, 1990).

In *Beyond Glasnost*, I argued that Arendt was in a sense the first post-totalitarian thinker, and that writers such as Adam Michnik and Václav Havel extend this tradition. In this work, I have considered their powerful insights in the present post-totalitarian situation. Especially important are Adam Michnik's *Letters from Prison and Other Essays* (Berkeley: University of California Press, 1986) and "Poland and the Jews," *New York Review of Books* ([May 30, 1991] pp. 11–12), and Václav Havel's "The Power of the Powerless," in

Václav Havel: On Living in Truth (edited by Jan Vladislaw, Boston: Faber and Faber, 1986), *Disturbing the Peace: A Conversation with Karoll Hvížďala* (New York: Alfred Knopf, 1990), and "The Future of Central Europe," *New York Review of Books* ([March 22, 1990] pp. 18–19). Timothy Garton Ash's *The Uses of Adversity: Essays on the Fate of Central Europe* (New York: Random House, 1989) provides a sound overview of the political and cultural context of Havel and Michnik as political writers and activists. George Konrád in *Anti-Politics* (New York: Harcourt Brace Jovanovich, 1984) presents a particularly fine Hungarian example of the post-totalitarian mentality.

I have maintained that the people of Eastern and Central Europe must not only try to undo the damage of communist rule, they must also confront persistent, perhaps universal, dilemmas of political practice and the demons of nationalist xenophobia and religious fanaticism, as well as a moral vacuum. With reference to Soviet Russia, Walter Lacqueur analyzes the dimensions of the problem in *The Long Road to Freedom: Russia and Glasnost* (New York: Charles Scribner's Sons, 1989). I have also used Liah Greenfeld, "The Closing of the Russian Mind," *The New Republic* ([February 5, 1990] pp. 30–31). The analysis of the Jewish question in Poland was informed by discussions with Kostek Gebert. He represents some of his views in English under his pen name, Dawid Warszawski, in "The Convert and Solidarity" (*Tikkun* 4, no. 6 [November/December 1989]: 29–30, 92–93). Also see Abraham Brumberg, "The Problem That Won't Go Away: Anti-Semitism in Poland (Again)" (*Tikkun* 5, no. 1 [January/February 1990]: 31–34, 93–94.

The ideal of Europe stands as an alternative to narrow chauvinisms. For an intriguing collection on the topic, see the special issue of *Daedalus* (119, no. 1 [Winter 1990]). In the text I quote from Jacques Rupnik's "Central Europe or Mitteleuropa?" on pages 249–278 of that issue. I also used the unpublished writings of Jan Urban, which he provided me. A key essay on the idea of Europe is in Milan Kundera's *The Art of the Novel* (New York: Grove Press, 1988).

In the discussion on the economy of existing socialism, I directly referred to Jeffrey Sachs and David Lifton, "Polish Economic Affairs," *Foreign Affairs* (Summer 1990), Jeffrey Sachs, "The Economist Heard Round the World, Part I," and Janine R. Wedel, "The

Economist Heard Round the World, Part II" (both in *World Monitor* 3, no. 10 [December 1990]). I also used David Ost's *Solidarity and the Politics of Anti-Politics: Opposition and Reform in Poland* (Philadelphia: Temple University Press, 1990) and some unpublished papers of Ost. On the limited leftist reaction to the beginnings of the Solidarity movement, see Daniel Singer, *The Road to Gdańsk* (New York: Monthly Review Press, 1981). My analysis of the Soviet Writers Union draws upon John and Carol Gerrard, *Inside the Soviet Writers Union* (New York: Free Press, 1990). I also referred to Alain Touraine, François Dubet, Michel Wieviorka, and Jan Strzelecki, *Solidarity: The Analysis of a Social Movement: Poland 1980–1981* (New York: Cambridge University Press, 1983). The quote by Jan Lityński appeared in Lyane Jones and Tomaz Mastak, "Democracy After Communism" (*New Politics* 3 no. 1 [1990]).

The closing chapters on culture and the importance of independent social institutions for democratic politics applies a convergence of American scholarly interests with Central European political practice and reflection. Some relevant examples of the American research include my own *The Cynical Society: The Culture of Politics and the Politics of Culture in American Life* (Chicago: University of Chicago Press, 1991) as well as Alan Wolfe's *Whose Keeper?* (Berkeley: University of California Press, 1989), and Robert N. Bellah, Richard Madsen, William M. Sullivan, Ann Swidler, and Steven M. Tipton, *The Good Society* (New York: Knopf, 1991).

INDEX

257